Milton and the Postmodern

. . . ce qui est resté d'un
Rembrandt
déchiré en petits carrés . . .

Jean Genet / Jacques Derrida

Herman Rapaport

Milton and the Postmodern

University of Nebraska Press

Lincoln and London

Copyright 1983 by the
University of Nebraska Press
All rights reserved
Manufactured in the
United States of America
The paper in this book
meets the guidelines for
permanence and durability of
the Committee on Production
Guidelines for Book Longevity
of the Council on Library
Resources.

Frontispiece: Rembrandt van Rijn.
The Blinding of Samson.
Oil on canvas. 1636. H. 236 cm,
w. 302 cm. By permission of the
Städelsches Kunstinstitut,
Frankfort on the Main.
Photo by Ursula Edelmann.

Library of Congress Cataloging
in Publication Data

Rapaport, Herman, 1947-
Milton and the postmodern.

Includes bibliographical
references and index.
1. Milton, John, 1608-1674 –
Criticism and interpretation.
I. Title.
PR3588.R355   1983
821'.4   82-21935
ISBN 0-8032-3862-2

For Alexander Gelley

Le travail de deuil, est-ce un travail, une espèce de travail? Et la thanatopraxie, technique de la pompe funèbre aujourd'hui enseignée dans des instituts, donnant lieu à des diplômes de qualification, la limitera-t-on à une corporation parmi d'autres, à l'intérieur d'une économie sociale? Tout travail n'est-il pas un travail de deuil? et du même coup d'appropriation du plus ou moins de perte, une opération *classique?* une opération violente de classe et de classification? une décollation de ce qui tient le singulier à lui-même? Ce travail de deuil *s'appelle*—glas.

("Is the work of mourning a work, a type of work? And *thanatopraxie*, that technics of the funeral rite taught currently in those institutions granting degrees, will one limit that to one corporation among others, to the interior of a social economy? Is not all work a work of mourning? and at the same stroke of appropriation of more or less a loss or lack, a *classical* operation? a violent operation of class and classification? a decapitation of that which keeps the singular to itself? This work of mourning is *called*—glas.")

Jacques Derrida, *Glas*

CONTENTS

Preface, xiii

Introduction, 1

CHAPTER 1 Milton and the *Thanatopraxie* of Writing, 11

CHAPTER 2 Milton's Epic *Trauerspiel*, 23

CHAPTER 3 Milton's Lady of the Flowers, 59

CHAPTER 4 Lycidas: The Poetics of Antherection, 103

CHAPTER 5 Samson Eikonoklastes, 131

CHAPTER 6 Milton and the State, 167

CHAPTER 7 Blessing the Text, 209

Notes, 241

Index, 267

PREFACE

Milton and the Postmodern was not originally composed with the idea of advancing a primer on either contemporary theory or Milton's works, for I was interested in attempting to use Milton as a test case for a poststructuralist reading that would assume familiarity with both Milton and poststructuralist theory. I am grateful to Murray Krieger for suggesting some practical approaches to the writing of such a study and to Joseph Riddel for his suggestions that eventually blossomed into Chapter 3 on the double scene in *Paradise Lost*. Louis Marin suggested that I work Milton into Jean-Jacques Rousseau, and though I feel that such a direction is worthy, I apologize for not having done it here. Many thanks go to Maria Ruegg, whom I consulted with my first drafts; to Harold Toliver, Hazard Adams, Dominique Desanti, and, of course, Peter Colaclides. I thank Cecile Lindsay for help with some of the French translations, and I am especially grateful to Alexander Gelley for his extreme kindness and thoughtfulness. It is for him that this book is written.

I consider myself fortunate to have studied with Geoffrey Hartman at the School of Criticism and Theory during the summer of 1978, and I thank him for reading and responding to my work on Milton. Similarly, I thank Jim Swan for his close reading of my manuscript and for his sensitive suggestions. Also, I have received a small grant from the University of California at Irvine which aided me with some aspects of researching materials, and this present form of the manuscript has been awarded a grant from Loyola University of Chicago. I am most grateful for such support and wish to thank those who have made that possible.

The rage for completion in the midst of other pressing projects has been enormously time-consuming, and I thank my wife, Susanne, for her patience and for helping me with text preparation. I am greatly indebted to her tireless and accurate work. Lastly I thank my mother, Betty M. Rapaport, for the kind of financial assistance that counted when I really needed it. Even if the writing of this study cannot repay what I owe her, it can at least acknowledge its debt.

A Note on the Text and the Translations

The text I have followed for Milton's poetry is the edition of Merritt Y. Hughes: *John Milton: Complete Poems and Major Prose* (New York: Odyssey Press, 1957). For his other works I have used the most convenient scholarly editions.

Unaccredited translations are my own, and all of the translations are only approximations, some more literal than others, as is always the case. These translations and their originals appear variously in the text and the notes, as I think will best suit the needs of most readers without greatly inconveniencing the rest.

INTRODUCTION

This text advances what Jean-Pierre Richard might call micro-readings, which appear highly fragmentary from the perspective of those who seek a study which develops a rationale for understanding the whole of Milton's oeuvre, the entirety of any given work, or the shape of Milton's thought or times. My texts do not totalize or summarize in such a fashion, and it would be a mistake to attempt to identify or extract the thesis of my approaches to Milton, though I think it will be apparent that the chapters which follow do provide some strong critical and thematic guides by which the various micro-studies can be related and considered as a whole. My aim is to uncover textual infrastructures in Milton's work whose relationships to the classical and humanist ideals often attributed to Milton—ideals which are logocentric and metaphysically committed—are highly problematic from the point of view of philosophical method, not only the kind of philosophical method which Milton would have known in his own time but in terms of contemporary philosophical issues as well. By studying Milton and situating his texts within a postmodern context, one comes to appreciate the strong philosophical relevance Milton's post-Renaissance and pre-Enlightenment texts have for the history of philosophy as we know it today and particularly as it has been reinterpreted by French intellectuals like Georges Bataille, Gilles Deleuze, Julia Kristeva, Philippe Sollers, Roland Barthes, Michel Foucault, René Girard, and Jacques Derrida.

2 Introduction

My readings of Milton are strategically focused in order that one can sight radically heterogeneous registers within what at first appears a homogeneous field, a heterogeneity that will not and cannot be reconciled with the traditional approach to Milton (headed by critics like Irene Samuel), which views the poet as the last great Renaissance apologist for humanism, despite his seventeenth-century modernism, expressing and upholding the ideology of classical, medieval, and Renaissance metaphysics (that is, Platonism, Augustinianism, Thomism, and Neoplatonism). No doubt one can focus upon a Milton who champions logocentricism and the onto-encyclopedic conception of a totalizing argument or syllogistic text written in a centered and recursive pattern, a structure accounting for all possible arguments or points and valorizing a single truth or master concept; one can align Milton with Dante, Plato, Virgil, and Homer and claim that the lifeblood of classicism ran through Milton's veins. However, one can already see in the essay of Lord Macaulay on Milton in 1825 a profound understanding of the problematics of inconsistency in Milton's oeuvre:

> Milton wrote in an age of philosophers and theologians. It was necessary, therefore, for him to abstain from giving such a shock to their understandings as might break the charm which it was his object to throw over their imaginations. This is the real explanation of the indistinctness and inconsistency with which he has often been reproached. Dr. Johnson acknowledges that it was absolutely necessary that the spirits should be clothed with material forms. "But," says he, "the poet should have secured the consistency of his system by keeping immateriality out of sight, and seducing the reader to drop it from his thoughts." This is easily said; but what if Milton could not seduce his readers to drop immateriality from their thoughts? What if the contrary opinion had taken so full a possession of the minds of men as to leave no room even for the half belief which poetry requires? Such we suspect to have been the case. It was impossible for the poet to adopt altogether the material or the immaterial system. He therefore took his stand on the debatable ground. He left the whole in ambiguity. He has doubtless, by so doing, laid himself open to the charge of inconsistency. But, though philosophically in the wrong, we cannot but believe that he

was poetically in the right. This task, which almost any other writer would have found impracticable, was easy to him. The peculiar art which he possessed of communicating his meaning circuitously through a long succession of associated ideas, and of intimating more than he expressed, enabled him to disguise those incongruities which he could not avoid.[1]

Macaulay has been one of the few readers of Milton to perceive a strategic wavering, or oscillation, between idealism and materialism, an attempt on Milton's part to arbitrate between two impossible grounds. Milton leaves the whole in ambiguity, by which Macaulay means something quite different from a formalist or New Critical figure or trope, for what is at issue here is a crisis, the impossibility of writing poetry that is decidably figural, concrete, and iconic, like Dante's *Divine Comedy*, since Milton lives in a time when culture has surpassed such naïveté, when philosophy has with its immateriality posited the abstract above the individual, what in the *Phenomenology of Spirit* Hegel would call the negativity of spirit. Milton himself is an iconoclast of a radical sort, something his political writings make very clear, and yet his iconoclasm does not simply turn against materialism and embrace idealism, for that too is a fetish. Milton takes his stand "on the debatable ground," as Macaulay says, and thus has to lay himself open "to the charge of inconsistency."

Macaulay knows that "the men who demolished the images in cathedrals have not always been able to demolish those which were enshrined in their minds,"[2] and this is particularly relevant to Milton, for his prose tracts and poems are committed to an evasion of both these errors—what amounts to the difficult philosophical project, still on the contemporary Marxist and poststructuralist agenda, of not simply transcending one idealism by means of another but of standing dialectically on a debatable ground that at once engages and disengages the metaphysical conceptual apparatuses that constitute Western philosophy (what Jacques Derrida terms the "white mythology"). Macaulay, of course, thinks that Milton's position or positions on the threshold between materialism and idealism is not defensible from a philosophical perspective, but that Milton may be forgiven on poetic grounds. The assumption of Macaulay is that poetry naturally belongs to a dark age and a civilization in its infancy, that Milton's difficulty is in having come at too sophisticated a time, when men have already abstracted ideas too much. Milton must, therefore, perform a regressive tactic by which he vacillates between philosophy and theology of his day and a much ruder poetic materialism, by which Macaulay means poetry's reliance upon incantation, or what Walter Benjamin terms *Sprachmagie* (in Macaulay, "the magical influence of poetry").[3]

Such romanticism, however charming, is blind to the possibility that philosophically what Milton achieves by taking his stand on the debatable ground is defensible as a legitimate philosophical activity and must not be discounted via poetic license as logically erroneous and merely contradictory from an enlightened perspective. To make such a defense, of course, one has to have access to a philosophical theory which is itself not an idealism, not in the process of merely transcending one idealism by means of another, but genuinely involved in deconstructing its own metaphysical presuppositions. Without such a theory, a critic's anti-idealist insights will always be recuperated or neutralized, as in Macaulay's essay on Milton, by the very presuppositions by which one's critique is initiated or motivated, that is to say, subverted by metaphysics proper. Certainly anti-idealistic theories can be sought in more than one place. We can go to Lucretius, Leibniz, Hegel, Marx, Nietzsche, Heidegger, Theodor Adorno, Lucio Colletti, and Louis Althusser, for example. However, I have found Jacques Derrida's deconstructive formulations most helpful, particularly as they are theoretically set forth in *La dissémination* and executed in *Glas*, for it is in such texts that the specific verbal operations of a deconstructive philosophy are exposed in greatest detail, where one can see how a text by occupying the debat-

Introduction 5

able ground between various idealisms manages by means of specific verbal economies to dislocate radically what one might ordinarily assume ought to be unified and coherent systems whose centers, or bases of support, pose as apodictic and therefore beyond question. It must be stressed that *deconstruction* is not a synonym for destruction, subversion, or culture assassination, but refers to the peculiar resistance and marginality of certain textual registers which occupy liminal zones, debatable grounds, or undecidable thresholds, registers which readers often pass over or manage to force into a logocentric alignment. An early Derridean formulation of deconstruction, and one I still find helpful, occurs in *L'écriture et la différence:*

Nous n'opposons pas ici, par un simple mouvement de balancier, d'équilibration ou de renversement, la durée à l'espace, la qualité à la quantité, la force à la forme, la profondeur du sens ou de la valeur à la surface des figures. Bien au contraire. Contre cette simple alternative, contre le simple choix de l'un des termes ou de l'une des séries, nous pensons qu'il faut chercher de nouveaux concepts et de nouveaux modèles, une *économie* échappant à ce système d'oppositions métaphysiques. Cette économie ne serait pas une énergétique de la force pure et informe. Les différences considérées seraient *à la fois* différences de lieux et différences de force. Si nous paraissons ici opposer une série à l'autre, c'est qu'à l'intérieur du système classique, nous voulons faire apparaître le privilège non critique simplement accordé, par un certain structuralisme, à l'autre série. Notre discours appartient irréductiblement au système des oppositions métaphysiques. On ne peut annoncer la rupture de cette appartenance que par une *certaine* organisation, un certain aménagement *stratégique* qui, à l'intérieur du champ et de ses pouvoirs propres, retournant contre lui ses propres *stratagèmes*, produise une *force de dislocation* se propageant à travers tout le système, le fissurant dans tous les sens et le *dé-limitant* de part en part.

("Our intention here is not, through the simple motions of balancing, equilibration or overturning, to oppose duration to space, quality to quantity, force to form, the depth of meaning or value to the surface of figures. Quite to the contrary. To counter this simple alternative, to counter the simple choice of one of the terms or one of the series against the other, we maintain that it is necessary to seek new concepts and new models, an *economy* escaping this system of metaphysical oppositions. This economy would not be an energetics of pure, shapeless force. The differences examined *simultaneously* would be differences of site and differences of force. If we appear to oppose one series to the other, it is because from within the classical system we wish to make apparent the noncritical privilege naïvely granted to the other series by a certain structuralism. Our discourse irreducibly belongs to the system of metaphysical oppositions. The break with this structure of belonging can be announced only through a *certain* organization, a certain *strategic* arrangement which, within the field of metaphysical opposition, uses the strengths of the field to turn its own stratagems against it, producing a force of dislocation that spreads itself throughout the entire system, fissuring it in every direction and thoroughly *delimiting* it."][4]

For Derrida, in "Force et signification," it is a matter of escaping metaphysical antinomies, of breaking with an endless dialectics of oppositions whose function is to close or round off an interpretation, to establish what from a logocentric system is a clear circumference of protocols and a decidable center of gravity for that circumference. Structuralism may be happy to engage binary oppositions, to consider systems within classical grids of symmetry, unity, and balance, as if those qualities were inherently part of a well-ordered theory and praxis. What interests Derrida is opposing by means of a strategic organization or arrangement (notice Derrida does not refer to chaos, annihilation, destruction, or culture assassination) a torsion from within metaphysics that serves to dislocate and fissure the coherence of a system, to delimit or break open the relays of metaphysical speculation. In doing so, however, *one does not exit metaphysics*, but stays on the margin, or limen, of metaphysical procedures, within the deconstruction and recuperation of terms like *origin, presence, trace, form,* and *force*. In that sense Alan Bass is not entirely justified in glossing the passage cited above in the following way: "According to Derrida, metaphysics can only be destroyed from within, by making its own language—which is the only language we have—work against it."⁵ The problem here is that Bass substitutes the word "destroyed" for "delimiting" or "fissuring." Geoffrey Hartman's reading of *Glas* in *Saving the Text* is far more accurate in positing the idea that the deconstructive act of realigning various series or registers does not result in a collapse or destruction of philosophy or literature, but in a "saving" of the text, the kind of "saving" Louis Martz sees at the beginning of *Lycidas* when he notes that "Yet once more..." is a phrase from the New Testament:

> Yet once more I shake not the earth only, but also heaven. And this word, Yet once more, signifieth the removing of those things that are shaken, as of things that are made, that those things which cannot be shaken may remain. [Heb. 12:25-27]

Or, to quote Derrida himself, "Quoi du reste aujourd'hui, pour nous, ici, maintenant, d'un Hegel?" ("Besides, what remains today, for us, here, now, of a Hegel?")⁶ That is, what is left? What is unshaken? What remains? What is saved (remaindered, treasured up, encrypted, exempted, rescued, salvaged, *Aufgehoben*, given salvation)? It is a question having to do with restitutions, a question that echoes into Goethe's *Faust* (Part 1) when the voice at the end of the drama cries out to Gretchen, "*Gerettet!*" ("Saved!"). Even in Derrida such a voice rattles forth, a scrap is saved, a remainder remains: the *gl* in *glas* perhaps, or Genet's vaseline tube, or the *gel* in Hegel. They are much the same, finally, and not necessarily to our surprise.

Thus Derrida's opening question on Hegel, "Quoi du reste aujourd'hui...?," or its echo in the Genet column, "Ce qui est resté d'un Rembrandt..." ("What has remained of a Rembrandt..."), sings however hoarsely in tune with Milton's "Yet once more..." These are more than just fortuitous affinities, but essential relations of great importance for the understanding of both Milton and Derrida. What is crucial is that we understand that Derrida provides a critical mode of access into what Macaulay calls the "debatable ground," that textual threshold which dialectically maneuvers textual registers or series out of alignment, imposes a contradictory crowbar or lever which produces a curious tilt in the operational devices of metaphysics. Not only *Glas* but Milton's *Lycidas, Paradise Lost, Samson Agonistes, Paradise Regained*, and the prose tracts strategically manage to oscillate between idealisms. If Derrida's *Glas* negotiates the idealism of Hegel with the sexual materialism of Genet, Milton's works too play off similar idealisms, as Macaulay noticed.

The following chapters will have to speak for themselves, and I only wish to remark now that if I have spoken mainly of Derrida as a critical mode of access to a study of inconsistencies which perplexed not only Samuel Johnson, Lord Macaulay, T. S. Eliot, but Christopher Ricks and other contemporary Miltonists, my study is not limited to an orthodox application of deconstruction. What is important to keep in mind is that no such orthodoxy is possible or in itself legitimate, for such an orthodoxy would only constitute a new formalism or academic dogma. Indeed, Jean-Luc Nancy points out in *Le discours de la syncope* that whenever one monumentalizes an index or vocabulary of subversive terms—an operation which goes into effect whenever critics find equivalences everywhere for philosophical or critical concepts, what amounts to so many practical applications—a "trans-substantiation" of even the most antilogocentric index will occur that results in a new concretization or fetishization: the replacement of one tyrannical doctrine by another. Nancy writes that such a "conversion" is "prescribed in the very economy of those initial discourses which advance such [deconstructive] indexes, and not only in the repetitions or pillagings of the epigones."[7] Thus the deconstructor is called upon to shift ground, mobilize an auto-critique, to engage in a *thanatopraxie* of writing.

And what is such a *thanatopraxie* but an economy of death, the production of a discourse which mourns and joyfully accepts the passing away of an antinomy: idealism-materialism, presence-absence, truth-falsehood, an opposition articulated in so many ways, recovering itself endlessly within a chain of repeated displacements? With *thanatopraxie* one is beyond the pleasure principle, that is, beyond aesthetics, certainty, and finality. With *thanatopraxie* there is no rest and no equilibrium; there is no peace or home. Deconstruction per se makes no sense in terms of anything absolute, as any sort of end to which a *thanatopraxie* might lead, but marks only the loss of stabilizing antinomies, of decidable certainties, of definite points of reference. However rigorous and determined the *thanatopraxie* may be to embrace a purifying holocaust, what critics of deconstruction call nihilism, it is a disillusioned and disillusioning embrace which knows that the holocaust always will hold back and renege, will never purify completely, that it will always save and restore something, even if it be but the letters *gl*——. For we are beyond the pleasure principle, the pleasures of presence *and* of absence. We are beyond the choice of life or death: the joy of living, the solace of dying. We are on Macaulay's debatable ground. The clapper in a bell is suspended and tolling the end of man and philosophy, but making us aware that even if it ends, it will not end, that we must, like the doomed figures in Beckett, go on, even if we cannot move any longer. And this is not a matter of choice, but of praxis, of *le glas*.

His ordinary rate of speech
In loftiness of sound was rich,
A Babylonish dialect,
Which learned pedants much affect.
It was a parti-colored dress
Of patched and piebald languages:
'Twas English cut on Greek and Latin,
Like fustian heretofore on satin.
It had an odd promiscuous tone,
As if he'd talked three parts in one;
Which made some think, when he did gabble,
They'd heard three laborers of Babel,
Or Cerberus himself pronounce
A leash of languages at once.

Samuel Butler, *Hudibras* (1678)

CHAPTER I

Milton and the *Thanatopraxie* of Writing

When T. S. Eliot attacks Milton's poetry in terms of a "dissociation of sensibility," he insists that poems like *Lycidas, Comus,* and *Paradise Lost* are examples of writing as *techne* (craft, artifice, sterility) and do not, as in the dramas of Shakespeare, make a firm commitment to *parousia* (presence), the living word. "Milton writes English like a dead language." The problem with Milton, according to Eliot, is that he severs signifier (word) from the signified (meaning, truth, presence) through the fabrication of an opaque style that effaces content and thereby anesthetizes the reader's feelings. In Eliot's words,

> A disadvantage of the rhetorical style appears to be, that a dislocation takes place, through the hypertrophy of the auditory imagination at the expense of the visual and tactile, so that the *inner meaning* is separated from the *surface*, and tends to become something occult, or at least without effect upon the reader until fully understood.

Shakespeare, unlike Milton, fuses surface and depth, and style and content and thereby composes a "living English" far closer to common sense and ordinary speech than Milton's or even Dryden's polished artificial phrases. In fact, it is Milton, according to Eliot, who is in large part responsible for the death of "living English," since he contaminates speech with music, "the auditory imagination." For Eliot, Milton's language is fallen because "the syntax is determined by the musical significance, by the auditory imagination, rather than by the attempt to follow actual speech or thought." Milton makes language into something abstract, stylish, and rhetorical and thereby violates the relationship between word (signifier) and meaning (signified), a relationship ideally preserved in ordinary speech, according to Eliot. Style is merely a surface and does nothing more than glorify the sound of words at the expense of content, spirit, the text's truth. Therefore, Eliot believes it is safe to view Milton's poetry as an "act of violence," a "perpetual sequence of original acts of lawlessness."[1]

Milton's transgression of what Eliot calls "actual speech" by the "auditory imagination," corrupted by book learning in general and rhetoric in particular, is very reminiscent of the kind of transgression that French poststructuralists address in terms of a writing that usurps or supplements voice. However much Eliot's opposition of the "auditory imagination" to "actual speech" appears to address merely a certain deafness to the colloquial in Milton, what underlies the criticism is actually quite akin to the "writing"–"voice" distinction which is so pronounced in a text like *De la grammatologie* of Jacques Derrida. For, as far as Eliot was concerned, Milton's auditory imagination is always already an internalized rhetoric or writing that is very much out of phase with natural speech, with an English consciousness which collectively embodies itself in spoken discourse. When Milton writes poetry, according to this way of thinking, he allows rhetoric or a bookish ear to transgress against actual speech and thus does violence to that English consciousness which internalizes itself in spoken discourse. In this way Eliot's objections adumbrate a critical distinction which poststructuralism takes up in the 1960s with its interest in those philosophers and critics who concern themselves with the manner in which "voice" (language as presence, spirit, consciousness, truth, speech) is usurped by "writing" (language as *techne*, material, tool, counterfeit, supplement), what amounts to a parricide conducted by the text against the symbolic father, the logos.[2] It is the slaying of content (spirit) by the style (the letter), and in the West this has always been a major concern to those critics who believe texts are holy relics, idols within which the gods reside. It is Milton's iconoclasm that Eliot attacks when he says that Milton writes a dead language and has virtually slain Shakespeare, a great poet of the living word, in the process (parricide). Milton's poetry transgresses English because it is a sterile production of words, a usurping of living texts written by the immortal poets, an entombment of living words within a catacomb of signs, such as *Paradise Lost*. What Eliot finds particularly disturbing is that Milton's dead language contaminates not only his own great epics but infects and sterilizes the poetry of his heirs, especially those in the eighteenth century. It seems that after Milton's original poetic sin, all poets discover themselves fallen and unable to return to the prelapsarian Shakespearean state.

Eliot's attack on Milton is intriguing not simply because it is a traditional attack on style or writing as a dead language that corrupts or poisons living speech but because it attacks a poet one would ordinarily suppose to be of Eliot's party, himself a poet who according to many readers appears to elevate speech above style, meaning above the word, truth above rhetoric. Yet this is not apparent, according to Eliot. Milton is not a poet of the logocentric, the theocentric book, but a poet who banishes the signified.[3] It is interesting that Eliot calls attention to Mallarmé as a poet in league with Milton, since Mallarmé has become in recent years the model poet of writing (*écriture*) from which presence has been banished, a writing that renders speech silent. Perhaps Eliot would have us ascribe Mallarmé's statement, "The poet's voice must be stilled and the initiative taken by the words themselves," to Milton. Just as Mallarmé signifies for modern French critics a linguistic crisis in which discourse is perceived as a heteroclite that cannot be enclosed within the fragile density of black marks on paper, but instead inhabits the white space between them, Milton signifies for Eliot a "dissociation of sensibility" arising from a linguistic crisis that similarly involves a discourse banished to the margins of writing, the elevation of the abstract *graphie*. According to Michel Foucault, "Mallarmé was constantly effacing himself from his own language, to the point of not wishing to figure in it except as an executant in a pure ceremony."[4] In other words, Mallarmé sought systematically to erase the voice, to create an "I" that is nothing more than a "shifter," or effect produced by writing.[5] Eliot accuses Milton of destroying the voice when he insisted Miltonic verse precludes "living English" and that Milton merely formed "what Butler called a *Babylonish dialect.*" This dialect is so didactic and allusive that it exists as a language outside of true communication, a ceremony from which the human has been excommunicated. Thus Eliot sees in Milton a firm connection with Mallarmé's belief that "thought consists of writing without pen and paper."[6] That is, Miltonic and Mallarméan language preempt the voice, the presence of the word, and opt for a Babylonish dialect, an agglutination of dead signs that are dispersed in the world only to be recollected within the poem. The origin of thought, language, speech, and poetry is not to be found within the imagination or within the elemental human drive to communicate, but is found scattered in the texts of others; it is a thought without an "I," a displaced thought Foucault has termed *la pensée du dehors*, thinking from without.[7]

Understandably, Eliot's modern existential concerns for the human finds this renunciation of the romantic *cogito* revolting. And, indeed, this accounts for Eliot's attack upon Milton as an unfeeling, unsympathetic man:

As a man, he is antipathetic. Either from the moralist's point of view, or from the theologian's point of view, or from the psychologist's point of view, or from that of the political philosopher, or judging by the ordinary standards of likableness in human beings, Milton is unsatisfactory.

Eliot, of course, assumes that Milton is an antihumanist and, even worse, an antipoet. Milton is a man "whose sensuousness, such as it was, has been withered early by book learning." The text, according to Eliot, has exterminated a great deal of what could have been the "human" in Milton, and its effect on future poets has been similar.[8]

Although one has to admit, as Miltonists often do, that Eliot's criticism is perverse and cranky, there is much to salvage from his attack, mainly the perception that Milton is, not a poet of presence, spirit, and idols, but an iconoclast who opposes such an orientation to the text. Eliot's vehement reaction to Milton at once discloses not only his own metaphysical prejudices but those of all critics who demand of poems the revelation of content, meaning, depth, or spirit, who think of poetry in terms of what Karl Marx would have termed fetishized objects. Eliot's negative criticism, then, not only points to the literary critic's own metaphysical assumptions but in doing so tells us much about Milton's decided antimetaphysical stance vis-à-vis the text. That critics like Eliot protest Milton's poems to the degree they do may be evidence in itself that the poetry is in some sense a violation of accepted norms, a transgression that ruptures the metaphysics of the book, a metaphysics which is the backbone of not only medieval scholasticism but Anglo-American formalism as well.[9] It is worth looking, therefore, into Milton's antimetaphysical, or iconoclastic, vision of what a text is or should be.

My working hypothesis for the essays that follow is that Milton does not accept the logocentric concept of the book, since he incorporates important resistances within his texts to prevent the word from acceding to an idolatrous notion of the Word, what Eliot would have considered the "living text." For Milton, Eliot's major concern that an English poet should not violate the English language with Latinate syntax, that he should not pollute the natural springs of his mother tongue with an artificial *techne,* is not as important as the risks involved in composing a text that appears to accede to voice, that ambitiously lays claim to the signified. We must never forget that Milton, unlike Eliot, was very much aware that, in using religious material in his poetry and prose, he would run the risk of appearing to duplicate the concept of a scripture in which the word incarnates spirit. Harold Bloom actually accuses Milton of challenging the authority of the incarnate word when he insists in *A Map of Misreading* that Milton did such an impressive rewriting of the texts of his great precursors (Homer, Virgil, Lucretius, Ovid, Dante, Tasso, and Spenser) that he fashioned a book to end all books: *Paradise Lost*. According to Bloom, "The ultimate ambitions of *Paradise Lost* gave Milton the problem of expanding Scripture without distorting the Word of God."[10] Since Milton was one who, in Bloom's opinion, "would not sunder spirit from matter," we can only assume that, for Bloom, Milton's ambition was to compose a book that would accede to the notion of scripture as the incarnate text, that he even wanted to expand the Word, without distorting it. Bloom insists that Milton attempted to do this through "transumptive allusion," a term that reminds one of alchemy, since Bloom uses it to define the way in which Milton "tropes on tropes" in order to turn the dross of Homer and Virgil, their fallen texts, into the gold of the expanded Word, the incarnate text, *Paradise Lost*.

But my argument is that Milton's texts carry insurance against such an arrogant alchemical project, that Milton's texts deconstruct themselves in order to ensure that they will not accede to this notion of scripture. In Milton, the linguistic horizon of the incarnate word, the point at which signified and signifier become one, is always undermined, sacrificed by script (*Écriture* by *écriture*, voice by writing); and it is this sacrifice or cutting off (which in later chapters I refer to as symbolic castration, death, *Allegorie, thanatopraxie*) that gives rise to an iconoclastic ideal of a true scripture that is not an idol or incarnate word, but rather a word divested of the divine, differed and deferred from the signified.[11]

This is not to suggest, however, that Milton simply rejects the notion of the incarnate word (presence) for the hollow signifier (absence), as Eliot would have it when he refers to Mallarmé as a poet in league with Milton, but that Milton locates his text within the space of the poet's "uncouthness," an "uncouthness" such as that of the swain in *Lycidas*, who is not merely "rude," but "estranged," "alien," "cut off," "distanced." It is in this uncouth space, or *béance*, between the word as presence (voice) and the word as hollow signifier (writing) that enlightenment occurs. It is within this threshold that the linguistic ideology in which matter and spirit are one and the ideology that maintains they are radically split apart are at once confused and separated. It is here that Milton displays his will to power, that he develops the Derridean "POTENCE du texte," which signifies by way of an intralingual pun at once the text as gallows ("POTENCE" as "gallows, decapitation, cutting, death") and as power or life ("POTENCE" as "erection, potency").[12]

In Jacques Derrida's *Glas* the strategy, or wager, that maintains the "double scene of writing" or "POTENCE" (potency / gallows) is *thanatopraxie:* "technique de la pompe funèbre," "travail de deuil" ("technics of funereal pomp," "the work of mourning"), and at the same time, "appropriation du plus ou moins de perte, une opération *classique*" ("appropriation of more or less a loss or lack, a *classical* operation"). Moreover, "ce travail de deuil *s'appelle*—glas" ("this work of mourning is *called*—glas"). But if this work of mourning calls itself, voices itself *glas*, the knell of death, the sound of that which cannot speak, cannot voice itself, it does so because such a work of mourning rides the margin of the "POTENCE du texte," that threshold between presence and absence, a threshold where the difference between the two is never established though always maintained. Lastly, and this is most important: "Le glas est d'abord (*clas, chiasso, classum, classicum*) le signal d'un trompette destiné à *appeler* (*calare*), convoquer, rassembler en tant que telle, une *classe* du peuple romain. Il y a donc du glas dans la littérature classique, mais aussi dans la lutte des classes:

classe." ("The death knell is first and foremost (*victory bells; clatter; fleet; clarion call, highest class of Romans*) the signal of a trumpet destined to call (*convoke*), summon, convene, assemble as such, a class of Roman people. There is then a death knell in classical literature, but also in the struggle of classes: *class*.")[13]

In the studies of Milton that follow, I take up this Derridean *Trauermotiv*, which is well developed in the "littérature classique" of *Paradise Lost, Lycidas, Samson Agonistes, Paradise Regained*, and so on. It is more than simply a motif, of course, but a motive, a strategy, resulting in "acts of violence" that T. S. Eliot would be most likely to call "lawless," for *thanatopraxie* is a calculated undermining of the ideology of the text as onto-encyclopedic book or scripture. Indeed, *thanatopraxie* produces a colossal or classical writing that can metaphorically be represented in terms of a Philistine temple crashing in upon the author of its destruction, a blinded, unmanned Samson who has forgotten the language of priests and has been condemned to speak the language of woman. Thus the emblem of my project: an iconoclast in the metaphysical house of language. Here the iconoclast is Samson, but in other instances it is Eve, a rude or uncouth swain, Christ, the blind Milton. They are all uncouth (in the sense of humble, but also estranged, cut off) practicers of iconoclasm, an iconoclasm predicated on the deconstruction of the ideology of text as presence.

My project takes a poststructuralist orientation whose task will be to facilitate a kind of peculiar immigration, the immigration of an English poet of the seventeenth century onto twentieth-century French and German critical soil. In itself this may seem a bit surreal, and the reader may well ask why one ought to allow Milton's classically oriented texts, in themselves so innocent of Hegel, Nietzsche, Freud, Bataille, but also of Benjamin, Lacan, Derrida, and Kristeva, to get mixed up with this strange crowd of modern and postmodern critical troublemakers, this strange group which has nothing in common historically with John Milton.

Although I feel the essays justify themselves, I do wish openly to acknowledge this kind of question by saying that Eliot was essentially correct when he noticed that Milton was, not so much an English poet, simply, but a man of letters who participates in the mainstream of European humanism and, as we shall see, antihumanism. He is not merely a poet, therefore, but a cosmopolitan poet-philosopher and politician, a figure who enters European letters at a very critical time when scholasticism was breaking down, when what Walter Benjamin called the symbolic was being undermined, perhaps even being deconstructed in the full sense of Derrida's term, by allegory. Milton's Protestantism does not simply revise bits and pieces of Roman Catholicism, but, I think, radically transforms theological tradition, and one of the ways he does this is by taking up a very Hebraic position in regard to Western metaphysics. Here Derrida's allusion to *classe* is not to be overlooked, for Milton's classical texts do carry a very strong political charge that relates to the issue of class, to the issue of attacking theological hierarchy both in the ideological and the political-ecclesiastical senses. In short, Milton's perspective on metaphysics is compatible (though not identical by any means) with that of the poststructuralists, particularly with that of Derrida, who, as we know, fashions a mode of philosophical or critical discourse not available to Milton, which, I feel, helps to expose those strata in Milton's texts of radical opposition to metaphysics that formalism, itself a replica of metaphysics, is unable to illuminate.

As we have already noticed, Eliot's criticisms of Milton point to some kind of foreign orientation that is suspicious of formalism, but point also to a kind of English provincialism that fails to recognize Milton's important place in an essentially Latinate tradition in which French philosophy, and here again Derrida is important, is itself very much engaged. Like Milton, Derrida and others in the poststructuralist movement are not only adamant about working within a highly classical tradition (Heraclitus, Empedocles, Plato, Aristotle, Lucretius) but write in a formal, philosophical style that is purified of the gratuitous and the vernacular.[14] Even in a work like *Glas,* in which there is much slang, or in much of Genet's vernacular, there is an artistic or philosophical working over of such a vernacular (what really amounts to lewd language) so that it becomes monumentalized, recuperated within a baroque or even mannerist rhetoric whose affectations (that is, elevated or idiosyncratic diction, literary or philosophical sentences rather than the imitation of spoken discourse, extended metaphors, highly abstruse allusion, copious quotation) distinguish a text as unnatural, artificial, elevated, sublime, classical. Moreover, there is compatibility between Milton and writers like Hegel, Nietzsche, Benjamin, and again Derrida in that they are all crossing the borders between philosophy, politics, and literature, and consciously so. That too is part of a Latinate perspective in which philosophy is at once stylistically monumentalized, made colossal, on a literary or aesthetic level which a classicist would probably call the rhetorical.[15] Thus Milton's *Areopagitica,* to take but a famous example, constitutes a radical crossing between politics, philosophy, history, literature, and (one has to admit) propaganda, and it is this kind of radical, classical grafting that Derrida and also Nietzsche, Marx, Bataille, Benjamin, and Lacan set up in their texts through their elevated styles. So in this sense one can with good conscience begin to consider Milton as an important figure within a cosmopolitan group of thinkers, a classical line, if you will, that does not easily absorb a Shakespeare, a Wordsworth, a Tennyson, or even an Eliot or a Yeats.

  In other words, I do not allow just any other English poet to occupy the kind of critical arena that I accord to Milton, though figures like Coleridge, Shelley, Joyce, Pynchon, and Ashbery can conceivably merit such approaches. What I wish to convey is the position that, exceptions aside, one cannot simply take any English poet and turn the poststructuralist critical machine loose on him or her in good faith, a point Marjorie Perloff has recently made.[16] For us Milton will be considered a special case, particularly since he is such a monumental figure, ranking in my estimation with Hegel and Marx. Milton escapes the gins and nets of easy English formalism and historicism, because he is working within philosophical and metaphysical traditions, but attempting, like a Hegel, a Marx, or a Nietzsche, to do something violent to this tradition, to affect it, with the strategic use of a radical style whose hardness has the purpose of puncturing or tearing the resistant, tough discourse that we know as Western metaphysics and that Milton knew as scholasticism and classicism. How Milton, like Heidegger and Derrida, no less than Nietzsche, worked to compose a classical style, a colossal writing, that turns upon classicism's ideology of the onto-encyclopedic book (that is, Homeric epic) is the main issue in these studies on Milton's oeuvre, studies that develop the Derridean *Trauermotiv* or *thanatopraxie* from various perspectives in order to show how Milton makes this peculiar classical turn.

Was da in Trümmern abgeschlagen liegt, das hochbedeutende Fragment, das Bruchstück: es ist die edelste Materie der barocken Schöpfung.

("That which lies here in ruins, the highly significant fragment, the remnant, is, in fact, the finest material in baroque creation.")

Walter Benjamin, *Ursprung des deutschen Trauerspiels*, translated by John Osborne

CHAPTER 2

Milton's Epic *Trauerspiel*

I

In *Ursprung des deutschen Trauerspiels,* Walter Benjamin writes, "Während im Symbol mit der Verklärung des Unterganges das transfigurierte Antlitz der Natur im Lichte der Erlösung flüchtig sich offenbart, liegt in der Allegorie die *facies hippocratica* der Geschichte als erstarrte Urlandschaft dem Betrachter vor Augen." ("Whereas in the symbol destruction is idealized and the transfigured face of nature is fleetingly revealed in the light of redemption, in allegory the observer is confronted with the *facies hippocratica* of history as a petrified, primordial landscape.")[1] It is from passages like this that much of Paul de Man's essay, "The Rhetoric of Temporality," is grounded, an essay that is very concerned with allegorical and symbolic landscapes and advances the thesis, essentially Benjamin's, that romanticism is heavily indebted to allegory and that its authentic voice, when it occurs, speaks forth out of the distance, out of the absence or space of the allegorical sign's *Dar-Stellung* ("re-presentation").[2] Unlike de Man, however, Benjamin is far more adamant about stressing the relationship of allegorical *Bedeutung* ("meaning") with *Tod*, ("death"), and in proximity to the passage from *Ursprung* above, Benjamin calls the *Antlitz* ("face") of allegory a *Totenkopf* ("death's head"). For Benjamin,

Das ist der Kern der allegorischen Betrachtung, der barocken, weltlichen Exposition der Geschichte als Leidensgeschichte der

24 Milton's Epic *Trauerspiel*

Welt; bedeutend ist sie nur in den Stationen ihres Verfalls. Soviel Bedeutung, soviel Todverfallenheit, weil am tiefsten der Tod die zackige Demarkationslinie zwischen Physis und Bedeutung eingräbt.[3]

("This is the kernel of allegorical reflection, of the baroque, worldly exposition of history as passion of the world; its significance exists only in the stations of its decay [fall, decline, ruin, decadence]. So much meaning, so much falling into death, because at the nadir of death the jagged demarcation line between *physis* and meaning buries itself.")

For Benjamin, then, meaning is nothing but the condition of its own fall, thus the formula: so much meaning, so much falling into death. But the last phrase is by far the darkest: "because at the nadir of death the jagged demarcation line between *physis* and meaning buries itself."

Even Paul de Man, who is sensitive to the crisis of language Benjamin expresses in the *Ursprung des deutschen Trauerspiels*, steers away from Benjamin's deeper sounding and from the *Barock* as well. He shifts, instead, to Hans Georg Gadamer, whose *Wahrheit und Methode* also considers the conflict of symbol and allegory in the romantic period, but, unlike Benjamin, without the slightest unease, not the merest hint that asserting the primacy of allegory not only signifies but is "so much falling into death."

It is in Milton, however, that Benjamin would have found a closer ally, not only because Milton was a baroque poet but because he was a writer who, I think, experienced Benjamin's deeper soundings, who perceived that jagged line between *physis* and meaning, that absence (death) that marks one's very being. In book 2 of *Paradise Lost* Milton uses an extended allegorical technique that has appeared to some critics to be uncharacteristic of the poem as a whole; but we will see that, in fact, this "allegorical set piece," as Addison preferred to think of it, is typical of a style that one finds throughout much of Milton's epic, a style situated within the problematic of death, of what Benjamin refers to as the *Totenkopf*. Just as the "allegorical set piece" in book

2 of *Paradise Lost* situates itself metapoetically within the problematic of language's relation to the economy of a fall, of death, of evil, of sin, many other sections of *Paradise Lost* similarly account for themselves in terms of what I call an allegorical style, because they too are inscribed within the problematic of death, loss, fall, and mourning.

I am, of course, extending and redefining the term *allegory* in such a way that allegory no longer means simply a narrative that consists of extended metaphors, of personified abstractions, but points, more generally, to a conception of language, a style that is adamantly antimetaphysical, that has no pretensions of any natural or any stable bonds between signifier and signified. I wish to use Benjamin's notion of *Allegorie* in order to provide access to a Miltonic conception of discourse that inscribes itself within the problematic of loss and death and in so doing sacrifices or slays itself by cutting itself off from what one might term "spirit." What one has, in short, is a script that is metaphorically dead, that is more like what Paul might have termed the letter rather than what he might have called the spirit. In this sense Milton is breaking away from the Spenserian notion of allegory in which the text presents itself as a veil within which is wrapped a truth or presence that only a few readers, experienced or initiated in a peculiar hermeneutical activity, can glimpse. Such allegorical texts are perceived as houses of being and, indeed, come close in spirit to a kind of Heideggerian notion of language as that which points to the proximity or relation of being to *Dasein*, a proximity which demands a hermeneutical deciphering.

Of course, at the end of the sixteenth century the Spenserian attitude towards allegory, one Spenser inherits from Pico della Mirandola as well as from well-known medieval and Roman sources, is challenged by critics who see largely an orational purpose to writing, who assume texts must aspire to voice and immediate or unmediated disclosure to an audience. Whereas the allegorical text can only be disclosed to a select few, oratory can be heard and understood by many. George Puttenham, Ben Jonson, and Thomas Wilson admonish those who write in dark conceits, for, as Jonson states, "the chief virtue of a style is perspicuity, and nothing so vicious in it, as to need an Interpreter."[4] Milton's use of *Allegorie* (versus *allegory*) is an inherent critique of Neoplatonic assumptions about allegory and the Jonsonian bias towards unmediated expression, for both schools of thought presuppose a metaphysics of language grounded in the living presence of a signified. Milton opposes such metaphysical conceptions, and precisely by introducing a script that is, not alive, but dead, one that is saturated with the problematic of sacrifice and loss. Thus Milton can be conceived of as not simply a Renaissance poet writing a continuous dark conceit but as a baroque poet in Benjamin's sense who is fully aware of how allegory contemplates itself as death and not as life (spirit).

Indeed, the story, or *Leidensgeschichte*, that Sin recounts to Satan, who has conveniently forgotten his daughter, is a metapoetic history about the origin of language as allegory. The story begins when Sin tells Satan that he gave birth to her parthenogenically, and that her presence in heaven was taken to be an emblem or a sign *for* something, a sign that the angels cannot quite make out at first. Sin tells Satan that she was taken as a "Sign portentous," a sign that excites wonder and amazement before that which is beautiful, but also possibly monstrous, since *portentous* is an adjective that can be used to describe one's awe before either magnificent or terrible things.[5] In the context of Sin as the "Sign portentous," this ambivalence not only points to the angels' initial bewilderment but implicitly points also to their eventual conflict over Sin, for great legions of angels will fight in her behalf, because to them she is wondrous and beautiful, while others will fight to expel her and the rest of Satan's allies; to them she is clearly awful and perverse. And it is here that one can already see the connection between the use of the word *portentous* describing awe before the magnificent and the terrible with the use of *portentous* to mean forecasting a calamitous event.[6] But what has to be stressed is that metapoetically the phrase "Sign portentous" casts a bad light upon the concept of the sign itself, upon the sign as something unstable or duplicitous, since it is at once attractive and repulsive, beautiful and terrible. That this is itself a judgment upon allegory will become, I think, clear shortly.

What is evident to most of the angels when they first see Sin is that if she is a sign, she is a sign *for* Satan. She was, she says to him, "Likest to thee in shape and count'nance bright, / Then shining heav'nly fair, a Goddess arm'd / Out of thy head I sprung" (2.756–58). She is the expression of Satan, a sign that resembles or re-presents him as a simulacrum. And it is because of this resemblance that "back they [the host] recoil'd afraid / At first, and call'd me *Sin*, and for a Sign / Portentous held me"; and yet, "familiar grown / I pleas'd" (2.759–62). That is, if at first Sin appears to the angels as a grotesque or strange simulacrum, a bad metaphor, she becomes, like all bad metaphors, acceptable with use, with familiarity. Like an allegorical figure, Sin at first displeases with her portentous similitude, her disparity with the real, in this case, the real angels, but in time is taken for this real; she is a counterfeit that is accepted as fiat.

The angels recoil because they recognize at first that beautiful though Sin may be, she is, after all, but a phantom proxy, and not a spirit; she has no being, only similitude. Satan's own anxiety over this is clear when he demonstrates his sudden desire to infuse Sin with his own seed, to inseminate her with a Satanic being that will prove to all that Sin is really a spirit, that she has being and that Satan, consequently, has the power to create life. Speaking to Satan, Sin says that she attracted the most adverse of angels, but

> thee chiefly, who full oft
> Thyself in me thy perfect image viewing
> Becam'st enamor'd, and such joy thou took'st
> With me in secret, that my womb conceiv'd
> A growing burden. [2.763–67]

Of course, the "growing burden" is not the burden of being, but the burden of a lack of being, "Death," and it is as the mother of Death that the sign now reveals itself to the reader. Unlike God's Son or living Word, Satan's daughter, the sign pregnant with Death, is merely a hollow phantom, a perverse similitude, a counterfeit. What becomes clear in the lines that follow is that Satan's narcissism, his desire to recreate himself in doubles, to repeat himself in portentous signs, does not result in a writing that resembles its author, but like an allegorical text, represents or repeats him in the most grotesque and hideous of characters: Sin and Death. Indeed, the fallen Satan cannot even recognize their allegorical connection to him and has to ask of Sin, "What thing thou art, thus double-form'd, and why / In this infernal Vale first met thou call'st / Me Father, and that Phantasm call'st my Son?" (2.741–43). Here the characters, or figures, of Sin and Death are to be understood not simply as the personages of Sin and Death but as the signs, the characters in which Satan's similitudes, or doubles, are expressed or written out. And Sin even reminds Satan of this double notion of character or figure when she calls Satan, "my Father, thou my Author" (2.864). Metapoetically, Sin is referring to herself and Death as not simply grotesque figures whose Father is Satan but as signs, characters who are defaced, fallen, and dead because they are the progeny of a perverted author, *of an allegorist.*

The connection between death and allegory is made most evident in the emblem that introduces us to Milton's extended allegory in book 2. We find Sin emblematically figured forth much as we might expect if this description were painted in the style of the most mannerist or baroque of painters, a style that Milton already hints is essentially a technics, a representation pregnant with death.

> Before the Gates there sat
> On either side a formidable shape;
> The one seem'd Woman to the waist, and fair,
> But ended foul in many a scaly fold

Milton's Epic *Trauerspiel* 29

> Voluminous and vast, a Serpent arm'd
> With mortal sting: about her middle round
> A cry of Hell Hounds never ceasing bark'd
> With wide *Cerberean* mouths full loud, and rung
> A hideous Peal: yet, when they list, would creep,
> If aught disturb'd thir noise, into her womb,
> And kennel there, yet there still bark'd and howl'd
> Within unseen. [2.648–59]

Not until many lines later does Sin explain that these hellhounds are the incestuous progeny brought forth by Sin as a consequence of her rape by her first offspring, Death. What Sin adds later is that the very identification of *meaning* of Death creates a "resounding" that brings about a growth or development of infernal signification, for the Mother, or sign, of Death is suddenly forced to suffer the "repetition" of her sin, the incestuous act out of which allegory is born.

> I fled, and cri'd out *Death*;
> Hell trembl'd at the hideous Name, and sigh'd
> From all her Caves, and back resounded *Death*.
> I fled, but he pursu'd (though more, it seems,
> Inflam'd with lust than rage) and swifter far,
> Mee overtook his mother all dismay'd,
> And in embraces forcible and foul
> Ingend'ring with me, of that rape begot
> These yelling Monsters that with ceaseless cry
> Surround me, as thou saw'st, hourly conceiv'd
> And hourly born, with sorrow infinite. [2.787–97]

What Satan saw, of course, is the emblematic portrait of Sin with her hellish brood at the gates of hell, the description quoted above, but what Sin explains to him here is that this emblem parodies, in terms of the most grotesque of allegories, Sin's own rape at the hands of Satan in heaven, a rape now repeated eternally in hell as Death, the son, takes over the father's role. Metapoetically, this repetition is the continuation of Satan's allegorical expression of himself, an expression that leads to doubles who re-present, but do not look like, their models, an expression that leads to doubles that even the fallen Satan cannot recognize without Sin's full allegorical exegesis.

Indeed, the emblem of Sin at the gates of hell only becomes intelligible to us as an extended metaphor or allegory, once we overhear Sin explaining to Satan that what he has seen is the very mode of production of allegory itself, not allegory as static picture, but allegory as a dynamic repetition automaton, a grotesque return to the primal scene in heaven in which Satan inseminates his double with his own sterile seed, this anti-logos. What we find in the emblem whose formalized contours appear only too sharp is in actuality, then, not merely a static representation, a symbolic scene that resembles the found condition of our being in sin at that moment we are facing death, but what Gilles Deleuze calls a "literary machine," the very productivity of language whose meaning is but a function of that productivity, of what in Milton is the productivity or reproductivity of technics (death) and not being (logos).[7] If Christ (Logos) is the manifestation of a true and pure resemblance as the living Word, which is not metaphorical, not different from that which it signifies, and yet still a word or sign for a signified, technics is the anti-logos, the making of a daughter, the literary machine, whose very productivity is perverse: allegorical in mode. What one has is not pure resemblance, but pure counterfeit.

This should alert us to the fact that the emblem as Milton uses it is breaking with emblem tradition in the Renaissance, a tradition that attempts, as Benjamin points out, to fuse the artistic influence of Greece with the mystical or hermetic influences of what was believed to be a long Egyptian tradition. That is to say, Milton is opposing the emblem as an allegorical portrait that supposedly contains, as a Henry Reynolds or Marsilio Ficino would have insisted, a sort of enigma, a single truth, and attacks this mystical notion of the emblem or ornate hieroglyph with the machinery of allegoresis as an economics of death. Indeed, Milton forces the reader to violate the contours of a static emblem at that moment he suggests through the mouth of Sin (violation, transgression) that what Satan is watching is, not part of a self-contained totality, but merely a repetition of something that does not mean latently within the emblem (that is, a truth different from and hidden in the emblem), simply a repetition of the machinery of counterfeiting, of allegory in terms of a prior scene that is only a repetition of a scene before that. What is important to recognize is that it is this mechanics of repetition, of the allegorical machine, that allows Satan and the reader to make allegorical sense out of the emblem, not any transcendental signified, not any hidden logos or truth.

If there is any truth or signified to be found in the allegorical machine, it can only be named in terms of process: narcissism, repetition, counterfeiting. But what we are talking about here is a truth, not in the sense of a delimited field or object, but in terms of truth as an antilogical counterplot. That is, Satan's narcissism, although it appears to originate with the birth of Sin, is really a process that has gone on long before even that moment, a counterplot hatched in Satan's mind at a point of origin that, like a limit in calculus, can only be projected, but never actually reached. What the emblem that introduced us to the allegory of Sin and Death reveals is not, therefore, *the* origin of an allegorical moment, that moment in which Sin springs from the head of Satan like Athena, but *an* origin, *a* moment in a chain of moments that regresses infinitely into the past and looks forward, is a portent for, an infinite progress into the future. Now this view of the emblematic picture and of the allegory in general in book 2 contradicts the usual assumption that an allegory must ultimately have a transcendental meaning, a thing that it points to, for Milton opposes to a terminal meaning, a "machine of replication," a "literary machine," as Deleuze would have it, whose meaning is its process, its mode of literary productivity. What we are forced to look for is, not something within the allegory that is represented, not sin, not death, not evil, not the Fall, but allegory itself, language as technics. That this process of language, this literary machine, is itself a machine of replication that is antitotalitarian, and from a Renaissance perspective antiallegorical, is quite significant.

But "antiallegorical" now means not simply what one might expect; for it is not so much an attack on allegory as an artificial technics, as a repetition automaton, as an attack also on allegory as emblem, as *Göttersymbol, parousia,* logos. Although Miltonists have been perfectly correct in assuming that Milton puts medieval allegoresis in hell in order to discredit it as a genre, they have not shown to what degree one finds here a deconstructive activity in which two kinds of allegory are at work, in which an allegory as repetition automaton explodes from within the presentation of allegory as emblem or hieroglyph, explodes the use of allegory as mode of symbolicity in which enigmatic truths are supposed to reside, as in that used by Dante, the church fathers, Gower. This deconstructive activity does not result in any *Aufhebung* in the Hegelian sense, a supremacy of allegory as automaton, as technics (the mode of allegory responsible for the fall of Satan), but in a double collapse in which the allegory-machine destroys the emblem and in doing so only asserts its own futility as repetition compulsion, or *thanatos* in Freud's sense.

What one has, then, is a *thanatopraxie* of writing, the praxis of death, or, more accurately, the death drive, itself a repetition compulsion, which represents itself by means of the Deleuzian literary or writing machine. *Thanatopraxie,* however, is a Derridean marker, and it is appropriate to mention it here, because Satan's allegorical technics, that praxis of writing which has no origin, is already a praxis of mourning, a praxis concerning loss. Satan, as we shall see, is the Freudian melancholic who cannot bear to accept any kind of absence and therefore introjects a presence (an imago) in order to supplement the loss he cannot bear. To exist in heaven, Satan believes, is to exist in a condition of being-without-something. It is to lack power, or in psychological terms, it is to be symbolically castrated, to have some kind of penis envy. Thus one has to make up for that which is missing, which is to recognize at the center of one's being a condition of death that has to be repaired, and Sin is precisely that supplementary recuperation, that symbolic phallus which denies what the melancholic obsessively considers: absence, lack, castration, powerlessness, and death.

Sin is part of a praxis of mourning, a *thanatopraxie*, in that she is the introjected imago, a kind of lost beloved (or presence divine) whom the melancholic is always disposed to project, to place before him, to represent in order to prove that there is no lack, that one is not castrated, that one possesses the symbolic phallus. It is, finally, to deny the Father whose presence always ensures that there is absence for all those who do not occupy his position as divine patriarch. It is, finally, to make oneself whole, complete, fully present, to deny one's imperfection vis à vis a totality. Ironically, the defense against lack or death is precisely a *Dar-Stellung* that Benjamin already recognized to be a slippage into the realm of the dead, a "Geschichte als erstarrte Urlandschaft" ("a story or history as frozen or torpid primordial landscape"). It is to discover that the re-presentation compulsion is a trap, a *mise en abyme*, or pit or hell, of infinite progress and regress, a chasm of illusions, which in *Paradise Lost* constitutes *le glas*, but also manifests itself in terms of *classe*, in the deconstruction of classical symbolic production and in the construction of class differences, of what in Benjamin is talked about in terms of the dialectic of history which allegory or *Trauerspiel* puts before us. Thus the *thanatopraxie* of writing takes us from pure being to signification, *Geschichte, glas / classe.*

II

But if allegory can be construed as a *thanatopraxie* of writing in book 2 of *Paradise Lost,* in the books following the Fall one can argue that Milton uses allegory in order to show us how to grieve properly; that is, he employs allegory as a mechanism to achieve what Freud calls the work of mourning: *Trauerarbeit*. And this too is *thanatopraxie*. In short, if allegory can be said to be a death drive or repetition compulsion that precludes the fulfillment of absolute knowledge and its ontological brood (truth, presence, being, signified), it can also be seen as the means by which the sorrow that accompanies the loss of origins and truth is recathected by the work of mourning, a work that is nothing less than a *Trauer-Spiel*.

Our advance is twofold. First, we must take up the Freudian notion of mourning (*Trauer*) in *Mourning and Melancholia* and show its work in *Paradise Lost,* and second, we must show how that work is essentially bound to the question of allegory and to the whole tradition Benjamin outlines in *Ursprung des deutschen Trauerspiels:* the funeral pageant, or play of mourning.

In *Mourning and Melancholia* Freud considers the reaction to the loss of the beloved in terms of how subjects substitute new love objects for old ones that have passed away. The melancholic subject, Freud says, internalizes the loss in such a way that the ego itself becomes the representation of the lost object:

But the free libido was not displaced on to another object; it was withdrawn into the ego. There, however, it was not employed in any unspecified way, but served to establish an identification of the ego with the abandoned object. Thus the shadow of the object fell upon the ego, and the latter could henceforth be judged by a special agency, as though it were an object, the forsaken object. In this way an object-loss was transformed into an ego loss and the conflict between the ego and the loved person into a cleavage between the critical activity of the ego and the ego as altered by identification.[8]

For the melancholic subject, the loss that occurs is either the result of outright rejection by the beloved, a rejection possibly triggered by the subject's own ambivalent feelings towards the beloved, as is often true in instances of divorce, or the loss interpreted as rejection of the subject, as in the case of death. In any event, the melancholic reaction to loss results in a narcissistic economy in which lover and beloved work out their love-hate relationship within the locus of the ego itself. Freud perceives this work in terms of denigration, or the process by which the subject is willing to accuse and humiliate himself, to denigrate himself openly before others. What is really happening, according to Freud, is that the subject is really accusing the beloved for whom his ego is standing in.

Mourning, in contrast, is a labor of recathecting, of slowly abandoning the illusion that the beloved is still there and turning one's libido towards another person or love object. Unlike the melancholic subject, the person who mourns does not have to cope with rejection, for the beloved has, through no fault of the subject, passed away. Here the libido does not have to withdraw for protection into the ego, but simply has, through the work of mourning, to redirect itself. "The fact is . . . that when the work of mourning is completed the ego becomes free and uninhibited again."[9] That is to say, the attachment between subject and beloved has been dissolved in such a way that the ego does not feel responsible for the dissolution or victimized by it.

The thematic of object loss, of course, is only too clearly a major concern, perhaps even the major concern, of *Paradise Lost*, and not only because *Paradise Lost* is a poem about the Fall, about Adam's reluctance to abandon Eve, about Satan's expulsion from heaven, about man's forfeit of his eternal life and his divine image, but because the thematic of object loss concerns the question of language itself. If T. S. Eliot called Milton a writer of a dead language, he did so because he recognized that *Paradise Lost* is a work of mourning and, it must be admitted, a work of melancholia as well. That these works have a bearing on the relationship of signified and signifier, that they determine an allegorical work or mode of literary productivity that can be summarized in Benjamin's phrase, "soviel Bedeutung, soviel Todverfallenheit," will become clearer as we proceed. But already one can see how

the economy of loss as expressed in Miltonic words—
"death," "expulsion," "erasure," "trace," "fall," "blank"—
forms a table of rather classical signs that ensures at least on
the thematic level the question of serious rupture is
broached.

Sown into the seams (semes) of *Paradise Lost*, the signs of
loss ensure that the work of mourning will take place, that
there will be a *Trauerspiel*. It is Satan who notices that the
lost host are sown into the barren region of hell:

> Princes, Potentates,
> Warriors, the Flow'r of Heav'n, once yours, now lost,
> If such astonishment as this can seize
> Eternal spirits; or have ye chos'n this place
> After the toil of Battle to repose
> Your wearied virtue, for the ease you find
> To slumber here, as in the Vales of Heav'n? [1.315–21]

It is as if the apostrophes signify cutting, loss, as if the
flowers are but "Flow'r," and heaven is similarly rent:
"Heav'n." Even choice carries its own tear as if to choose is
to fall, as if the devils have really chosen to inhabit this
place of doom, have chosen to have their names erased
("ras'd" [1.362]) from the books of life.

Satan's work, of course, is initially meant to effect mourning. If heaven is lost, Satan wishes, not to lament its passing away, but to affirm joyously the landscape of hell and in that manner recathect his passion for a new love object. That this attempt to mourn is quickly transformed into the work of a melancholic is only to be expected, since the new love object, hell, is not exactly an object, not exactly a something that can be appropriated. Rather, it is a lack, a no-thing. More importantly, it is clear that Satan is essentially a narcissist and therefore prone to melancholy in the Freudian sense. Thus he will boast:

> Hail horrors, hail
> Infernal world, and thou profoundest Hell

> Receive thy new Possessor: One who brings
> A mind not to be chang'd by Place or Time.
> The mind is its own place, and in itself
> Can make a Heav'n of Hell, a Hell of Heav'n.
> [1.250-55]

Here Satan, as we mentioned earlier, is internalizing loss and performing the work of melancholy, for he allows the mind to make an identification with that which has rejected him, heaven, and actually goes so far as to say that there is nothing else but this identification. Yet, if it is clear that the mind can make a heaven of hell, can recuperate the loss of the holy landscape, it is also clear that Satan reserves great hostility towards this heaven, this mind. That is to say, a hell can be made of heaven; the subject (loss) can denigrate its ego (the love object which has passed out of sight). This is no place to psychoanalyze Satan, of course, and even if one had the space, it should be undesirable to reduce a character as rich as Satan to a Freudian disorder. All I wish to demonstrate here is that this work is founded upon narcissism, or what we have already termed sin.

It should already be clear in terms of the contexts of the passage we have been discussing that integral with the work of melancholy is the work of allegoresis whose narcissism has been the focus of section 1 of this chapter. If Sin and Death recount the birth of allegory through their reactions to the loss that has taken place, the fall from heaven, Satan opens the way for allegory when he asserts his solipsistic creed that the mind is its own place, that things are whatever you decide they are, that signifier and signified no longer have a special relationship. Again, the passage from book 10 in which the devils undergo theriomorphosis is not only a reaction to the problematic of loss but is a very allegorical passage, perhaps even, as A. J. A. Waldock says, a "cartoon scene." The reason such a scene is merited here, I suggest, is that Milton appears to make a connection between the work of melancholy, that deviant reaction to loss, and the repetition compulsion inherent in allegory itself. He appears to understand that allegory is appropriately suited to render the psychological economics that follows rejection by the beloved, that accompanies the Fall.

But if allegory is bound with the work of melancholia in hell, it is bound with the work of mourning, or *Trauerarbeit*, in the last two books of *Paradise Lost*, and here the term *allegory* must not be restricted to a limited sense of a highly metaphorical analogy that is to be drawn out point by point, as is more commonly seen in such passages as Sin and Death before the gates of hell, but must be understood to signify the use of language as representation or repetition by means of an analogue, of a metaphor. To recall Milton's *Christian Doctrine*, human discourse is allegorical to the extent that it is an accommodated language corresponding to a higher reality we cannot see or understand. Milton is referring to God's manner of revealing himself in Scripture, and we may well expect an allegorical explanation at this point in *The Christian Doctrine*'s argument. But does such an allegorical approach hold true when language is not being used as scripture?

In the last two books of *Paradise Lost*, Milton clearly shows how the sin that Adam and Eve commit initiates the fall of language, causes signifiers and signifieds to break their natural bonds. This fall of language, I maintain, directly imitates or repeats the linguistic fall that occurs at the moment Satan gives birth to Sin, a fall that is, as we have seen, the fall into allegory itself. However, the fall of language on earth is, unlike the fall of language in hell, not bound with the work of melancholia, but with the work of mourning: *Trauerarbeit*. That this earthly fall of language is really a happy fall, and that this happy fall resuscitates the notion of allegory by way of mourning, a work concerned with death as we have outlined so far, is the line we will follow from here out.

That a fall of language does indeed occur after Adam and

Eve sin is most evident in book II of *Paradise Lost,* for

> Nature first gave Signs, imprest
> On Bird, Beast, Air, Air suddenly eclips'd
> After short blush of Morn. [11.182–84]

That is to say, things are no longer signifieds, but signifiers; things are not archetypes, but only copies of archetypes. It is as if nature suddenly turns into a book and man into a reader or interpreter of the signs written in that book. Things have faded, and all that remains is their residual semiotic significance. Adam appears to realize this transformation caused by the Fall when he says,

> O *Eve,* some furder change awaits us nigh,
> Which Heav'n by these mute signs in Nature shows
> Forerunners of his purpose, or to warn
> Us haply too secure. [11.193–96]

Just as Satan's daughter, Sin, is taken by the wise host as a forbidding "portent," Adam sees his sin in terms of natural signs that are omens. These natural signs are "forerunners," or adumbrations, that point to unhappiness and suffering; they "warn / Us haply to secure" in the same way that Sin warns the host in Heaven that great sorrow and suffering will shortly become the lot of many securely residing in the vales of holiness. More specifically, the natural signs, like Sin, not only point to the Fall, which has already taken place at that moment when Sin is born in heaven and which has already taken place before Adam notices there are opaque signs, but point to their own breaking apart of signifier and signified and foreshadow expulsion. Adam, of course, is more sensitive than Satan to the warning afforded by the portent of suffering to come. In fact, at the precise moment Adam notices the split between appearances and realities, the signifiers and their hidden signifieds, he begins to suspect the source of this change: Death has been released.

> And what till then our life,
> Who knows, or more than this, that we are dust,

> And thither must return and be no more.
> Why else this double object in our sight
> Of flight pursu'd in th' Air and o'er the ground
> One way the self-same hour? why in the East
> Darkness ere Day's mid-course, and Morning light
> More orient in yon Western Cloud that draws
> O'er the blue Firmament a radiant white,
> And slow descends, with something heav'nly fraught.
> [11.198–207]

Suddenly the world has become an allegory into which the parents of mankind are thrust. The firmament changes color, and this signifies the birth and death of all things. The animals begin to hunt, and the double object of birds of prey and fierce mammals hunting also signifies the intrusion of death into the world. Certainly it is death that has given birth to the mute signs, or emblems, that Adam interprets for Eve as best he can. It is death that has given birth to writing.

In *Ursprung des deutschen Trauerspiels*, Benjamin writes that "die Allegorie sie darstellt, als einer blossen Weise der Bezeichnung. Allegorie—das zu erweisen dienen die folgenden Blätter—ist nicht spielerische Bildertechnik, sondern Ausdruck, so wie Sprache Ausdruck ist, ja so wie Schrift." ("Allegory represents itself as the exposed method of symbolization. Allegory—as the following pages will show—is not a playful technique of illustration, but is expression, just like speech, yes, just like writing.")[10] What Benjamin elsewhere calls the "Schriftcharakter der Allegorie" is meant to point up the fact that, as Fredric Jameson puts it,

> script rather than language, the letter rather than the spirit; these are the fragments into which the baroque world shatters, strangely legible signs and emblems nagging at the too curious mind, a procession moving slowly across a stage, laden with occult significance.[11]

In book 11 of *Paradise Lost*, Adam definitely is faced with such fragments, such mute signs or writings that are laden with what must seem to him an occult significance. He is faced with the *Schriftcharakter*, or what we have called, after Benjamin, *Todverfallenheit*, and *Allegorie*, and as in the dramas Benjamin is investigating in his study, Milton associates Adam's sudden confrontations with death-writing-allegory in terms of *Trauer*.

In *Paradise Lost* the work of *Trauer* ("sorrow"), or mourning, is itself facilitated by Michael, who appears, curiously enough, as himself an emblem. Indeed, just as Sin is an allegorical figure who has to explain herself as part of an allegory to Satan, as *Schriftcharakter*, Michael reveals himself to Adam, not in his angelic form, but rather in emblematic shape and garb. Thus after death (this *Todverfallenheit*) has been unloosed through the practice of sin, the angels, like the demons, have to engage in shape changing:

> And th' Arch-Angel soon drew nigh,
> Not in his shape Celestial, but as Man
> Clad to meet Man; over his lucid Arms
> A military Vest of purple flow'd
> Livelier than *Meliboean*, or the grain
> Of *Sarra*, worn by Kings and Heroes old;
> . . . .
> His starry Helm unbuckl'd show'd him prime.
> [11.238–45]

Michael appears as a signifier, an emblem, a *Schriftcharakter*, though one whose signified becomes rather obvious even to Adam, who can discern the meaning of the ornate military equipage in terms of magnificence and power. Here, the mere surface and shine of Michael's glamour reflect what is meant by the signifiers. It is within this reflection of the signifier that Adam will always be able to discern the traces of God, and Michael tells Adam as much when he says,

> Yet doubt not but in Valley and in Plain
> God is as here, and will be found alike
> Present, and of his presence many a sign
> Still following thee, still compassing thee round

With goodness and paternal Love, his Face
Express, and of his steps the track Divine. [11.349–54]

Michael's statement is intended to facilitate an Adamic work of mourning by showing Adam in what way he can recuperate the loss of the love object which Adam expresses when he asks, "Where shall I seek / His bright appearances, or footstep trace?" (11.328–29). The loss of presence, of the Father, is to be recuperated precisely through his works which have become signs: *Schriftcharakter*. But if the world has become writing, has become an *Allegorie*, we are not to assume that it is a repetition of the allegorical landscape of hell, that Adam, like Satan, is condemned to a narcissistic repetition compulsion. For Adam is not condemned to melancholia; he is, rather, encouraged to participate in a *thanatopraxie*, a *Trauerarbeit*, a working out of sorrow that provides for recathexis, for a reinvestment of love in a love object that is eclipsed yet still present. What is crucial for Milton is to show in what manner Adam is saved from despair, in what manner Adam's fall does not constitute an eternal damnation in which mankind is suddenly plunged into a Satanic repetition compulsion that signifies only narcissism, error, melancholy, death, evil, but opens the way for a more positive working through of sorrow in the Freudian sense of *Trauer*. That is, the loss of God's presence and the expulsion from paradise is to be recuperated in terms of emotional and spiritual reinvestments in God's traces, his grace, Christ's sacrifice, and finally, man's "paradise within." How man is to turn away from the problematic of the loss of his happy estate and look toward the appropriation of other gifts which may be happier far, though gained at the cost of sorrow, suffering, and unhappiness, is the burden of the last two books of *Paradise Lost*. Indeed, it is Michael's task to make sure that Adam and Eve do, indeed, avoid despair and embrace the *Trauerarbeit* as prescribed by Providence in a most positive, affirmative manner.

That Michael himself appears as an emblematic creature

and that he explains the *Schriftcharakter* of God's works is particularly important, for Michael is showing how the world of signs is to be taken as the matter upon which a *Trauerarbeit* must rest. Indeed, Michael's reflections on the *Schriftcharakter* of God's works differ from those of Raphael in the earlier books to the degree that after the Fall, the *Schriftcharakter* has taken on a materiality which it did not have before. We recall that in book 5, when Raphael uses the analogy of the "bright consummate flow'r" in order to relate the notion of a great cosmic scale of being and at the same time to explain in what manner man's body and mind is itself a replica of this grand scheme of nature, Adam is being given a talisman by means of which analogical verities are disclosed. Reason is the being of the bright consummate flower, its presence or spirit, and this reason is both "discursive" and "intuitive." But if there seems a rift, Raphael is quick to add that these modalities of reason differ only in degree; they are "of kind the same" (5.490). The analogue of the bright consummate flower is, not so much a material sign which excludes penetrability, which marks a line between *physis* and meaning, but a spiritual talisman of which Adam's discursive habits are inherently a part; it is a fusing of intellect and image, truth and sign.

Michael's signs, on the other hand, are taken from the material relations into which Adam has fallen; they represent, not a natural affinity with man's reasonable soul, but an alienated script which appears incomprehensible and exterior from the perspective of man. Upon viewing the historical sights which Michael presents, Adam will be able to react only from the perspective of one who, even when told the significance, can only comprehend with disbelief, with a dubious knowledge. Even when Michael speaks of a "paradise within," it is not so much explained to Adam as proclaimed to him in the voice of one who reads a verdict or sentence. And when Michael says to Adam, "Thou hast attain'd the sum / Of wisdom," it means, not so much that Adam has regained his unfallen intellect, as that the angel is nearing the end of his disclosures, that Providence has revealed what it is going to reveal. Clearly the emphasis in the last books is, not so much on Adam's ability to understand intellectually what has been presented to him, but on Adam's comprehension of what the Fall has meant and what it will mean in the future. Michael's purpose is first and foremost to console Adam and to effect a *Trauerarbeit* so that when Adam and Eve leave Eden, they will look to Providence as something good and not as something evil which has unfairly judged two hapless creatures placed in a situation whose end was inevitable and beyond human control.

If Satan's melancholia is linked to an allegorical landscape in which there is only repetition and narcissism, Adam's mourning is linked to a landscape of signs whose allegorical *Schriftcharakter* is not simply a punishment but a divine recompense. If Adam and Eve have brought about a division of signifier and signified through their sin, if they have loosed death into the world and have brought about allegory, and if this results in suffering, *Trauer*, Michael makes certain that Adam understands such suffering is the spur that will lead him to regain the love object as well as his blissful seat. The fall of language is therefore in part a happy fall, at least on earth, because it ensures that a work of mourning will take place.

More importantly, however, the *Schriftcharakter* of this fallen language functions as, not merely a motivation, but a means by which such a *Trauerarbeit* is to be carried out. For it is through the "traces," and "tracks" divine that Adam can at once let go of the presence in some other manner. This can occur only because the writing that is the world neither contains presence nor is wholly removed or cut off from presence. It is liminally situated between presence and absence and functions at once as an agent of estrangement (separation) and identification (confusion).

The undecidability of signs is precisely the problematic of the trace, the problematic of a presence or signified which at once conceals and reveals itself, which appears without even making itself fully present, which frustrates, perhaps even denies the difference between life and death, while, in fact, maintaining that distinction in the most pitiless way. What Michael suggests to Adam after the Fall is that man will no longer be able to experience God in epiphanies, such as Adam recalls when told of the Expulsion to come, but will experience God in terms of a loss or a lack. This is to suggest, not that Adam must face the absolute absence of God, but that he must relate to God in terms of his concealment, his disappearance, his traces. Michael's suggestions are very much in line with Jacques Derrida's analysis of the sign as trace in *De la grammatologie*, when Derrida says that the trace belongs to an "économie de la mort" and that the degree to which one drifts towards death, towards a loss of the subject, towards a fading of consciousness and an effacement of presence determines to what extent one will resuscitate traces of that from which one is falling away. This view is expressed again in *Glas*, when Derrida insists that something always remains, that death cannot effect a complete consumption of presence, meaning, signified. Death is not a "dépense sans reserve" ("expenditure without reserve"). It is for this reason that the sign, the residue or reserve or remainder, is always to be considered as a threshold, or limen, between presence and absence, death and life. The trace is the "hinge" ("brisure") that at once divides presence and absence, appearance and disappearance, and at the same time confuses them. In *Paradise Lost* Adam is told the fallen signs are traces because they are the hinges where the sacred and the profane come together without touching; they are the undecidable spaces where separate orders can coexist.

That Michael reveals to Adam that the fallen world is a writing in which the signs are traces at precisely the time he has delivered the parents of mankind an eviction notice is significant because it not only reinforces the theme of loss but assuages Adam's and Eve's suffering while at the same time carrying out God's harsh doom. In fact, the revelation of traces is meant to ensure that Adam and Eve do not despair, but engage in the more positive work of mourning that will lead to their (and, by extension, our) salvation. It should be clear that only because fallen language is a trace can Adam and Eve be removed from the presence of God without at the same time being entirely rejected or cut off as Satan is. Rather, the traces ensure that man can still hope, and this is, to be sure, the first important stage of the *Trauerarbeit* to follow the realization that one has suddenly experienced loss: death.

This is not the place to embark upon a phenomenology of hope, but I merely point out the importance of understanding the trace as the necessary precondition of hope, as the starting place for hope. Certainly, it must be in that undecidable space, or break, between God's self-concealment and his revelation that man experiences the expectation of an authentic encounter with the Godhead (epiphany) grounded on the experience of loss, of a being where God is not. Hope signifies the process whereby loss is recuperated as a sign for restoration, not rejection, as the mark for a full restitution of the authentic encounter with the Godhead that man once enjoyed. The traces, or signs of loss or God's concealment, act as beacons that point man's distance (Heidegger's *Distanz* comes to mind here) from God, but at the same time light the path toward him. The traces are accusative signs signifying man's disobedience, what Paul Ricoeur would call part of a symbolism of evil, but they are at the same time the signs of consolation, the signals of what Kierkegaard calls "repetition": the recuperation of the sacred. By means of the trace, man can recathect his emotions in terms of hope, in terms of the certainty that man's fidelity to God, his careful interpretation of the traces, will ensure repetition.

Michael's task in books 11 and 12 is to show Adam an economics of consolation—that is, hope, promise, waiting, restoration, grace—that depends upon the happy fall, upon the positivity of loss, upon the opening created by the trace.

And it is in this way that Michael assists Adam in the work of mourning, in a work that turns away from despair without compromising the pain of sorrow and suffering, the punishment God forces man to bear.

The history lesson that Adam receives from Michael is, of course, meant to complete the work of recathexis by showing Adam the new love object, Christ. Indeed, the historical progress which is well known to us through the Old and New Testaments is allegorical to the extent that it too participates in a work of mourning that depends upon the elements of death, sin, loss, and evil but also upon restoration, recompense, consolation, and hope, upon the fact that events are signs, or a writing, that at once show man's distance from the signified, the truth, and at the same time reveals through that distance traces, or shadows, of that truth. The first of the scenes in the long pageant of mourning that Michael introduces begins with the problematic of death, appropriately enough. It is the story of Abel and Cain, and after Adam has seen murder, he asks, "But have I now seen Death?" (11.462). And Michael answers, "Death thou hast seen / In his first shape on man; but many shapes / Of Death, and many are the ways that lead / To his grim Cave, all dismal" (11.466–69). Clearly, the Abel and Cain scene is only one *shape*, one metaphor for Death, who, as we all know, is born in allegory.

Next we are shown a lazar-house where great numbers of the diseased are to be found, and here again allegoresis is most prominent. "Despair / Tended the sick busiest from Couch to Couch; / And over them triumphant Death his Dart / Shook" (11.489–92). Adam's reaction is one of shock and despair. "O miserable Mankind. . . . Better end here unborn" (11.500–502). But Michael attempts to convince Adam that man suffers, not because he is being cruelly punished, but because he has willfully debased himself. If death seeks out men and puts an end to their lives in a most cruel and hideous manner, it is because such men have lived indecently. Accepting Michael's revelation of the depravity of man, his debasing of his own image and with it the destruction of any correspondence between himself and God's image (what amounts to the Satanic fall into allegory), Adam wishes to know whether this rift can be assuaged, particularly with reference to death. Although Adam is willing to submit to the archangel's arguments, he is not wholly convinced, even at this point, that if man is condemned to a *thanatopraxie* of allegory, it would not be best to die without further ado. Thus Adam asks:

> But is there yet no other way, besides
> These painful passages, how we may come
> To Death, and mix with our connatural dust?
> [11.527–29]

"These painful passages" refers, of course, to the plight and error of mankind, to this deviant history that offends God and heaven. Considering the dismal progress of man, would it not offend God less simply to die, to put all this error to rest? And Michael answers:

> There is, said *Michael*, if thou well observe
> The rule of not too much, by temperance taught,
> In what thou eat'st and drink'st, seeking from thence
> Due nourishment, not gluttonous delight,
> Till many years over thy head return:
> So may'st thou live, till like ripe Fruit thou drop
> Into thy Mother's lap, or be with ease
> Gather'd, not harshly pluckt, for death mature:
> This is old age. [11.530–38]

It is clear to Adam that he must simply live out his life as best he can to the end, that he must accept old age, and with it the difference between what he is now and the decrepit man he will be. Here too *thanatopraxie* is in effect, but it is a *praxis* of death which, as Michael dourly notes, is not merely negative but, in fact, in accordance with God's plan. Adam is asked to accept and submit to a *thanatopraxie* which fulfills God's scheme for the salvation of mankind, a *thanatopraxie* which works counter to the *thanatopraxie* in hell.

As the historical scenes multiply, Adam begins to see not only the suffering of man but the promise of a restoration of his lost status. The restitution of men in the story of Noah, the covenant God makes there never again to destroy the earth by flood, and, in the later recollection of this by Moses on the mount in book 12, the informing of men by shadows and types—all look forward to man's recuperation of an authentic revelation of divine presence. Of course, it is finally in the story of the Crucifixion that Adam sees the repetition of sorrow, death, evil, sin and restoration, hope, consolation, salvation, and grace. Here the triumph of man over death, sin, and sorrow is finally realized. The traces of Adam's unfallenness are suddenly revealed, manifest. And it is to the Son of man and of God that Adam is finally directed to fix his love, to direct his hope for the salvation of all that Eve lost when she ate of the forbidden fruit. And it is here that the *Leidensgeschichte*, the story of man's sorrow and his passion, what Benjamin would call the *Trauerspiel*, comes suddenly to the fore as not merely a thematic, a work, but as a literary genre.

III

It is particularly in the last two books of *Paradise Lost* that the labor of *Allegorie* is used to facilitate the work of mourning, just as in book 2 it is intimate with the work of melancholia. This is not meant to say that there are really two kinds of *Allegorie* operative in the epic, but that there is inscribed within the problematic of loss and death a *thanatopraxie* of writing that can follow the economics of a repetition compulsion, a literary machine of the same (narcissism) and also, as in the writing of books 11 and 12, an economics of mourning, of reading traces and vestiges, of redirecting one's love, a redirection that exits paradise and begins to fix upon Christ. In both instances we are talking about a discourse that Benjamin would have called *Trauer*.

My position in this chapter is that Milton's *Paradise Lost* is not simply an epic but in large part a *Trauerspiel* and that it is no accident that an economy of loss, death, expulsion, sin, and fall is linked to the thematic of sorrow and that this is expressed through the use of *Allegorie*.

So why the delay? Why not just state this from the beginning? Because my major intention is not so much to force upon Milton another historical reading that takes as its context the literary history of the seventeenth century, to make another connection of literary influence, which indeed could be strongly argued in this case, to use history as some sort of proof for something, but to show how the various networks we have exposed in Milton that refer to the matter of allegory, to the *thanatopraxie* of writing, to *Trauer*, lead us to ask the question whether the epic is composed of a large internal network of themes, terms, phrases, passages, and even whole books that call attention to themselves as *Trauerspiel*, as a kind of German drama.

Such a thesis would sound forced were it not for the fact that Milton wrote an Ur-*Paradise Lost*, entitled "Adam Unparadized," in the early 1640s that mapped the writing out of an allegorical, tragic drama that appears modeled upon the kinds of dramas that men like Andreas Gryphius, Johann Rist, and Daniel Caspar von Lohenstein were writing in Germany at approximately the same time. What characterizes Milton's "Adam Unparadized" and the *Trauerspiel* written by seventeenth-century German dramatists is the fact that these works attempt to present a Protestant rewriting of the miracle play tradition, a rewriting that preserves allegorical representations on stage while at the same time attempting to secularize or humanize them. That Milton had such an idea in mind when he sketched out "Adam Unparadized" is clear, for the long list of dramatis personae in the third draft of the Trinity manuscript mentions the presence of mutes, such as Labour, Grief, Hatred, Envy, War, Famine, Pestilence, Sickness, Discontent, Ignorance, Fear, Death, Faith, Hope, and Charity. The speakers include

Michael, Gabriel, Adam, Eve, Justice, Mercy, Wisdom, and Lucifer. Also, and this is most important, Milton intended a chorus to relate action to the audience, such as the Fall and the revolt of the angels in heaven. Milton's conception of the chorus and the allegorical mutes was intended to relate not so much the tragedy of the Fall as the suffering that followed, and it is in this sense that Milton stresses the humanizing, or secularization, of a religious theme. For the sorrow, mourning, or *Trauer* of Adam involves his human and, ultimately, our human crises vis-à-vis the problem of evil and death, the recognition that fallen man is part of an economics of death, labor, grief, hatred, envy, war, and sickness from which he cannot separate himself, an economy that, as we saw in book 11, metonymically represents him, defines him. The function of the chorus is largely, Milton seems to indicate, to shift our attention away from the falls of Lucifer and of man, and conveniently it brings us face to face, not with the tragedy of the descent into evil, but with the suffering of evil after the event, the Fall itself. The allegorical mutes are meant not to distract us from the human drama by presenting sterile, abstract concepts in human dress, but are intended, as in the *Trauerspiel* tradition, to bring about a "Verweltlichung des Ewigen" ("secularization of the eternal"), as Herbert Heckmann in *Elemente des barocken Trauerspiels* makes clear.[12] Indeed, the tradition of the *Trauerspiel* is based on the splitting of man, the presentation of a hero who has to come to terms with his many reflections, which are allegorically presented. In comparison with the miracle plays of the High Middle Ages, the *Trauerspiel* creates characters who are more highly self-conscious about their encounter with themselves, and consequently the audience of the *Trauerspiel* becomes, in its own way, anxious about its relation to itself as fallen man. Allegory here does not perform a function of merely making stories didactic, or conceptual in a sterile manner, but functions to harass the complacent spectator by bringing him into relation with his own fallenness and his own salvation with his *Tugend,* or virtue. We recall that it was Michael's aim in *Paradise Lost* to bring this about in Adam after his fall from the prelapsarian state.

There are, of course, many connections between *Paradise Lost* and the *Trauerspiel* of Gryphius, Martin Opitz, Rist, and Lohenstein besides the emphasis on suffering, mourning, melancholy, and allegory. We have little space to consider them here in detail, but shall mention a few instances. For example, one finds in both *Paradise Lost* and the *Trauerspiel* a conversion of the secular history into sacred history; an emphasis upon stoicism and cruelty, the folly of man and the end of days, war and politics, fear and pity (though not in the Aristotelian sense); and the stress upon the world, the heavens, and the regions of hell as part of one entire *Schauspielhaus,* or arena, in which the spectator situates himself. However, it is to Benjamin's deeper sounding into *Trauerspiel* and *Allegorie* that I wish to return, since this is most relevant for our discussion.

Benjamin, unlike the others who have written on the *Trauerspiel* tradition, is not so much interested in the convention of the *Trauerspiel* as he is in the significance of its allegorical technique for Western culture. Fredric Jameson observes that Benjamin sees in allegory the dissolution of consciousness, the psychological impairment of man, a vision of a world in ruins and fragments.

Benjamin's work seems to me to be marked by a painful straining toward a psychic wholeness or unity of experience which the historical situation threatens to shatter at every turn.[13]

Martin Jay, in *The Dialectical Imagination,* summarizes this problem of maintaining psychic wholeness in terms of Benjamin's suggestion that there are two processes of name-giving at work that are in opposition to one another: the empirical name-giving of man (signification) and the sacred name-giving of God (revelation). It is the fall from revelation to signification that Benjamin uses as the starting point for his analysis of allegory in the seventeenth century.

In *Ursprung* Benjamin writes,

Das adamitische Benennen der Dinge war so weit davon entfernt, leeres Werk spielender Willkür [zu sein], dass vielmehr gerade in diesem der paradiesische Stand aufs hellste als ein solcher sich bestimmt, der mit der mitteilenden Bedeutung der Worte noch nicht zu ringen hatte: als in denen vielmehr unverkennbar die Ideen sich gaben. Wie sie Adam intentionslos beim Benennen sich geben, so müssen in gleich reiner Anschauung dem Philosoph im Erinnern sie sich zu erneuern streben. Diese Erinnerung ist eine die in den alten Worte[n] wieder auftaucht.[14]

("The Adamic naming of the things [of the world] was at the furthest possible remove from a hollow and arbitrary play of the will; rather it was precisely here that the paradisiac state showed itself as what it was in the most illuminating manner: not yet engaged in a struggle with the communicative meaning [signifying operation] of words, for in them the ideas revealed themselves unmistakably. Just as they reveal themselves without intention in Adam's naming, so must they strive to be renewed in a similarly pure intuition in the philosopher's act of recollection. This recollection is one that emerges again in the ancient words.")

Benjamin's point is that Adamic naming, unlike philosophical signification, does not require any human intentionality, any will to meaning, and therefore his speaking does not have to grapple with the problem of representation. Adam's words simply participate in the givenness of ideas. In the draft for *Ursprung* that I have just quoted from, Benjamin says that the sacred givenness of ideas is given through an *Ursprache* ("original language"), but in the final version this is modified. The givenness of ideas is not to be found in any *Ursprache,* but in an *Urvernehmen* ("original understanding"), in terms of what one might call sacred revelation rather than philological archaeology. Benjamin's view is expressed by Paul Ricoeur in "Religion, Atheism, and Faith":

Language is less and less a work of man. The power to speak is not at our disposal; and it is because we are not masters of our own speaking that we may be "gathered in," that is to say, joined to what gathers. In this light our language becomes something more than a practical means of communication with others and of mastering things: when speaking becomes "saying," or better, when "saying" abides in the speaking of our language as a gift and of thought as the recognition of this gift. Thought gives thanks for the gift of language, and this is once more a form of consolation. Man is consoled when in language he lets things be, or be shown.[15]

Ricoeur is using Heideggerian terms, and Benjamin would probably have not wished to associate himself with concepts like "gathering" and "saying"; yet Ricoeur's statement, "The power to speak is not at our disposal," is essentially what Benjamin means when he writes that the truth is the death of intention ("Die Wahrheit ist der Tod der Intention"). Adam knew how to speak in the Heideggerian sense; he did not have to signify, but simply say what was already revealed to him by God. However, this psychic unity of an intentionless saying, based upon the closeness of man and God, is impaired after the Fall. Once fallen, man can signify in the sense that he can represent things and ideas in signs. That is, man is suddenly reduced to symbolizing that which he means. Man is suddenly required to intend or mean something, and he needs symbols in order to carry out these intentions. The symbol, according to Benjamin, provides man with only the ruse that a sign can actually present or make present a meaning or truth; it holds out the promise that man can signify in such a way that the *intellectus archetypus* can be incarnated in marks, that man can actually appropriate that which he intends. However, for Benjamin, the symbol only ensures that we never let go of a mechanical substitute for the kind of intentionless naming man enjoyed before the Fall, and it does so precisely by seducing us with a mythology of organicism, unity, intentionality, and presence, with the promise that symbolicity can, indeed, effectively substitute itself for intentionless naming.

Allegorie, on the other hand, does not promise us the illusion that signifiers and signifieds are really connected, does not maintain that we can ever mean that which we intend, but maintains, instead, the essential disjunction between sign and referent. *Allegorie* is a mechanical means of naming that only approximates, often in the most unsatisfactory terms, what one means. Ironically, it is through encountering what appears as the most mechanical, most inadequate, most uncouth signifying machine that one comes closest to recuperating the Adamic state, since *Allegorie* brings us most negatively to the threshold of paradise by severing the symbol's tyranny of intention. Benjamin believes that if one looks carefully at the *Trauerspiel* tradition, one finds dramatists actually taking this point of view, for they turn against the symbol; they fragment the world by means of *Allegorie*; they harass intention:

Das Bild im Feld der allegorischen Intuition ist Bruchstück, Rune. Seine symbolische Schönheit verflüchtigt sich, da das Licht der Gottesgelahrtheit drauf trifft. Der falsche Schein der Totalität geht aus. Denn das Eidos verlischt, das Gleichnis geht ein, der Kosmos darinnen vertrocknet.[16]

("In the field of allegorical intuition the image is a fragment, a rune. Its beauty as a symbol evaporates when the light of divine learning falls upon it. The false appearance of totality is extinguished. For the *eidos* [idea, form] disappears, the simile ceases to exist, and the cosmos it contained shrivels up.")

In Benjamin, the way to psychic wholeness is often not, as in Heidegger, a retreat from the machine, the city, the simulacrum, but an acceptance of these mediations. Just as the film is responsible for a destruction of the aura in "Das Kunstwerk im Zeitalter," and is therefore a means of restoring authenticity precisely because it does such a good job of defetishization, and just as the city in Baudelaire is the site where man undergoes his most radical dehumanization, but is for all that the place where correspondences are produced, *Allegorie* produces psychic wholeness precisely because it too does such a good job at defetishization, dehumanization.[17] Here the word *Trauer* must be recalled for the last time in Freud's sense, for it should be apparent by now that Benjamin's analysis of *Trauerspiel* is a *Trauerarbeit*, that Benjamin, like Milton, uses allegory in order to cut us off from our *Liebesobjekt* and at the same time provides for a restoration, a Kierkegardian repetition.

It is in this sense that *Allegorie* is akin to the Derridean notion of *différance,* of the undecidable mentioned in *Positions,* and if Derrida has used the voice-writing distinction in *De la grammatologie* to deconstruct metaphysics, we can add that Benjamin in his *Ursprung* essay foreshadows grammatology by strategically dismantling the symbolic-allegorical dialectic in the context of seventeenth-century German drama. What is important for this study, of course, is to highlight Benjamin, not as the greater thinker who diminishes Derrida, for this is certainly not the case, but as a textual site that facilitates our bringing Milton's writings into the orbit of modern European criticism. Indeed, once the lines of contact are delineated between a work like *Paradise Lost* and Benjamin's *Ursprung,* it becomes possible to see Milton's poetry in terms of a philosophic tradition, even a long-range project, whose aim is to test and assess the boundaries between presence and absence, life and death, meaning and nonsense, and prelapsarian and postlapsarian.

How Milton tests such a threshold, or boundary, what Derrida terms the *limen* in *La dissémination,* becomes the subject for the next chapter, in which we examine closely the notion of the Fall, the *praxis* of death par excellence; and we will do so thinking through, not allegory, this time, but something not so removed from allegory: metaphor.

Der Unterschied zwischen Mann und Frau ist der des Tieres und der Pflanze; das Tier entspricht mehr dem Charakter des Mannes, die Pflanze mehr dem der Frau, denn sie ist mehr ruhiges Entfalten, das die unbestimmtere Einigkeit der Empfindung zu seinem Prinzip erhält. Stehen Frauen an der Spitze der Regierung, so ist der Staat in Gefahr, denn sie handeln nicht nach den Anforderungen der Allgemeinheit, sondern nach zufälliger Neigung und Meinung. Die Bildung der Frauen geschieht, man weiss nicht wie, gleichsam durch die Atmosphäre der Vorstellung, mehr durch das Leben als durch das Erwerben von Kenntnissen.

("The difference between men and women is like that between animals and plants. Men correspond to animals, while women correspond to plants because their development is more placid and the principle that underlies it is the rather vague unity of feeling. When women hold the helm of government, the state is at once in jeopardy, because women regulate their actions not by the demands of universality but by arbitrary inclinations and opinions. Women are educated—who knows how?—as it were by breathing in ideas, by living rather than by acquiring knowledge.")

G. W. F. Hegel, *Grundlinien der Philosophie des Rechts, Zusatz* 166, translated by T. M. Knox

CHAPTER 3

Milton's Lady of the Flowers

I

For the modern reader, Jean Genet's comment, "There is a close relationship between flowers and convicts," may have an interesting bearing upon Renaissance art, for it suggests that we may, if we look closely, find a dark side to pastoral imagery, particularly flowers, a dark side from which even Milton's epic may not be excluded.[1] In order to explain what we mean by such a dark side to pastoral imagery, it may be useful to turn for a moment to the work of Genet, since for him the image of the flower is a metaphor for the *voleur*, or thief, who takes what does not belong to him and metes out to others what they do not deserve or ask for. This flower is always a violator of sorts: a rapist, a burglar, a pickpocket, a counterfeiter, a person whose language is always deviant and, as in *Pompes funèbres*, sexually perverse. Ultimately, Genet cannot decide what flowers really are (symbols? signs?), since their nature is to be what they are not.

If the flower is beautiful for Genet, it is because the flower is antisocial, a kind of tramp for whom the work of everyday man is an "unreal city," to recall Baudelaire, whose "flowers of evil" should never be too far from our thoughts. A promiscuous outlaw, the flower always takes detours or back alleys and always has to hide his true identity behind masks or screens which for him are but an array of metaphors used to escape detection by the police. Thus "Our

Lady of the Flowers" is a man in drag, an escape artist par excellence who dodges not only society, the police, and the reader's sympathy but also the binary opposition of male-female implicit within the question of sexuality itself. A true flower, Our Lady is an undecidable, a "différance," as Jacques Derrida would have it in *Glas*, whose deviance, or undecidability, reveals itself in terms of the "not itself," in terms of distancing: metaphor. Our Lady's liminal sexual status, like the flower's bisexuality, harasses the distinction between the sexes at the same time that its confusion is predicated upon sexual difference. Not simply a thief who enters houses in order to take goods, Our Lady is a thief of identities, a robber of the feminine, and as such is the proper paradigm for all metaphorical activity. Such mimetic disturbance is, for Genet, the key to a drama or prose of screens, of illicit borrowings, of illegal masks that is intimately associated not only with the illegitimacy of theft but with the sexual deviation of homosexuality itself. For Genet, to be a man in drag is not simply to be an outlaw, a thief of prohibited identities, but to exist metaphorically. Derrida, of course, recognizes that such a conception of metaphor as a transgressive activity based upon illicit modes of exchange (the taking on of identities that do not properly belong) not only confuses but threatens the distinction between binary oppositions like masculine-feminine which can analogically be compared to presence-absence, reality-appearance, meaning-sign, and so on. For Derrida, Genet's flowers of rhetoric, such as Mimosa, the Plantagenet, and the Rose, are images of this transgressive activity, an activity that Derrida terms *dissémination*.[2]

However, for Genet this transgressive activity is fundamental to what he calls a mystical vision. That is, the undecidability of flowers is rooted in the well-known Western formula: that sexuality is mystery, that it is at once forbidden and offered, hidden and revealed, pleasurable and painful, criminal and holy. Botticelli and Milton, of course, were only too well acquainted with this mystery and allow it to give expression to what we might call a double scene in writing, which is to say, the simultaneous vision of woman, sexuality, and nature as at once prelapsarian and postlapsarian, a double scene in which a figure like Eve may be the principal player, or Flora the main visual attraction. Indeed, if Derrida exposes so many screens in Genet, fractures his prose and drama into so many scenes, undecidable and doubled, indeterminate and folded, catastrophic in René Thom's sense, it is not a morcellation that can be localized in Genet alone but implicitly involves a literary tradition within which Genet belongs: decadence, symbolism, romanticism, and, of course, tradition pertaining to the Renaissance and back unto classical times. This is not the place to outline a whole history of the literary conception of flowers and undecidability, deviance, promiscuity, and all the rest, just the moment to mention that it would be profitable to look at just two important Western figures, Botticelli and Milton, using an approach compatible with Derrida's on Genet.

Certainly the relationship between the promiscuous flower which passively receives all admirers and disseminates its sexuality, more or less freely and openly, and the figure of woman is a most classical topos. Beautiful yet wild, flower and woman resemble one another in the writings of more than a few authors, and without doubt it is the figure of Aphrodite that most strongly establishes this connection in ancient literature, for there she is Aphrodite Urania (queen of the mountain) or Erycina (of the heather). She, like so many fertility goddesses (Pomona, Persephone, and others) reminds mankind that nature and culture are contradictory and cannot be strictly separated, that with even the beauty and urbanity of an Aphrodite there is also promiscuity, transgression, and illegitimacy, and those are what characterize her nature too. Her wildness is associated with Adonis as well as with the Hermaphrodite, and already here

"Our Lady of the Flowers" would make a suitable companion of sorts. Renaissance painters and poets were quick to seize the apparent contradictions between the promiscuity of nature and the properness of culture; thus Lucas Cranach the Elder stresses Aphrodite's urbanity but also her naturalness in the counterpoint between the fashionable hat she wears and her otherwise unclad figure. This can be viewed in Cranach's *The Judgement of Paris* (1530), in which there is the strong suggestion that Aphrodite is to be associated with the first of all women, Eve. In the *Adam and Eve* (1526) the unclad female figure stands in a purely wild or natural setting and seduces man rather self-consciously and, one might even add, urbanely, under a tree, and this scene strongly reminds one of *The Judgement of Paris*, in which Paris sits under a similar tree trying to decide important matters. In both paintings the tree scenes are epiphantic sites which determine man's fate with regard to not only woman but the divine as well. For Cranach, seduction-temptation is essentially a property of woman's nature, a property which bodes ill for man's state (Adam's innocence, his relation to the *locus amoenus*, Eden) or empire (Paris's Troy). For Cranach, however, the conflict between nature and culture, reason and desire, and law and transgression remains on the level of the paradox which from his perspective is articulated in the figure (the ambivalent trope) of woman.

But what in Cranach remains on the level of contradiction or paradox is more highly complicated by other Renaissance painters and writers, pushed beyond mere logical inconsistency, mere metaphysical speculation. This is my argument concerning the work of Milton and Botticelli, whom we will consider in this chapter. In both *Paradise Lost* and the *Primavera* we find that Eve and Flora, respectively, are not merely ambivalent female figures but deconstructive ones articulated by way of what Jacques Derrida calls the "double séance," the double scene or session. What will concern us is how such figures are themselves part of a pastoral tradition which problematizes the question of mimesis and visibility by way of posing an abysm of scenes whose purpose is to destabilize the reader's gaze and to make invisible the mise en scène even while displaying its spectacle. It is the figure of woman which is itself subject to such a logic of appearances and disappearances by means of a double scenery which Derrida in *La dissémination* develops by way of the nonconcept of the hymen, a partition which makes undecidable certain mimetic features in the text or painting and thereby lays claim to a peculiar unrepresentational quality which in *La dissémination* is evident in Mallarmé, and in *Glas* is developed by way of Jean Genet. It is with the latter that we will begin in order to establish the connection between the flower girls of pastoral and undecidability. We will then discuss the relation between Eve and the Fall in *Paradise Lost*, which is to say, the Fall as undecidability, and then consider how this double session or double scene of the Fall can be reinterpreted more existentially in George Bataille's sense of the sacrifice, thus making our link between woman, fall, and, of course, flower (pastoral) with a sacrificial moment that is not only undecidable but unrepresentable. From there I move to considering visible objects in Milton's epic to uncover a specific dream work in the poem which by way of the Fall, woman, flower, and sacrifice phantomizes the mise en scènes of the poem. And finally, we turn to Botticelli to demonstrate how what we have noticed in *Paradise Lost* is already anticipated by one of the greatest artists of the High Renaissance. The purpose of such a series of rather restricted readings is to show to what extent the usual eighteenth-century mode of reading *Paradise Lost* by means of a gaze that is omniscient, all-knowing, and all-seeing—a gaze that depends upon the presence of an objective and manifest mise en scène—ignores certain deconstructive registers of *Paradise Lost* which simply do not conform to such a ubiquitous and logocentric reading.

II

We recall that when Milton names Eve an "unsupported Flow'r," he not only puns on the word "unsupported" and throws into question whether Eve is sufficiently standing or engaging in the freedom to fall but is throwing Eve into a long catalog of analogues, is already strewing that feminine flower of Eden, as if the "storm so nigh" were itself a metapoetic reference to the nature of words in *Paradise Lost*, a reference we will follow up at a later time:[3]

> He sought them both, but wish'd his hap might find
> *Eve* separate, he wish'd, but not with hope
> Of what so seldom chanc'd, when to his wish,
> Beyond his hope, *Eve* separate he spies,
> Veil'd in a Cloud of Fragrance, where she stood,
> Half spi'd, so thick the Roses bushing round
> About her glow'd, oft stooping to support
> Each Flow'r of slender stalk, whose head though gay
> Carnation, Purple, Azure, or speckt with Gold,
> Hung drooping unsustain'd, them she upstays
> Gently with Myrtle band, mindless the while,
> Herself, though fairest unsupported Flow'r,
> From her best prop so far, and storm so nigh.
> [9.421–33]

It is Satan, of course, who is approaching Eve, whose wish-fulfillment dream is being realized as he sights Eve alone among the flowers. We remember that in the first book of *Paradise Lost* Satan and his crew are described as the former "Flow'r of Heav'n" (1.316) shortly after the famous simile concerning the autumnal leaves "that strow the Brooks / in Vallembrosa." We notice too that Eve is "veiled" by the waist-high roses, and the gynecological suggestions these roses have for readers familiar with the *Romance of the Rose* are unmistakable. We notice further that Eve is here equated with the interdicted tree, for just as the tree and its fruit will ultimately tempt Eve, albeit with the aid of Satan's rhetoric, Satan here is visually seduced by Eve. She is so alluring that Satan is "abstracted" from "his own evil"

(9.463–64), tempted by her to be good, led astray by this feminine flower. But if by way of analogue Eve is the interdicted tree, she is also the "bright consummate flow'r" of the fifth book, and she at once embodies the blend of corporeal and spiritual qualities of that flower, and also disembodies that identification, for she is lacking in any real sapience. The pun on "mindless the while" (Edward Le Comte interprets this as "not regardful" versus "mentally careless or light") makes this clear in the passage from the ninth book quoted above.[4] In addition to these analogues, Eve is a synecdoche for the flowers she props up, and in that is the dramatic irony of the passage, one filled with sorrow and gentle consolation. We are to remember, above all, that in the third book God tells the Son he made man just and right, "Sufficient to have stood, though free to fall" (3.99). As unsupported flower, Eve represents this man, stands in for "[him] and his faithless Progeny," Adam and the other patriarchs. Analogues continue in the lines following the quotation above, for Eve is further compared to goddesses who inhabit pagan gardens and the women associated with the gardens of Solomon.

My citations point to a rich network of relations in which Eve's status oscillates between fallen and unfallen modes of spiritual existence, a conflict of interpretations that goes far beyond mere ambivalence or paradox, terms too general to specify the economy of oscillations we experience at numerous points such as these in the poem. The phrase "though fairest unsupported Flow'r" is a condensation of this oscillating movement, one of a vast dispersion of Freudian nodal points in the epic, and it harasses the ability to choose which of two terms, "supported" or "fallen," most suits Eve. It repeals the law of contradiction that underlies these kinds of oppositions (fallen-unfallen, experienced-innocent, and so forth) by suggesting that although the terms are distinct, they can be confused, and the context in which this passage occurs only serves to support this contention, for at every point in the immediate context, Eve's status is being fractured into numerous analogous relays, many of which in and of themselves are freighted with indeterminacy, an indeterminacy which is the consequence not simply of contradictory puns but of the hermeneutics involved in the production and decipherment of analogues: Eve as tree, rose, consummate flower, pagan fertility goddess, genius of nature, or Edenic poesy.

The question is, how are we to read Eve? Certainly the description of her as the "fairest unsupported Flow'r" suggests that what appears at first to be a clear-cut distinction or bar between terms like *fallen* and *unfallen* turns out to be an interval that puts into relation the difference and resemblance of the terms. In pursuing this line of thought, we will be moving towards a dialectical and poststructuralist model, and this model differs sharply from Donald F. Bouchard's interesting reading of the labyrinth which he pursues in *Milton: A Structural Reading*, for what concerns me is the relational capacities a metaphor or pun can arbitrate: the positions of a relatively marginal element and how such positions are recursively redistributed on different textual registers.[5] In seeking to discuss such issues in a dialectical and poststructuralist manner, I am led to conclude the text is, not a labyrinth, an opaque or impenetrable mass of words, resistant to interpretation, like some new novels or new-new novels (one thinks of Sollers's *Paradis*), but interpretable within a Derridean or grammatological mode.

In "La double séance," Derrida calls the bar between oppositions the "undecidable," an operation which at once places contraries into confusion and yet maintains itself between contraries ("opération qui 'à la fois' met la confusion entre les contraires et se tient entre les contraires").[6] Derrida's point is that one can find binary terms in philosophy and literature that refuse to succumb to the logic of either-or and both-and, that operate according to another kind of textual economy: undecidability, an economy that takes a detour around either-or and both-and distinctions. Such an economy is predicated on the assumption that the partition that separates and confuses terms is always a syntax that operates like a hydraulic clutch that can engage and disengage at the same time two terms, letting them operate (or rotate) together, a clutch that fuses different terms into identities while conserving their difference, maintaining the gap that separates them. Thus the Aristotelian law of contradiction which we are taught to assume automatically when such oppositions are raised is repealed. The bar between terms like *good* and *evil, innocence* and *experience* turns out to be an interval that *at once opens and closes the passage from one term to the other, an interval that puts into relation the difference and resemblance of the terms.*

Undecidability is, obviously, not a synonym for the New Critical concept of paradox, since paradox constitutes a stabilizing logic that solidly affirms the presence of mutually exclusive terms: the possibility of the impossible. Paradox clearly decides on synthesis, reconciles what one ordinarily assumes cannot be reconciled. Paradox yokes dissimilars and homogenizes them, converts difference into identity. If two souls are one, if riding westward is riding eastward, if the bell which tolls for the dead is really tolling for the living, it is absurd only to those of John Donne's readers who are not spiritually awakened, to those who cannot see beyond mere appearance. Through the figure of paradox and its comprehension, however, one is led to see beyond mere appearance, to become illumined and to join in the brotherhood of similarly illumined or spiritual people. Again it is a matter of making identities, of bringing different people together under one truth, of transforming the heterogeneous into the homogeneous. Paradox thus serves to center us in a present truth which is metaphysical, whether metaphysical refers to a spiritual position or whether it refers to a transcendent conceptual framework by means of which contraries are resolved or yoked. Finally, the manner in which paradox serves to ameliorate contraries by means of a new synthetic concept of unity in diversity nominates paradox to a logocentric position: a centralizing strategy by which two diverse positions can be relocated within the space of a single point: a circle's circumference is always already at one with its center, an example Donne uses in the well-known "Valediction Forbidding Mourning."

When Milton says that Eve is the "fairest unsupported Flow'r," it is not *simply* a paradox or logocentric figure that is being introduced, for although the pun on "unsupported" yokes a contradiction, it does so by means of calling attention to the wildly divergent analogues cited earlier, analogues that refuse to resolve themselves in the way a conceit might in a Donne poem. A sensitive reader will notice that Milton's marginal inscription of Eve into the garden of Eden opens up onto a series of relations that will not stabilize or focus Eve, but serves to destabilize and unfocus her in the reader's eye. Such an iconoclastic figure of the mother of mankind makes her less comprehensible or comprehensive than would a metaphysical conceit, for Milton produces an oscillation in which the difference of mutually exclusive terms is preserved, the identity refused or foreclosed. And yet this foreclosure is mortgaged, indebted to identifications which are, strictly speaking, illicit.

Milton's metaphor of Eve as "fairest unsupported Flow'r" is certainly what Aristotle would call a bad metaphor, since it cannot bring us to know what Eve or woman is. Instead, this metaphor gives us a perverse syntax and only serves to frustrate the clear and certain knowledge of woman's theological, ethical, and ontological status as she moves closer and closer to plucking the apple. Yet it is precisely such a syntax that contains the ingredients out of which a discourse of transgression can emerge, a syntax based upon the deconstruction of the binary opposition already established in the text of the epic. The metaphor of the flower can deconstruct these oppositions, because it insists that woman is situated in the syntactical margin that separates and confuses fallen with unfallen, good with evil. In fact, there is not simply transgression here, but a double crime, for not only does woman cross the margin between good and evil, but she does so in such a way that the problematic of good and evil is wrenched out of an acceptable theological perspective. By confusing good and evil and by denying their dialectical economy, woman overthrows theology and in *Paradise Lost* jeopardizes the epic's logocentric structure as well. The figure of woman does not, as the theologians do, respect the opposition of binary terms as a dialectic in which two distinct concepts work against each other to produce a synthesis, in which good gives way to evil only to be sublated again in the resurrection of Christ in the Last Judgment, for Eve is the criminal syntax that destroys dialectical economy by casting the terms into an indistinct economy in which such terms themselves are sacrificed or mutilated, their meanings lost. Already by making contraries into doubles, Eve, the radical iconoclast of paradise, inaugurates an economy that only works against (or plays against) the meanings of good and evil that are given in a Protestant theology, a theology so basic to the epic's formal structure.

As Derrida points out, it is not so much that metaphor is in the text; rather, these texts are in metaphor.[7] What appears in *Paradise Lost* as a simple, sensuous, and passionate metaphor for the alluring Eve, a marginal ornament slipped into the text, is very much a condensation in the Freudian sense of an ordered pattern of comparisons which all serve to undermine one another, a pattern which carries an entropic force. The metaphor of the unsupported flower is but another detail within a context of conflicting analogies; yet it is, in the passage we have been considering, a synecdoche for the surrounding comparisons, a synecdoche that cannot decide, that wavers already here between purity and sin, that knows so much of evil while being wholly innocent, so unconscious of the conflicts that only postlapsarian awakening can resolve within those texts what finally we term theology. Not only wavering between prelapsarian and postlapsarian, the "unsupported Flow'r" wavers between metaphor and synecdoche and leaves even that kind of literary distinction hazier than one might at first assume. But for now let us be content with studying more closely the violence of the metaphor, of this wavering between innocence and experience.

One of the problems arising in this regard can be thought about in terms of the Fall and the point at which that occurs. What has perplexed Miltonists, as well as every serious reader of *Paradise Lost*, is that the structure of the poem demands that we see Adam and Eve in two very different states, prelapsarian and postlapsarian; yet it is hard for most readers to believe that Eve is not in some sense fallen before the Fall, a reading which is, to be sure, an uncomfortable contradiction, one that Wayne Shumaker, who sees himself as an "orthodox Christian," reproaches the mischievous Millicent Bell for bringing up in "The Fallacy of the Fall in *Paradise Lost*."[8] According to Shumaker, Bell goes against "three centuries of correct interpretation" when she maintains that Eve has transgressed long before actually plucking the apple and in doing so has violated what the poem demands we accept, that Eve does not fall before line 781 of the ninth book: "She pluck'd, she eat:/Earth felt the wound." For Bell the question of fallenness before the Fall, this fallacy of the Fall, as she calls it, is already an issue determined in Augustine's *City of God*: "Our first parents fell into open disobedience because already they were secretly corrupted; for the evil act had never been done had not an evil will preceded it."[9] Not only Eve, but Adam too is fallen before the Fall, corrupt in will. Whether Milton's epic glosses this famous reading of Genesis will never be something one can prove, nor would it convince us that there is not a fundamental and great difference between Adam and Eve in *Paradise Lost*, that however much Adam may dote too much on Eve before the Fall, it is a crime that in itself does not deconstruct anything; Eve's criminality differs substantially in that regard.

What we know in terms of the passage quoted from *Paradise Lost* above is that the metaphor of woman as flower mimics and anticipates the contradiction of the Fall, suggesting that there is at once a confusion and distinction between two states. Certainly, this metaphor overthrows the violent hierarchy of good's supremacy over evil, not by simply reversing it, as Satan does, but by making the question of one term's superiority over the other an indeterminate matter. This is not to say the metaphor neutralizes or takes out of play the question of supremacy and subjection, of master and slave, but that it destructures their hierarchy by allowing one term to dominate and now another to take over.

This destructuring, or deconstruction, is most obvious in those passages Stanley Fish cites when he notes the reader is "surprised by sin," those passages in which the innocent garden and the innocent Eve are described in terms that for us have fallen or evil import. Thus Eve's "wanton" ringlets or the garden's "mazy" contours signify what a poststructuralist like Derrida would call a double scene of writing, in which a bifurcated text is in play, in this case, a text in which the prelapsarian is described or perceived in terms of the postlapsarian. Fish writes,

> By confronting the reader with a vocabulary bearing the taint of sin in a situation that could not possibly harbour it, Milton leaves him no choice but to acknowledge himself as the source, and to lament.[10]

The error in Fish's book from a Derridean point of view (and today Fish might agree) is the attempt to locate a source or origin in a text that is cloven, whose terms are, as in the metaphor of woman, in play in the ribbon that at once separates and confuses them. But even more disappointing is the fact that, attractive as Fish's argument seems—that this double scene of writing is meant to ambush an unsuspecting reader—it fails to come to terms with the problematic that concerns us here, Eve's fall. What Fish assumes is that it is the reader's own perversity that forces him to violate the law of contradiction operative in *Paradise Lost*, that allows him, even forces him, to entertain the notion that innocent

Eve is really fallen before she falls. What I would argue in defense of the guilty reader is that it is this double scene of writing itself that opens up *Paradise Lost* to an economics of transgression or sin that begins with repealing the Aristotelian law of contradiction. Indeed, Fish shows in *Surprised by Sin* how Milton's epic folds contraries over into doubles when in fact it should not do so, according to strict logical expectations; however, this doubling does not occur, as Fish believes, because the reader is simply ambushed, because he is tricked into making faulty assumptions about what words mean, but because the text itself is engaged in a deconstructive discourse that transgresses or trespasses from one state to another, that makes confusion and distinctions at the same time between a prelapsarian tongue and a fallen one. Indeed, to talk about states becomes itself erroneous, a misguided manner of reification, in this Miltonic economy of strategic twisting or torsion, what amounts to a violent skidding movement in which fallen and unfallen columns of language are put into relation. It is this putting into relation that is, on a miniature scale, reflected in the metaphor of woman as flower, a metaphor that bifurcates what is the whole of *Paradise Lost* in terms of the double scene of writing, a double scene which can already be glimpsed.

Unlike Fish's static-state theory, whose differences are always clearly marked or decidable, the poststructuralist's notion of a double scene is not an effect of a logocentric conception of thought, no matter how psychologically or aesthetically modulated, for a double scene always implies a bifocal vision in which the fold or space or angle between sides acts as a threshold that is unable to decide the question, "What is?" Such a threshold cannot fix relations by aspiring to the lexical or conceptual status of a term. Indeed, in even Derrida's texts the sign that represents the limen is always shifting: "blanc"—"pli"—"coin"—"e/antres" ("blank"—"fold"—"corner"—"between[s]"/"caves"). That is to say, the space that represents the threshold is *irreducible*. It does not gather meaning or fix meaning, and most certainly not like the New Critical notion of ambiguity which does precisely that, which, as Sigurd Burckhardt says, is based on the premise that "many meanings have *one word*," for the double scene scatters and disseminates meaning, fragments the text, explodes the relays of coherence, produces so many analogues that any concept of logocentricism that may attempt to install itself in the text is subverted.[11] Thus for the poststructuralist, the double scene of writing, which is nothing less than *écriture* itself, is precisely that which ensures the text will not become corporealized, as critics like Burckhardt and Murray Krieger would have it, is precisely that which prevents ambiguity (no matter how incompatible in Empson's sense) from arising as a limiting or determinate factor in the text.[12]

What I am stressing here is that the most far-reaching and deconstructive of the analogues of the "fairest unsupported Flow'r" metaphor is the Fall itself, for Eve as the unsupported flower is falling though sufficient to stand. Still but a kind of textual hint or foreshadowing, a tiny elegiac moment, the metaphor draws our attention to the possibility that the Fall may be nothing more than an undecidable space that separates and confuses good and evil rather than a clear historical break that places an unbridgeable gulf between innocence and experience, sacred and profane, but, more importantly, literature and truth. What the flower metaphor suggests is that the Fall may not be a thing so much as a "blanc" or "pli" that puts in relation the prelapsarian and postlapsarian without deciding either their difference or their identity. As everyone knows, the Fall never appears in *Paradise Lost*, although it happens. All we have for such a fall are but the signs for it: the plucking of the apple and Eve's tasting of the fruit, the withered garlands, the wound that earth feels, and so on. The Fall itself, however, is never present; it is only represented (re-presented or repeated) in terms of simulacrums that stand in for the Fall, that mimic the Fall, which in itself is not there or present. As the metaphor of the flower, itself a stand-in of this sort, suggests, the Fall is a transgression that never appears in itself, but whose effects are disturbing. It is, like the metaphor of Eve as flower, participating as an oscillating movement between various options, as a movement or free play which allows for the difference and identity which makes poetic language possible and which makes moot the kinds of debates that marked Milton criticism in the early fifties, debates premised on a reified Fall, a static poetics in which critics fight it out for firm and definite epic territory, for a certain place within what amounts to a very naïve plot model.

III

In considering the metaphor of the "fairest unsupported Flow'r," one may profitably turn to Francis Ponge, who in *Le parti pris des choses* writes the following in a characteristically telegraphic style:

> Un ensemble de loi[s] compliquées à l'extrême, c'est-à-dire le plus parfait hasard, préside à la naissance, et au placement des végétaux sur la surface du globe.
> La loi des *indéterminés déterminants*.
>
> ("A body of the most excessively complex laws, pure chance, in other words, presides over the birth and distribution of plants across the globe.
> The law of *undetermined determinants*.")[13]

The excess or surplus of energy which Ponge notices is characteristic of flowers, among other beings, and is an excess expressing itself botanically in a "vomiting of green"; such excess accounts for the "excessively complex laws" by which plants disseminate and replicate. This notion of excess is also to be found in Georges Bataille, particularly in *La part maudite* and its working papers, *L'économie à la mesure de l'univers*, writings which describe the effects of surplus energy in nature and economy.[14] Bataille would have seen Milton's paradise as exemplary of the idea that every system is blessed with a surplus or overload of energy whose tendency is suddenly to explode into a moment of pure release, the spasmatic liberation of bound energy. As William Blake may have agreed, the Fall in Milton is nothing else if not that. But this moment, however much we might attempt to define it, escapes strict bounded discourse, for the moment can only be marked with words: sacrifice, *jouissance*, violence, and, in Milton, Fall. Such moments (and this word is already but a marker or metaphor) are what Ponge calls the "undetermined determinants" or "chance."

Like Ponge's conception of flowers, Eve too is subject to an economics of excess, what Derrida might term supplementarity, and in *Paradise Lost* it becomes a question whether Eve can or ought to curb this overspilling of energy in herself as well as in the garden she must tend. Eve's zeal to divide the labor with Adam so that she can more efficiently bind the plants points to a subversive inability to control and police the deviant flowers and curb their desire to grow wild and express themselves in floral bursts, extensions of excess. For Eve is a compatriot of flowers, and the pun on "unsupported" suggests, in addition to so much else, a tension between something self-contained (standing up in its proper place) and uncontained (drooping and transgressing its natural station, overextending because of luxuriant growth). The pun also points to the elevation of a surplus energy in terms of the stiffened stem and the discharge of energy in the stem's slackness, a motif reflecting upon the theme of uxoriousness (Eve in Adam's role) and one that appears again in *Lycidas* in terms of the Derridean *anthérection*. What is most relevant in the context of these analogues is Bataille's sentence, "L'excès a toujours lieu mais l'énergie retrouve sa liberté première."[15] Satan notices this too when he views Eve in the garden: that excess always takes place, but this energy will recover its initial freedom.

Many are led to believe that because Milton lets us see so much through Satan's eyes, the inevitable expenditure of energy invested in Eve by nature will constitute her Fall, that Eve is originally depraved or prone to evil. However, the energy that she must release, this surplus, is itself neither good nor evil. It is merely energy and erupts in the interval, a moment, when nothing is decided and everything is left up to chance within the economy of a double scene. Just as we must not confuse the pun on *Eve* (Eve as evil, or as Heva: serpent) with her fate, link her inextricably with death, evil, and falling, we must not confuse her surplus of energy or beauty with corruption as if the two were bound. For we must recognize a *béance*, or opening, a place where and when the "fairest unsupported Flow'r" exposes itself to the unknown, throws or sacrifices itself to whatever fortune or peril might befall it. In this Eve is truly like a flower, for just as the erect flower disseminates its pollen and just as flowers scatter their seeds, sacrificing themselves and their progeny by exposing the future of the species to contingency, Eve rises to the occasion of her own fall, exposes herself and her progeny (the seed) to a contingent future. However, this future, though certain from God's perspective, is still one that is always open: left to chance, probability, and wager. The self is in suspension, even in this Calvinist universe, and nothing is certain until it happens.

In *Sacrifices* Bataille begins,

I exist—suspended in a realized void—suspended in my own distress—different from any other being and the diverse events that may affect any other and not me, cruelly banishing this self outside of a total existence. But at the same time, I consider my coming into the world—which depended upon birth and upon the intercourse of a certain man and woman, and then upon the moment of that intercourse—Indeed, there exists a unique moment in relation to the possibility of a self, a me—and thus there appeared the infinite improbability of this coming into the world.[16]

When one considers the violences, improbabilities, and contingencies to which the self is subject, the certainty invested in the notion of a homogeneous "I" determined in an Aristotelian sense collapses. "The total improbability of my coming into the world poses a total heterogeneity in an imperative mode," Bataille writes.[17] To be born is to belong to a catastrophe (and this even applies today in René Thom's sense of the word), an undecidable occurrence, to recall Derrida, in which something exceeds the purely rational and causal. The "I" cannot be exhausted by any homogeneous conceptual grid, by any totality of thoughts, any system. In short, medicine simply cannot account for *me*, however much it can account for anyone in general. What is referred to as the self, Bataille says, is an impasse, a reified term that represses what really matters: all those possible selves that *could have* existed. What "I" am is precisely everything other than what might have constituted me as well as all that I might never have become. Thus in *Sacrifices* it is clear that the self is to be considered as a difference or deviance, the arbitrary actualization of potentials in some form or construct that defines itself in terms of its distance from other probable and actual manifestations.

More importantly, the self is a remainder, whatever scrap chance leaves over, and even that scrap is living in a suspended relation between life and death. It is a remainder estranged from itself, its own heterogeneity, and that estrangement expresses itself as homogeneity: the ability to represent oneself as oneself and not an other. The idea of sacrifice is crucial, for the self is always hollowed out by its own negation, crossing itself out or being crossed out in a violent and contingent existence which constitutes the suspension, or hiatus, in which a future is asymmetrical with the past. It is a condition we see again in Blanchot's *L'arrêt de mort* or *Le très haut*, a condition that opens for Blanchot the *entretien infini*, or infinite dialogue. But already in 1936 one could read this in Bataille:

The self raising itself to the pure imperative, living-dying for the sake of a boundless, bottomless abyss, this imperative defines itself "die like a dog" in the strangest part of being.[18]

In Bataille's work, the self is supported-unsupported, rising-falling, living-dying. And it does so for *the sake of (pour)* an abyss (*abîme*), a moment or interval when everything is suspended, undecidable, undefinable, between two scenes, an interval where the homogeneity or possibility of representation as presenting something that is present to itself is threatened. There is just the imperative, "Die like a dog!"

Such Satanic suggestions hold their tongues during Eve's temptation, although she is also in suspense and condemned to "die like a dog," to be sacrificed. A self is in suspense, undecidably between life and death, for God has made that the enabling condition for man and woman's existence in paradise. And now in book 9 of the epic a woman or flower is poised on the threshold of annihilation, a condition of the self which exceeds homogeneity, the ability of mere representation to recuperate a self. More than ever, Eve, like the flowers, is plural, heterogeneous, disseminating. Her self cannot be represented as something final, shackled to a transcendental signified, but has to be understood as that which eludes strict representation, since the self is a differing, an oscillation within a dynamic of perpetual suspension, like the clapper in a bell which must sound the knell of death and transfiguration. At best there can only be figures which approximate this situation of the self, the structural relations with regard to the condition of existence or placement in the life world, of which Blanchot's *l'arrêt de mort* is exemplary.[19]

With this in mind, let us consider Eve before the tree of knowledge with its surplus of forbidden fruit, pausing for a moment, suspending the action of the epic. She has heard Satan out, even though not exactly aware that a temptation scene is in progress and that she is starring in the role of victim. And so far all Eve knows is that another friendly intelligence has been discovered in Eden, another opinion heard, and that a little empirical demonstration has been made: a serpent has eaten of the forbidden apples and now can speak. She is through listening, and now there is a pause: "Pausing a while, thus to herself she mus'd" (9.744). An ordinary reader might easily skip over this pause, of course, reading ahead into Eve's speech of amazement and perplexity on all that she has heard. Yet some of us might be tempted to ask, how long is this pause in "Pausing a while"? And what occurs here? Critics have noticed the fruit tempts Eve only after she has decided to eat, that suddenly the apples smell fragrant after Eve's mind has been corrupted. Has her mind been made up during this pause? Has a decision been made? Alastair Fowler's edition of *Paradise Lost* points out in the voluminous footnote apparatus that it would have been "improvident or provoking" of God to allow Eve to be tempted by the fruit itself. But since Eve is corrupted, the blame rests with her. Fowler also adds, "The pause is indispensable: Eve must have time to resolve deliberately before acting."[20]

But what is resolved here? What has happened? Is Eve fallen after this pause, as the annotations in Fowler's edition suggest? Has the Fall occurred already, forty-two lines before Eve actually plucks and eats? Or must one acknowledge prelapsarian corruption? To say that the notion of a single Fall is fallacious goes without saying. At issue is not a decisive rupture, but, rather, moments in the epic which are curiously suspended, lapses which are charged with undetermined determinacy: an undecidable violence which refuses such easy resolutions as the Fall fallacy critics have proposed. Such suspended moments, or pauses, if you will, are heterogeneous and threaten the cogency of the usual either-or and fallen-unfallen logic and with it the cogency of an "I" identical with itself from one moment to the next. In the pause we are considering Eve is herself undetermined, in flux. We see no reason why she might not just coyly go back to Adam, refreshing herself at his side and not Satan's, since she is free to leave the scene in which her crime will be performed.

And if much is in suspension here, we might inquire also into the speech which follows the pause, a speech which may or may not belong to the moment of the pause itself. Indeed, Fowler's annotations can at best only assume a difference between the pause and the speech that follows, can only assume a resolution has taken place in the mind before it is represented in words and deeds. But such an assumption cannot be proven, never made determinate. Whether the pause constitutes an action in the plot is exceedingly more complicated to decide than one might at first presume. And the speech that follows the pause is difficult to interpret because we are not sure to whom it is addressed: Satan? Eve? God? or the reader? the tree? My point is that a reader can only jump or leap to a conclusion in order to decide and stop the free play of possibilities from all suggesting themselves at the same time. Traditionally, such leaping is done with the venerable authorities in mind whom Milton supposedly consulted at such moments in his text. But this kind of historicism, crude as it is, never acts as anything more than a contextual frame whose purpose is to stop dissemination in the text, as a brake for interpretation.

Bataille would argue that such a pause as we are considering constitutes a sacrificial moment in which Eve raises herself to the pure imperative of a "living-dying" for the sake of an abyss, a suspended relation in which the self is at once supported-unsupported, rising-falling, living-dying. Such a relation, pause, or abyss is undecidable and therefore cannot be represented, but only repeated in the structural terms of a double session or scene, what amounts to an interval where the homogeneity of self-identity is discarded or sacrificed for the sake of the plural, a sacrifice Derrida calls *dissémination.* The sacrifice is the abyss which constitutes the self, not as a cogito, but as the fallen residue of an excess of energy, of an overspilling. Just as the flowers in Eden are marked by a surplus of energy and beauty, of what Ponge calls the excessive complexity of indeterminate determinacies characteristic of all flowers, a complexity which has everything to do with a build-up of force which seeks sudden release in a disseminating moment which cannot contain or predict how energy will be spilled, in Eve, too, there is a similar force in tension with the structure of her existential and moral condition, a supplementary force whose overspilling is that sacrificial moment in which the self is cast in radical suspense and made unrecuperable, unrepresentable. Such sacrifice can only be marked by metaphor, like the trope of an unsupported plant, a pause, a theory of sacrifice or double sessions. The overspilling of the floral and the feminine into a catastrophic moment of dissemination signifies the point at which the distinction between form and force becomes itself undecidable, an operation in which the text and its relations are fractured by means of cleavages which occlude the reader's ability to homogenize all the registers of the text into a uniplanar reading construction.

That is to say, *Paradise Lost* is not a text meant for an eighteenth-century reader whose gaze or perception is omniscient and trained by way of mathesis to turn a text into a similacrum of continuous and self-evident relations. Rather, the text is perforated by moments which frustrate such rationalistic readings. In the following section, where I take up the question of representation in terms of a certain dream work in *Paradise Lost*, we come to terms with how a seventeenth-century text situates itself in a readerly *imaginaire*, to borrow a term from Jacques Lacan, which cannot presuppose a Cartesian and rationalist *cogito*. It is through flowers and women, then, that we come to appreciate this deconstruction of the self in *Paradise Lost*.

IV

If we have noted the indeterminacy of a pause in which sacrifice occurs, we must consider at more length what sacrifice signifies in terms of temporality and the status of vision and representation in *Paradise Lost*. What will concern us in this section is how sacrifice can be referenced with the Derridean notion of the hymen in "La double séance," thus demonstrating how in the epic a present moment can be understood as the effect of moments which are strictly speaking not present or there. The scene of the now is, therefore, always an effect of scenes elsewhere. That is to say, the sacrificial present is always repressed or deferred in the text. The scenes are displaced and occluded. In this sense the text achieves a dreamlike quality, for at work are so many double scenic strategies which allow us to see what is there only by way of looking at or considering something that is elsewhere. Indeed, if the trauma of sacrifice is dissimulated, we notice that such dissimulation concerns not only gaps or pauses in the text but represented figures as well, that is, the "unsupported Flow'r" and Eve. Notice that the seductive and alluring figure of Eve can be read from a Freudian view as the mother who cannot be seen in her nakedness by our gaze without being displaced. Eve is what Jacques Lacan might term the Freudian thing, that feminine enigma which vanishes as it appears. In making this case, we elaborate upon previous sections and move forward an analysis of a feminine infrastructure in *Paradise Lost* whose deconstructive potential should not be overlooked from the standpoint of mimesis and visibility. In this way we prepare for an examination of Botticelli's art in which a flower girl once again puts representation in jeopardy.

We begin with Derrida's explanation of the hymen as not simply a spatial but as a temporal marker.

Grâce à la confusion et à la continuité de l'hymen, non pas en dépit de lui, s'inscrit une différence (pure et impure) sans pôles décidables, sans termes indépendants et irréversibles. Telle différance sans présence apparaît ou plutôt déjoue l'apparaître en disloquant un temps ordonné au centre du présent. Le présent n'est plus une forme-mère autour de laquelle se distinguent et se rassemblent le (présent) futur et le (présent) passé. Ne sont marquées dans cet hymen entre le futur (désir) et le présent (accomplissement), entre le passé (souvenir) et le présent (perpétration), entre la puissance et l'acte, etc., que des différences temporelles sans présent central, sans un présent dont le passé et l'avenir ne seraient que les modifications. Peut-on dès lors parler encore de *temps* et de différences *temporelles?*

("Thanks to the confusion and continuity of the hymen, and not in spite of it, a (pure and impure) difference inscribes itself without any decidable poles, without any independent, irreversible terms. Such difference without presence appears, or rather baffles the process of appearing, by dislocating any orderly time at the center of the present. The present is no longer a mother-form around which are gathered and differentiated the future (present) and the past (present). What is marked in this hymen between the future (desire) and the present (fulfillment), between the past (remembrance) and the present (perpetration), between the capacity and the act, etc., is only a series of temporal differences without any central present, without a present of which the past and future would be but modifications. Can we then go on speaking about *time, tenses,* and *temporal* differences?")[21]

Without the mother form of the present, the real never offers itself up in the plenitude of a now. Everything becomes much like the pause we have considered in book 9, a moment which is not saturated with any central present and which frustrates our sense of time, tense, and temporal difference. Derrida insists that by way of considering a double scene, particularly as it is marked by the hymen, the question of perception is put into jeopardy, since one perceives in the present when something is offered up. Indeed, the double scene or session with its hymen can and must be thought of in the following manner:

L'hymen illustrant la suspension des différents, que reste-t-il? plus que le Rêve. La majuscule frappe l'inédit d'un concept qui n'appartient plus à la vieille opposition: le Rêve, étant à la fois perception, souvenir et anticipation (désir), chacun dans l'autre, n'est vraiment ni l'un ni l'autre.

("What does the hymen that illustrates the suspension of differends remain, other than Dream? The capital letter marks what is new in a concept no longer enclosed in the old opposition: Dream, being at once perception, remembrance, and anticipation (desire), each within the others, is really none of these.")[22]

We are not too distant from Jacques Lacan's well-known formulation of the *imaginaire,* and if Lacan was touchy about Derrida's appropriation of Lacanian psychology, such passages justify the father of French Freud's sensitivity. Derrida's interest is also in formulating a mimicry without imitation, what he calls the miming of an appearance which has no real (*le réel*) behind it. The present is but a false appearance, the effect of a not-there which is nevertheless constructed, produced out of the traces of surrounding moments or displaced times.

This is noticeable in *Paradise Lost* to the degree that Milton disarticulates the mother form of the present by way of calling up so many analeptic and proleptic moments, thus perforating the now with a fictive trace structure whose effect is to dissolve or erase the present as such. Already in the first two books of the epic, Satan and the hellish throng try to ascertain themselves as present by way of constructing a Cartesian now in relation to a past. However, in book 2 it is clear that the now is just a hypothesis, that the devils cannot perceive themselves yet as anything other than drastically changed. Not until book 10 will history assign the devils a temporality by which they can know themselves in relation to a fall which is, incidently, not theirs, a scene which happens in the dreamlike paradise. But if the devils must know their present sin by way of man's first disobedience, Adam is given proleptic admonitions by way of being told about the disobedience of Satan and the war which ensues. Again, one is expected to ascertain a moment by way of reflecting on a scene which is not of a mother form of the present. It is as if everyone were being asked to see double or by way of displacement in *Paradise Lost*.

Some familiar instances of this doubling or displacing of scenes which accompanies the formation and dissolution of a centered present includes the dream in which Adam tells Raphael about God's creation of man and woman; Eve's well-known dream which doubles the Fall in book 9; the odd discussion God has with the Son in book 3 about man's redemption through the sacrifice of the Son, this news which cannot be *news* to the Son; and the history that is told Adam in the last books of the epic. Although these latter histories are supposed to concretize a fallen perception on Adam's part, they repeat accounts like the war in heaven, producing more of an emotional than an intellectual effect, a dreamlike or, in this case, a nightmarish perception which knows no now.

T. S. Eliot was aware of such a disarticulation of the mother form of the present when he insisted in *On Poetry and Poets* that visualizing *Paradise Lost* is indeed a disturbing experience for the reader, since what one sees and hears in the poem frustrates perceptual synthesis. Eliot believed that this disjunction between seeing and hearing occurred because Milton's vision was defective, that, like James Joyce, Milton was compensating for bad eyesight with a surplus of poetic *melos*.[23] Empirical explanations aside, one could better argue that Milton uses analeptic and proleptic scenes in order to render Adam and Eve as subjects who have never been initiated into what Lacan calls the real. In other words, for the parents of mankind, paradise is all in the *imaginaire*, or imaginary. It is a place where the difference between self and other is not yet experienced fully as an absolute split, where objects and consciousness are not yet bifurcated. In the real (*le réel*), of course, absolute repressions take place. We are situated in an alienated present whose ground is predicated upon a refusal to see an abyss. Thus out of foreclosing the abyss, what amounts to Bataille's notion of sacrifice, the empirical comes to be.

If Eve is attracted to her reflection in the water shortly after her creation, it is not simple narcissism, but a scene in which a mother form of the present is refracted in a double sitting, session, or scene. Although Eve appears as mother form of presence, she is anything but articulated in the certainty of a now or presence. In her self-perception there is a suspension of difference and identity that makes the self and the now but an effect of dreamy reflection, a now without present, presence, or place. This is the condition of the imaginary (*l'imaginaire*) which counters the baseness of Satanic enlightenment, "The mind is its own place, and in itself / Can make a Heav'n of Hell, a Hell of Heav'n" (1:254–55). For Satan the presence and present of mind is immutable. It is always grounded in the real and absolutely represses acknowledgment of an abyss or suspension in which the self is defetishized, the now of a will to power threatened.

For the paradisal couple, the real is kept far away, because Eden is not yet a world that can be perceived in terms of the historical now. Notice that the function of prayer, discussion, and narrative is mainly to retell and foretell, to place man and woman in an iterative mode which does not know how to arrest itself in a single moment or time. Even after the Fall of Adam and Eve, narrative still accedes to the level of echo, for even in the last books, prosaic or flat as they may sound, history is not yet quite history. For even as Adam and Eve leave paradise, they walk through a ruin which is still a dream unrecoverable by historical consciousness. Though Adam and Eve have changed, and drastically so, they are still more or less innocent in very significant ways, caught in a hiatus between having lived in Eden and knowing no other kind of life in the wilderness. Where history is felt most, perhaps, is in hell, since it is there the devils have been languishing and have been finding themselves more and more reified. It is in this materialization of the self with its concomitant investment in evil and ruin of the creation (something Satan believes can happen in one stroke) that hell finds itself temporally in a present whose very construction or constitution reduces consciousness to merely a crass essentialism and empiricism. It is here that John Locke is anticipated and critiqued by way of a poem whose double sessions deconstruct Enlightenment thinking at the moment of its very dawn in Western civilization.

The impossibility of the present is not only evident in the action code which makes up the plot but is manifest in terms of objects we are likely to visualize in the poem. Again the "unsupported Flow'r" is exemplary. The trope disconcerts vision because it offers a view of Eve, invites us to see her, but also occludes her figure through the filter of temporal transpositions. We see Eve, not in the present, but in terms of the difference and identification of prelapsarian and postlapsarian. The "unsupported Flow'r" is analogous to the (non)concept of the hymen in "La double séance," because it marks the impossibility of a space in which a present can appear per se. The "unsupported Flow'r" mimics but does not imitate a mother form of the present. Perception is perforated, then, because of the manner in which a trope such as the "unsupported Flow'r" fractures the locus of the gaze's object, refracts the reader's glance. Since Eve is identified so closely with this pun which locates and dislocates her, sees and occludes her, we notice that her presentness becomes but a matter of dissimulation through other scenes. Her now is deconstituted by a temporal conflict or trace structure out of which her present is composed.

We have already noted how the "unsupported Flow'r" is disseminative with regard to the sacrificial in the previous section of this chapter. What I wish to stress now is how by prolepsis the "unsupported Flow'r" shifts to another scene: from the sacrifice of Eve which is anticipated by the word "unsupported" to the foreshadowing of the sacrifice of Christ on the cross. The trope raises the suggestion that Eve is like Christ, since the flower itself looks forward to the cross upon which Christ falls and rises. Like the stalk of the flower, the cross is that place where falling and rising, the unsupported and the supported, is figured forth. Like Christ, Eve is immortal and yet mortal, strong and yet vulnerable, holy and yet defiled. She is, like Christ, asked to experience a death that will have significance for all mankind, and like Christ is sacrificed by way of being asked (in Bataille's sense) to die like a dog. Of course the "unsupported Flow'r," the tree of good and evil, the cross, and other botanical figures in Scripture work to make such typological connections by way of metalepsis. Without forcing the point too much, we might simply point out that in the anticipation of the Fall, the "unsupported Flow'r" trope also recollects from a very distant future yet another sacrificial moment which will make of Eve's fall a felix culpa. By way of such displacement the "unsupported Flow'r" sublimates psychic pain and produces a resistance to the sacrificial now whose present is the effect of a double sacrifice or diptych. The trope of the flower is thus structured to show and veil sacrifice.

Perhaps it is no accident that, when Eve approaches the serpent, she will not know to whom she is speaking, for she, like the reader, is not privileged to see the sacrifice which is in progress. For her there are only recollective and anticipatory moments which derealize the present. Although she converses with the serpent, she has only other and imaginary scenes by which to comprehend him. Perhaps the serpent as representation is to Eve what the "unsupported Flow'r" is to the reader: a tropological vision which remembers and anticipates in order that the present remain imperceptible as mother form of presence, a vision which remains but what Derrida calls dream.

What is represented? It is the hymen as sacrificial membrane which Eve is privileged to offer the reader, a hymen always already rupture and veil, a nonconcept and nonappearance whose marked-unmarked being intrudes and leaves alone. Perhaps René Girard would caution us that there is nothing odd about the fact that in Genesis the sacrifice is hidden even at the beginning of time, that in *Paradise Lost* the hymen is the hymn of the scapegoat who knows no present, whose sacrifice is narrated but never unveiled. What one knows is only the effect of the representation (the re-presentation or iteration) of sacrifice, but never the mother form of its presentness. Rather, the now is hidden, faded, and dissolved into so many dreams and phantasms; the now is what cannot be represented or viewed in the fullness of its being.

The scene, then, is the sacrifice and dissimulates or displaces because of the violence which is the representational or mimetic apparatus, the trauma of the scene. No wonder

Paradise Lost is visually and psychologically disturbing. Yet it is also pleasurable and wondrous, for its spectacles elicit a passive gaze upon the originating scenes of sin whose deferrals and deconstructions of the origination captivate the reader's desire to see. And how is this captivation produced if not by way of visual detours? We are captivated only because representation is displacement, because the trauma of the Fall is pleasurably displaced or repressed into a textual unconscious which is produced by the phantasmic effect of the double scene. Hence we note the appearance of a dreamwork in *Paradise Lost*.

The epic, then, is a speaking picture which we can only see indirectly by a visual deferral, and from a Freudian orientation the text becomes much like a woman's body which dissimulates beneath the captivated gaze of a voyeur, a body that can never be seen except as that which it is not. Lacan's title for one of his seminars, "Encore," makes a playful pun, however forced, between signifying "in the body" (*en corps*) and "again" (*encore*), a point stressed by Sanford Ames, and thereby suggests that any desire to see into the body ("Encore" is about female sexuality) only forces us to look again.[24] Seeing therefore turns into repetition compulsion. In *Paradise Lost*, the body of Eve as well as the flower trope are both supported and unsupported by a compulsive gaze in precisely this manner, a compulsion which my text acts out. *Paradise Lost*, then, is the textual body as feminine form which exacts from us a gaze trapped between *en corps* and *encore*. It is the performance which we as readers all must repeat in order to fulfill our desire to see.

Eve is the mother form of the present which is but an effect of a double seeing which Lacan explores in great detail by way of puns like "encore." But Lacan also recognizes in the body of woman a "Freudian Thing." This is Diana from mythology who as "la chose elle-même" ("the thing herself") speaks to Actaeon: "Je suis donc pour vous l'énigme de celle qui se dérobe aussitôt qu'apparue" ("So for you I am the enigma of her who vanishes as soon as she appears"). Moreover, the Freudian thing insists that,

Moi la vérité, contre vous la grande trompeuse, puisque ce n'est pas seulement par la fausseté que passent mes voies, mais par la faille trop étroite à trouver au défaut de la feinte et par la nuée sans accès du rêve, par la fascination sans motif du médiocre et l'impasse séduisante de l'absurdité.

("I, the truth, would be against you, the great deceiver, since it is not only through falsehood that my ways pass, but by the hole or veil too narrow to find for want of pretence and through the inaccessible cloud of the dream, and through the motiveless fascination of the mediocre and the seductive impasse of absurdity.")[25]

That is to say, the ways of truth-deceit pass through not only falsehoods (*la fausseté* = faithlessness) but by or through *la faille,* the crack, hole, tear, but also the veil of coarse silk which covers the hole and which the Freudian thing wears. To recall "La double séance," the *faille* is analogous to the hymen, and not any less deconstructive.

Let us conclude this part of our discussion on the following points. The Derridean hymen is very much the Freudian thing whose truth is articulated as specular deceit herself, the impasse of the scopic drive's faith in recognizing truth as truth where one sees it, the absurdity of an empirical gaze. This deceit-truth is based on "la fascination sans motif du médiocre" which can be translated as the "motiveless fascination of the mediocre," or as "the fascination without mediocre motive," my supplement to Alan Sheridan's rendering. The reason for Lacan's syntactic punning is that fascination can be at once captivated and yet oddly inattentive to what is really there; it can be a motiveless fascination which looks at things, however mediocre or uninteresting. And yet fascination can at the same time be strongly engaged, caught up in *l'emprise* (seizure, captivation, expropriation, and so forth). Fascination sees through the crack or slot but is distracted by the veils or coverings. From a Lacanian perspective this is how phobic objects are produced, what the Freudian thing amounts to, and thus one must consider far more than Derrida does in "La double séance" a certain unconscious attention which outsiders will always see as "the seductive impasse of absurdity."

Without doubt, there are those who read the great matter of *Paradise Lost* as seductively absurd, however willing they may be to suspend disbelief. But to do so is to recognize and miss the marvelous phobic quality of the poem's mimetic register. For if the Freudian things in the poem resist penetration of a reader's gaze, it is because the reader is trapped in an encore whose supplement will never constitute the performance. Lastly, what guarantees the hold of the phobic representation is the loss of a certain time, the now, which the encore wishes to restore. In that loss of the present the phobic nature of representation is maintained, its captivation secured, the absurd seductiveness of woman and text with all its tropological displacements kept safe, while all sights are veiled and kept secret, as if we were but in the inaccessible cloud of a dream which fears not to look at what it fears to see.

V

In spectacle there is always sacrifice, since, as Louis Marin has argued, the representation is a trap or snare for the viewer whose end is the immobilization of the gaze in a pause which is unable to decide what it is one is *really* looking at. Marin has argued this position quite effectively with respect to French culture during the time of Louis XIV, arguing that especially with the trompe l'oeil, the viewer is trapped within the radical ambiguity of a representation which poses itself as both imaginary and real, thus immobilizing the viewer in a moment which renders one wholly passive.[26] It is at this zero degree of action, this perplexing moment of surprise in which imagination and reality compete for truth status in the mind of the viewer, that the representation reveals its dominance over the viewer. Marin believes that in this manner, the representation raises the question of death, since what is real is precisely the figure or outline of something that is not there. The real is death, but the imaginary steps in as a defense mechanism which phantomizes the portrait or scene, reinscribing it with a living pretense: the so-called likeness of the representation. Here again the abyss is covered over by the veil which is the representation; the real is denied by the viewer, who defends himself against the terrible truth that the viewer himself is fated to die, that the cogito is but a representation for a presence which is not wholly present to itself, a presence which can only imagine a now or present by means of recollecting and anticipating. The now is false; the self is false; one's sense of one's substantiality and subjecthood is false. Only representations support and unsupport these illusions whose necessity none of us can deny. As Descartes himself noted, "Masked I go forward" ("Larvatus prodeo").[27]

The historical affiliation of French seventeenth-century culture with English culture of the same period is in itself a complex issue, but no one can deny that Milton could have been acquainted with the kinds of mimetic questions which preoccupied his contemporaries on the Continent. If in the Netherlands painters like Vermeer, Saenredam, and Rembrandt were articulating a highly sophisticated visual subversion of common perceptual assumptions, and if Poussin, a French painter, developed even more subtle ways to fool the eye, it is unlikely that, however poor his eyesight, Milton would not at least have known about the rendering of spectacles whose scenes put the subjecthood of the viewer into a doubtful relation between that which is certain and uncertain. Michel Foucault has demonstrated how in *Las meninas* (1656) by Velázquez "no gaze is stable, or rather, in the neutral furrow of the gaze piercing at a right angle through the canvas, subject and object, the spectator and the model, reverse their roles to infinity." Foucault continues by insisting that with the painting's back or reverse side towards us, by which he means the inversion of the scene upon which we look, the painting is "stubbornly invisible." Thus "it prevents the relation of [the] gazes from ever being discoverable or definitely established."[28] The choice of *La meninas* by Foucault is made to demonstrate to what extent the seventeenth century produced spectacles in which the now was bracketed by the illusion of presence. And it is interesting from our point of view that in *Las meninas* there is a double scene which Foucault elaborates and in doing so touches very much on Derrida's point that by means of the double scenes, sessions, or sittings the imitated presence gives way to a mimicry without a mother form of presence.

The problematization of the mise en scène did not occur simply in the seventeenth century, of course, but occurs much earlier in the High Renaissance. We see this already in the very famous painting of Van Eyck, *Giovanni Arnolfini and His Wife* (1434), and again the well-known painting of Hans Holbein the Younger, *The French Ambassadors* (1533). What will concern us, however, is but another of these famous works, the *Primavera* (1478) of Botticelli. It is most probable that Milton actually saw this painting on his Italian journey and that its influence may have exerted itself on *Paradise Lost*, though like any such historical connection we can only make a hypothetical link. Still, there is the interesting fact that in the *Primavera* one has a double scene operative which concerns not only pastoral imagery but an unusual flower girl who is like Milton's Eve at once deviant and innocent. In some ways we are closer to Genet than to Milton, since the question posed by the figure of Botticelli's flower girl raises the status of her sexuality, one that is usually subsumed within the larger question of just trying to establish who or what this figure in Botticelli's painting is. This ambivalence may not be due simply to ignorance of Renaissance tradition, but Botticelli may have desired to disturb what Renaissance art historians have perceived as the fixed relationship between symbol and reference. However, we can be sure that Flora is a more or less feminine representation of a promiscuous proliferation of flowers induced by the potent breath of Zephyr. Flora represents dissemination. Whether she is really a girl is another question, one we will take up shortly.

In Ovid's *Fasti*, a probable source for much of what is represented in the *Primavera*, Flora tells the reader she was the first to scatter the new seeds among countless people.[29] Unlike the goddess of love, who is diffident, self-contained, motionless, or the three Graces, further emissaries of culture, of social behavior, Flora is not statically positioned. She does not stand, like Venus, in a motionless, weighty posture, nor does she revolve, as the Graces do, around a center. Instead, Flora as the emissary of nature traverses the canvas as she scatters her flowers, or herself, about. Like the arrows the blind cupid shoots, the flowers of Flora are dispersed in a careless, haphazard manner. For she represents not only the floral but the spring as well, the climate of dissemination. Indeed, the flowers are thrown, as Plato would say, in a "holiday spirit" that is reckless and deviant.

And certainly such deviance goes far beyond Flora's mere act of strewing flowers, for it marks the indiscriminate tossing off of her bountiful gift with unchaste enthusiasm, reflected partly in her smile. That not merely the act of tossing the flowers but Flora herself are perverse is seen in her face, which manifests some qualities that commentators find disturbing. For example, Jan Kott in *Shakespeare Our Contemporary* notes that Botticelli's Flora is sexually ambivalent, not unlike Genet's "flowers," for

Flora looks like a tall, fair-haired boy who has been disguised for the purpose of the carnival procession, dressed in a transparent veil with flowers, his hair combed and curled. He has a sad triangular face, still almost Gothic. He seems to be ashamed of his participation in this masquerade. He turns his head back at the sight of girls, tempting and tempted, present and absent. He smiles with the corner of the mouth, but the smile is like a grimace.[30]

Perhaps in itself a deviant interpretation when seen in the light of extensive documentation by E. H. Gombrich, Edgar Wind, and Charles Dempsey—that Flora is a transformation of the frightened Chloris—Kott's insight is less concerned with classical allusion than with pastoral genre, which he sees, in the chapter "Shakespeare's Bitter Arcadia," as disturbed and troubled from within.[31] Indeed, he is right when he notices that Flora's face is not like those faces of the Graces or Venus, but far more angular, sharp, masculine. There is not the expression of feminine grace, no sympathetic diffidence as in the faces of the other females. Rather, Flora's smile communicates an ironic gesture that undermines our confidence in both her innocence and her femininity. She communicates the message that she may not be what she appears to be, that her garb is not wholly suited to her.

Like Genet's inmate flowers and Milton's Eve, Flora is a deconstructive outlaw whose transgressions are easily identifiable. Like Our Lady of Genet, Flora's sexuality is ambivalent and indeterminate, a violation of what should be a clear distinction between male and female. Eve too is a usurper of man's role, a metaphor for Adam, or being *for another*. Thus when she postures before the beguiling serpent, she is only carrying through her natural inclinations, which in theological terms are perverse and transgressive. Moreover, Flora, like Eve, is uncivilized in her manner of indiscriminately strewing about her bounty, a strewing of excess that trespasses on civilized codes of order, whose representatives, Venus, the three Graces, and even the errant cupid, are present in the painting. In Botticelli the strewing of flowers reminds one in Milton of the dishevelment of Eve's hair that "in wanton ringlets wav'd / As the Vine curls her tendrils" (4.306–7). More importantly, in Ovid's *Fasti* there is reason to call Flora a thief, for she cleverly tricks Zephyr into giving her the mantle of flowers, a mantle that does not properly belong to her. As in Genet's novels, this form of thievery is really the robbery of an identity, an illicit borrowing or taking on of an alias that results in a visual personification or metaphorization whose double scene, the figure known as Flora before the transformation (or transgression) as seen through the figure of Flora after the transformation, confuses at the same time that it straightens out identities. But if Flora steals the mantle, Eve steals the forbidden fruit and similarly broaches the matter of a double scene, one that Genet too becomes familiar with in far more hideous and malevolent terms. In all of the pastoral flower girls we have noted, the question of dissemination is connected to the question of the mixing or pollution of identities, one that results when seeds are randomly cast about and hybrids cultivated, that results when Zephyr capriciously casts his floral mantle on Botticelli's ambivalent flower child.

The associations made by Botticelli between woman and flowers, and goddesses and their respective gardens, already foreshadows in the late fifteenth century a skeptical vision of the *locus amoenus,* a vision in which the garden, personified by woman, becomes a *locus* for transgression, dissemination, redoubling, and, it must be admitted, symbolic castration. But more interesting is the suggestion that, in addition to this, Botticelli situates Flora in a double scene that throws into question the query, "Qu'est-ce que?" I am referring to the fact that Flora is often considered the transformation of Chloris, Chloris's double. Again, the gap that separates the doubles, the transformation, is really a partition, or screen, analogous to the concept of transgression we have been considering in *Paradise Lost.* Like the Fall, this transformation in Botticelli never presents itself as itself, though its effects are obvious. What this transformation produces is a mixing, or pollution, of one identity with another, a grafting on one figure with another, and it is this pollution that leads one to suspect that the transformation itself is very much a part of what we call dissemination: that which the figure of Flora is actually represented as enacting. The strewing of the flowers itself immediately suggests a cutting off, or decapitation, of the blooms as well as a mixing, or confusion, of them with one another, and this decapitation and confusion are nothing less than an imitation of the undecidable transformation that at once separates Flora from Chloris at the same time that it mixes their identities. Indeed, the image of Flora scattering the blooms is but an emblem for this transformation, an emblem for a process of dividing and confusing, for what Derrida has termed the economics of undecidability, the double scene of writing. It is this economics of undecidability that is, even in Derrida's terminology, seen as a literal dissemination by Botticelli and similarly by Milton in *Paradise Lost* in terms of nature's wanton vitality, which distinguishes and confuses the contraries of nature-culture, master-slave, dependence-independence, for such a vitality at once submits to Adam's reason and the civilized vision engendered through the discussions between Adam and Raphael even while it surpasses and oversteps such rational bounds.

What is striking in Botticelli, of course, is that the double scene is visually represented as two scenes painted on the same canvas next to one another and that it is the meaning of these two scenes that has thoroughly eluded all spectators who are critically minded. E. H. Gombrich suggests there may be a purposeful attempt on the part of Botticelli to harass the clear referential path between sign and meaning, and certainly this justifies the hypothesis that perhaps Botticelli intended the kind of double scene we are suggesting takes place in the *Primavera*. But if this scene eludes strict referentiality, is it not because such a scene is itself metaphor?

Certainly Flora is a metaphor for Chloris, since Flora represents her as an other and vice versa. This constitutes the paradigmatic reading of what could be read syntagmatically and leads us to ask whether one ought to consider metaphor as, not merely a trope within the text (the painting), but rather as a text within a trope. In terms of the *Primavera* this means subordinating so many pictorial signs to the suspended relation of Flora to Chloris and thereby broaching the Derridean problematic of the border or fold, that is to say, metaphor as the threshold that maintains the place of a relation it denies at once. For to say that Flora is Chloris is to fabricate a lie, to dissimulate or disseminate a truth. In "La mythologie blanche," Derrida shows that the radiance of metaphor, its power of illuminating or disseminating the connections between things, is an extinguishing of one identity in another and at the same time a purposeful "misrecognition" ("méconnaissance") of identities (an awareness of differences) that maintains the original obscurity of connections. In this sense the radiance of metaphor puts itself out, produces what Derrida calls an "effacement of the visage of being" ("effacement du visage de l'être").[32] And what does one have in Botticelli if not just such an effacement of the face, the radiance of two faces (of Chloris, of Flora) that by means of their both being present at once obscures their reference? And certainly this is not surprising, for as Derrida points out, metaphor is a calculated risk, a double scene that basks in the loss of an original or prior meaning, which in the arts is something of an investment whose profit is the aesthetic, that "je ne sais quoi" whose articulation is always the matter for critics.

Following this line of thinking, one can add that the double scene in Botticelli not only produces a surplus value of beauty but preserves, even as it attempts to dispel, a sense of depth, of hiddenness, of the mystery of what we might term woman, the sexual, or desire. Botticelli's double scene illuminates and makes most visually accessible that which is being effaced, and this phantasmic erosion of the visual is most evident in the figure who represents dissemination, as if to say that Flora (and the name itself is cloven, representing flowers, spring, pleasure, and wantonness, but also the representation of a figure re-presented in the painting) is the visual space where sight is obscured, the disseminating locus where reference, analogy, and meaning are buried in the service of sense, logic, and spectacle. And yet, having said that, we must recognize Flora is merely the reflection of an other, not something in her own right, not a proper figure, but merely a screen facing another screen. Like Eve, she does not exist for herself or in herself; rather, she exists *for an other*. And similarly, Chloris. What separates these two (or this one) is nothing less than death, loss, and change, a *thanatopraxie* that we experience as the Fall in *Paradise Lost* and which we can appreciate here as crucial to metaphoricity.

It is not fanciful to say that in the *Primavera* Botticelli anticipates the phantasmic quality of *Paradise Lost* by way of the double scene, that although there is so much to look at in the *Primavera*, so much remains concealed from the eye, as if the painting were censoring itself. And one wonders whether that occurs because in pastoral itself there is not something obscene or traumatic, something which brings about a repression by way of dissimulation or displacement: the double session? Perhaps it is time to reconsider Jean Genet.

In *Glas*, Derrida points out that Genet's novels and plays work through double scenes. The heterosexual becomes the homosexual because Genet recognizes in the homosexual the capacity for a doubleness whose fall is not just from innocence, but from even the basest experience, a fall that makes hell seem heaven by comparison. It is as if Genet's flowers cannot burst to enough evil excess, that their only unhappiness is in not falling deep enough into perversity. In this manner Genet looks for a negative *Aufhebung* which opens onto a level of degradation unknown by even the worst devils. And it is by way of such a fall that chains burst into flower and hoods look like malevolent but dainty beings. To fall means to cross sexual borderlines and to find oneself where one is not. At issue is not merely sexual ambivalence but a radical undecidability which can no longer distinguish what one is. Genet's point is that disguise is criminal, that dissimulation is already an acceptance of a fall. But in Genet this sacrificial fall in which one gives up one's liberty in the act of crime must be enacted so that it can be fantasized in a time which is not a present. The pastoral elements in Genet are not just ornaments, of course, but the necessary accoutrements of evil, the fetishes by which sexuality is at once determined and undetermined. The fetish, then, is a place where an anxious gaze fixes itself; that is to say, where one has fetish, one also has phobia. It is again a matter of double scenes. And it is a question of the dream.

After Eve has fallen, she is still irresistible to Adam; in fact Genet might argue that it is because she is a criminal that she suddenly attracts so much attention from Adam. Where there is perversity there is also great beauty. However we wish to take sides on that issue, if indeed there are sides at all, given the doubleness of scenes, it has to be recognized that in the pastoral tradition the various thematics we have discussed are highly problematized and that Milton inherited what were not mere conventions but extremely complicated mimetic, ethical, and sexual questions which articulate themselves, not as ideas ready to be discussed in the narrative line, but as part of a pastoral endowment which has to be considered in the dream work that is inscribed in the hymen of an innocent fall among flowers. Although I have not been able to offer an extensive study of pastoral, since that would transcend the scope of this book, it is already possible to see some outlines by which such an approach might proceed, an outline which nurtures the flowers of evil, those unsupported flowers strewn everywhere for the pleasure of saucy girls.

Le jeu (l'érection tombe) s'annonce comme cérémonie mortuaire ensevelissant l'autre sous les fleur mais le faisant du même coup bander sous les figures de rhétorique et les voiles en tout genre.

("This play [the erection falls] makes itself known as a funereal ceremony entombing the other with flowers, but also wrapping it in and under figures of rhetoric and veils of every sort and at the same time makes it rise.")

Jacques Derrida, *Glas*

CHAPTER 4

Lycidas: The Poetics of Antherection

I

In "Analysis Terminable and Interminable," Sigmund Freud defines a complex as a "psychic theme," and it is precisely such a theme this chapter will develop further.[1] Indeed, it was already apparent in terms of the comparison in *Paradise Lost* between Eve and the "unsupported Flow'r," a comparison we have already analyzed. However, in the earlier poem, *Lycidas*, this theme is more fully developed in terms of a *thanatopraxie* of flowers. If *Lycidas* has an elaborate funeral rite of flowers, it is not simply because Milton is following the destiny of classical elegiac convention, simply repeating Latin tradition and preserving in his poem a botany of death, but because he is using classical tradition in order to deconstruct the classical metaphysics of death, is, in short, turning classicism against itself by not merely repeating the funereal pomp but also engaging in a *thanatopraxie*, which is to say, a praxis of death that goes beyond a simple presence-absence dichotomy. In other words, *Lycidas* is not at all a typically classical poem, particularly when one becomes aware of a certain nodal point, the relationship between pastoral imagery and undecidability which in *Lycidas* is manifest as symbolic castration.

We will proceed by analyzing *Lycidas* in terms of what a Freudian might call a primal scene, which is not to say an originating scene, but a scheme that succinctly defines a complex, or constellation, of relationships that are repeated or displaced in terms of other scenes. That primary scene is the shepherd's plucking of the berries and leaves at the opening of *Lycidas*, a scene that is always already a repetition of that which escapes memory or memorialization, and its meaning is nothing less than the economy of the castration complex, which we will situate mainly within Derridean problematics, though we will have recourse to Lacan also.[2] It is fitting that we dwell for some time on this opening scene, because the economics of castration involves itself here most directly with the important thematics of the Fall, loss, death, cutting, transgression, theft, dissemination, impotence, belatedness, mourning, pastoral, and access to poetic power, as well as with the more complicated situation of the "uncouth Swain" who acts out the role of Oedipal son or would-be poet. Lastly, this primary scene defines most clearly the function of the poem in terms of what Derrida calls *écriture*, discourse that is belated, ruptured from presence, and cut, since it is the economics of castration that is operating here to dismantle the difference between presence and absence, father and son, past and present, life and death. In short, this primary, or opening, scene of plucking already ensures a poetic that is antimetaphysical.

Section ii of this chapter looks at the repetitions or displacements of the primary scene, or, more appropriately, the return of the castration complex, and certainly readers familiar with the poem can already guess what they will be: the decapitation of Orpheus, the shipwreck of Lycidas, the two-handed engine, the flower catalog, and, finally, the "uncouth" position of the shepherd at the end of the poem, the odd role of the shepherd as one who remains forever rude and estranged, a profane wanderer. What will become evident is not only that the shepherd's Oedipal condition is maintained throughout *Lycidas* but that his discourse, which is metaphorically associated with the numerous instances of cut flowers (the berries, the leaves, the sedge of Camus, the flowers strewn on the laureate hearse), is itself dictated according to the economics of cutting, castration, and that the poem is, finally, a repetition in toto of the castration complex, what amounts to an obsessive poem.

In *Lycidas* the pressures of a poetic impotence weigh heavily upon the self-conscious poet, who, like the writer of *Glas,* wishes for a potency of the text, or power of the word. "Ce que je voulais écrire, c'est POTENCE du texte." ("What I wanted to write is potency of text, the gallows or scaffold of the text.")[3] What the speaker in *Lycidas* contemplates is an unripe fruit whose reproductive capacity (sexuality) has not yet matured and whose eventual development or potency he will abruptly cut off. It is with this recognition that the poem begins.

> Yet once more, O ye Laurels, and once more
> Ye Myrtles brown, with Ivy never sere,
> I come to pluck your Berries harsh and crude,
> And with forc'd fingers rude,
> Shatter your leaves before the mellowing year.

The shepherd is plucking the berries himself and gathering the leaves to commemorate the drowned Lycidas, to imitate his premature fall, and to recognize the loss of what would have been his mature poetic fruit. In short, Lycidas performs homage. However, the act of shattering the leaves and plucking the berries also signifies the manner in which the speaker steals for himself the glories that ostensibly are put in reserve for Lycidas, an act in which the speaker raids the immortal groves in order to confer upon himself the poetic power and authority of these laurels, myrtles, and berries. But, as we already know, the fruit and leaves are not yet mature; they are powerless.

We are told that it is "yet once more" that the speaker comes to pluck the berries and the leaves, an action that we might call, after Lacan, an "automatisme de répétition."[4] As Lacan elegantly demonstrates, it is because something is broken off, because a space or absence has been created that an "automatisme de répétition" can function at all. Or, to put it another way, it is because there is a falling or breaking of some kind (in this case, death) that the notion of a new start, a new beginning, can come about, indeed, must come about, and it is man's obsession with this need for the new beginning that causes him to repeat, re-act, rethink. Thus the speaker in *Lycidas* finds himself, as Milton the epic poet does so many years later, musing a terrible rift (death, absence, fall) that dictates one begin anew at the same time that it signifies the very futility of that act, since the Fall is always there to remind one that a prior state, whether it is that of prelapsarian man or Lycidas as living poet, must be recuperated even though one's best efforts will be consigned to failure. What is involved, of course, in *Lycidas* is, above all, that the speaker recognizes Lycidas's death, his fall in relation to the speaker's own expressive importance, realizing that all his restarts are false starts, that his song is doomed to a premature fall, that it is, at best, a song cut off from a living poesy, the living Lycidas.

It is precisely the speaker's acknowledgment that his song is but another false start in an interminable history of such starts that opens *Lycidas,* an acknowledgment that immediately involves the image of plants and their fruit. One cannot help noticing the similarity between this opening scene and Eve's rash act in *Paradise Lost* when she too plucks with forced fingers rude the fruit of that forbidden tree. Can we not also say that the speaker in *Lycidas* approaches these berries, these leaves, as interdicted fruit as well, fruit that like Eve's apple signifies a fall, death, and loss? Is it not possible that the speaker's picking of the leaves and berries, like Eve's picking of the apple, marks a fall, or gap, that dooms the speaker in *Lycidas* to an "automatisme de répétition," the false start, and that poetry hereafter can only be considered as at best an abortive activity, an arrogant sterile act in which the poet robs the fruit while it is not yet mature? Again, it is the "POTENCE du texte," the power that is made possible only by violence, cutting, or rupture, a power that rests on the guillotine.

In order to speak, the poet of *Lycidas* must first mutilate or shatter the leaves, abort the reproductive process by plucking the fruit too soon in the same way that the writer of *Glas*, before he can discourse, must cut up the texts into "morceaux." It is to affirm that the "POTENCE du texte" is really founded upon a violent act of cutting out of which emerges "l'érection [qui] ne se produit qu'en abyme" ("the erection [which] only produces itself in the abyss").[5] That is to say, the column of words which erects itself in the abyss can only produce itself in such a space. That space is nothing other than the place of castration, the place where one is at once cut off from potency forever only in order that one may become powerful. The model for such an economy is sexual and Freudian, but here it is being used in terms of the text which some poststructuralists, like Jacques Lacan, Julia Kristeva, and Roland Barthes, refer to metaphorically as the phallus.

This is not to reduce *Lycidas* simply to a sexual mise en scène, an unconscious or archetypal truth, but to clarify the complex problematic of poetic or textual composition in *Lycidas* in terms of certain psychological models of power developed in the works of Derrida and Lacan. Since the thematic of text and potency is so strong in *Lycidas*, it seems appropriate that we pursue this line of thought further, even if it will eventually demand of us explanations in terms of concepts like *castration, thanatopraxie, potence*. What the insistence of a break, or shattering, at the beginning of the poem suggests is that one can expect to be concerned with the relationship between two conceptions of writing, the living text and the dead letter. What the *coupure*, or breakage, signifies at the beginning of the poem is that there is a praxis of death at work and that its potency is not so much that of the living word, of the voice of the pastor who has drowned, as that of the Fall itself, the death blow, the shipwreck, the plucking of the berries. The question, of course, is whether we can say such a dead text can have any power at all. Is it not merely a *potence* in the sense of being a gallows, a gibbet, a cutter? Is not such a text merely castrated? Or again, is not such a text merely a *pompe funèbre*, a funeral rite?

Here it is useful to consider potence-castration, the *pompe funèbre*, in terms of what Derrida calls the *anthérection:*

> Il ne faut pas simplifier la logique de l'anthérection. Ça n'érige pas *contre* ou *malgré* la castration, *en dépit* de la blessure ou de l'infirmité, en châtrant la castration. Ça bande, la castration. L'infirmité elle-même se panse à bander. C'est elle qui, comme on dit encore aujourd'hui dans la vieille langue, *produit* l'érection: une prothèse qu'aucun événement de castration n'aura précédée. La structure de la prothèse appartient à l'intumescence. Rien ne tient débout autrement.
>
> ("One must not simplify the logic of antherection. It does not erect itself *against* or *in spite of* castration, *in despite of* the wound or the infirmity, castrating castration. It binds, castration [*ça bande, la castration;* the placing of the comma makes subject and predicate interchangeable here]. The infirmity itself is bandaged or bound [*se panse:* pun on *se pense* = "is thought"] to bind itself. That it is which, as one still says in the old language, *produces* erection: a prosthesis ["all theses are prostheses," Derrida writes elsewhere in the book; or any *Satz* (sentence or proposition), *ersatz* (242b)] which no event of castration will have preceded. The structure of the prosthesis belongs to intumescence. Nothing stands up otherwise.")[6]

Metaphorically the *anthérection* is the flower whose very cutting results in exfoliation. More precisely, it is the *coupure* that at once castrates or cuts off in order to provide access to power, potency, force. In *Lycidas*, the *anthérection* is nothing less than the cutting of the berries and leaves, a cutting that represents at once the inferiority of the shepherd to Lycidas (the shepherd's impotence, his castration complex) and his superiority. To cut off the berries and leaves is thus not simply to render oneself impotent but to make the necessary incision that will give rise to a binding or bonding, a breaching of the Fall: "l'anthérection du style en abyme" ("the antherection of style in the abyss").[7] The text or poem is initiated in terms of "une coupure re-coupée," of a cutting off that *impairs* at the same time that it *repairs*.

For the speaker in *Lycidas*, the drowning or fall of the poet does not spell the end of poetry, but the affirmation of it; as in *Paradise Lost*, there is the working out of a felix culpa, or happy fall, in which a serious rupture or impairing is at the same time seen to be recuperated in terms of a bonding, binding, or repairing. Thus, just as Lycidas is "sunk low, but mounted high," the power of poesy is, even though cut off, perpetuated through the shepherd's song.

But we are getting ahead of ourselves. For we must still consider the act of plucking the berries and leaves, an act that is, for us, associated with castration, as we have seen, but that also must be seen in terms of two other related ideas: dissemination and criminality. We note, after Derrida, that the process of dissemination is always considered in terms of a transgression, a deviance, and it is here that we can see how deviance is connected with the problematic of castration, of the illicit and terrifying *coupure* that opens the way to death, absence, perversion, sin, and, of course, language.[8] In *Lycidas* the violating of the immature berries, the appropriation of sacred fruit, is an interference with nature's normal reproductive process in the same way that Christ's descent in the "Nativity Ode" spells the sterilization of the earth, the law of the Immaculate Conception, for the plucking of the berries and fruits signifies an errant propagation, a kind of reproduction that is controlled, not by the laws of nature, but by the laws of chance, a process we are calling dissemination. Just as the seeds of thistles spread by way of dehiscence, by way of scattering, the leaves in *Lycidas* are "shattered by Milton's singing before they have an opportunity to reach mature exuberance."[9] An unnatural intrusion that interrupts the natural reproductive cycle without negating it entirely, this intrusion results in a scattering or strewing, a dissemination whose productivity is based upon the *coupure*, or cut, upon the fall which gives way to the *anthérection*. And, of course, it is the dissemination of the text we are considering, the "POTENCE du texte" that is created out of this initial violation, cut, castration.

What becomes only too apparent as one reads the poem is that Lycidas himself, like Christ in the "Nativity Ode," becomes a model for dissemination. Indeed, like the plants who suffer the arbitrary severing of their parts, the dissemination of their leaves and fruits, Lycidas too appears endlessly tossed beneath the water stirred by fierce winds. Like seeds that have been thrown onto stormy waters, Lycidas is not only violently cut off from his safe enclosure, the bark, but thrown into nature's inhospitable current, only to reemerge, to regenerate much later in the same way that the day star, the sun, "flames in the forehead of the morning sky," after being sunk beneath the watery floor.

Indeed, the identification of Lycidas with the sun, an identification much like Christ with the "rays of *Bethlehem*" in the "Ode," allows us to consider Lycidas as an important part of the economics of dissemination, of an economy based upon the *anthérection*, whose primary condition is the double effect of impairing and repairing. Such castration simultaneously makes one powerless and opens the way to productivity, potency, which is never potent in the normal sense of possessing a power, of enclosing a force like presence, but potent in the deviant sense of belonging to an economics of errant dispersion, an economics based upon an initial cut that at once distances us in an unbreachable gap and at the same time bonds us between two severed pieces. Like the poet's vegetative *coupures*, Lycidas's drowning forms the nexus where fall and restoration meet, where presence and absence are not merely pitted against each other, or synthesized, but kept at bay by a third term, *anthérection*.

If Samuel Johnson, as is so well known, found *Lycidas* an uncomfortable poem, it was not simply because it violated what he considered to be decorum or human sensitivity but because the poem offers one, not living poetry, not words that bleed, but a poetry that is castrated, whose potency is that of a *thanatopraxie,* of the simulacrum, of the mask whose reality is the truth of castration, the truth that castration is not simply a breach but an *anthérection.*[10] This is the *béance* without which words cannot disseminate.

But we said that dissemination was only one other aspect of castration and that criminality was another, and certainly Johnson's negative response to *Lycidas,* like Eliot's response, is expressed in terms of these "original acts of lawlessness," as Eliot called them. Such "original acts" refer, of course, to Milton's style, but there is a sense in which such original acts of lawlessness are inscribed thematically into the poem as well. For, just as a letter in one of Poe's stories is purloined, the berries and leaves in *Lycidas* are purloined by the shepherd. They have to be, because they cannot otherwise become fitting decorations for the laureate hearse, since the poet, in order to give the gifts of honor, must first use them himself to fashion the poem within which they are given. Although the leaves and berries are not rightfully the speaker's, they have to become enlisted into the poet's project. Such a theft is always one the poet has to make, of course, for without it he could not compete with the fallen poets he is praising, a competition that he dares despite the anxiety of knowing in advance that he is interdicted from outdoing his predecessors.

The anxiety that marks the plucking of the berries or poetic fruit can be stated in Oedipal terms. We might, after Harold Bloom, say that this anxiety is an "anxiety of influence," an anxiety created by the crime of competing with symbolic father figures. Certainly, the shepherd occupies an Oedipal position in relation to the drowned Lycidas, for the plucking of the berries involves the Oedipal recognition of a power (call it authority, voice, poetic strength, or sexuality) that naturally belongs to the symbolic father or pastor figure while at the same time suggesting the Oedipal son's illegitimate appropriation of that power for himself. Ironically, the only way the Oedipal son can appropriate the power of the father is by symbolically effecting the ruse that the son has not got it, by paying homage to the father through the symbolic ritual of plucking, or castration. That is, by cutting off the berries, the shepherd admits his own castratedness, his own distance from the power of the pastor's voice. However, at the same time, he is stealing the fruit and appropriating poetic power for himself. He is, like Eve in *Paradise Lost*, partaking of forbidden fruit.

The plucking or theft of the fruit and leaves, then, is a metaphorical reenactment of the castration complex in the sense that this scene of cutting confirms at once that the shepherd is belated, secondary, and inferior while simultaneously hinting this admission of inferiority is only a ruse.[11] Certainly the shepherd pays homage to Lycidas and elicits the recognition that Lycidas is the one who really has the power. However, it is abundantly clear that in itself this process of paying homage, a process in itself poetic that is initiated by the Oedipal child, constitutes a hiding of the power that the Oedipal son himself has. Thus the cutting off or castration of the berries functions to pay back the symbolic father, to recognize his authority, at the same time that it authorizes the son. This is commensurate with what Derrida calls the logic of the *anthérection* in the sense that paying homage, giving back, and losing authority, power, and prestige will result in a gain, in a surplus of power.

Indeed, the instability of this relation between the shepherd and Lycidas is antherected at every point, even when both shepherd and Lycidas are represented like twins *nursed* on the self-same hill, when their mimetic rivalry is greatest. We recall that, according to the shepherd, both he and Lycidas once "fed the same flock, by fountain, shade, and rill," that they once appeared "together both" on the "high Lawns" and "under the opening eyelids of the morn." Such kinship suggests nothing less than a smoothing over of any harsh rivalry, and yet we must bear in mind that such a representation serves to idealize a relation in such a way that the shepherd can put himself in the place of his friend.

The image of the twins nursed on the self-same hill suggests harmony and gentle fraternity, but it also insists that a certain interchangeability exists, that the living shepherd can take the place of the one who has died, since the living shepherd has always occupied that space, has always wished to be where the other was (that is, has always harbored a death wish for an other). It is a clever assumption to power which the shepherd makes, and precisely by playing at being the double of the drowned Lycidas, by insisting upon a kinship and identity that is undermined by the recognition, ambivalent though it may be, that Lycidas "hath not left his peer," which is to say, has not left anyone as great as himself, but also, has not left the shepherd. Here paternal and fraternal relations are curiously mixed.

II

Si *Fall* marque le cas, la chute, la décadence, la faillite ou la fente, *Falle* égale piège, trappe, collet, la machine à vous prendre par le cou.

("If *Fall* marks the case, the fall, the decadence, the bankruptcy, or slot, the *Falle* equals the trap, pitfall, snare, noose, the machine that seizes you by the neck.")
Jacques Derrida, *Glas*

"L'anthérection du style en abyme." Derrida's phrase alerts us to the condition of the text as antherected, as itself decapitated or decapitalized. In *Lycidas* not only the shepherd, but the text suffers the "l'infirmité [qui] elle-même se panse à bander" ("the infirmity [which] itself is bandaged or bound"). The decapitation of the text from its source, from the wellsprings of being, is most clearly represented in the shepherd's recollection of Orpheus's severed head floating down the river of Hebrus as it makes mournful sounds. Thus Ovid writes, "And the banks echoed / The strains of mourning." The voice of Orpheus is not the voice of the living, but the knell of the dead, the passing bell, that floats to the Lesbian shore. It is not presence, not something happening at its source, but an echo, a melody that is distanced from itself, cut off. It is the fall, the inauguration of a *thanatopraxie*, a text that is neither living nor dead, the inauguration of a liminal song whose point of inception is nothing other than an incision, a partition, a gap. It is this law the Orpheus reference in *Lycidas* asserts most loudly: that in order to name, to speak, to signify, one has first to cut the throat, to trap the voice in its chamber and to slit the chords.

Cette institution, loi qui pose le nom en déposant la tête, ne se passe pas d'un cou.

("This institution, a law setting up the name by cutting off the head, cannot do without a neck.")[12]

The citation of the beheaded Orpheus in *Lycidas* inscribes the Derridean notion of a *thanatopraxie* and of an *anthérection* most clearly into the economy of the text itself. For Orpheus's song represents a discourse whose power is confirmed precisely in terms of its own castratedness, its cut vocal cords. Orpheus's decapitated and gory head is, of course, a metaphor for Lycidas, and it signifies to us that Lycidas's power can be measured in terms of his wreck at sea. However, the metaphor also relates to the speaker's condition as well, and to his poetic act that is in the process of being made at the moment, the poetic act that we actually encounter. In short, the Orpheus myth is a displaced return of the repressed, a repetition of the castration complex that the shepherd himself is subjected to. The manner in which the complex is presented, of course, is not in terms of the shepherd but in terms of an other. Here something that is most familiar to the shepherd is perceived in terms of something that is unfamiliar, terrifying, gory, other. Apparently, the Orpheus myth is functioning in such a way that the problematic of cutting is preserved while at the same time the difference or space that separates Lycidas and the shepherd (and, too, the space that separates the discourse of Lycidas and the text of the shepherd-poet) is curiously effaced. What one has is at once an assertion of splitting and its denial.

Sigmund Freud traces the circuit of the castration complex in terms of what he calls the "Unheimlich" or "uncanny" in his essay "The Uncanny," and he describes this circuit in terms of a repetition compulsion, a confrontation with something fearful and intimate that occurs over and over again, but that always appears in the guise of something foreign and unfamiliar.[13] The decapitated head of a mythic figure, the severing of the immature berries, the drowning of Lycidas are all appearances of this uncanny experience. And they are recalled, I suggest, by the poet out of his own self-conscious fear of experiencing a symbolic castration of the poetic act and, even worse, of realizing that it may not even be the activity of the poet that is in peril, but perhaps the activity of language itself. After all, the speaker makes reference to "lucky words" shortly after he implores the Muses to make another beginning: "Begin, then, Sisters of the sacred well . . . / Begin, and somewhat loudly sweep the string." But we quickly realize that the Muses are unable to preserve the lucky word from decapitation, that Calliope herself cannot prevent the cutting of Orpheus's throat and the maiming of language as presence, voice, and being. So even this invocation to the Muses to begin (line 15 and following) singing with "lucky words" is to be taken somewhat ironically, with an eye toward the problematic of poesy, song, melody: as uncanny, divorced, and fallen.

Lycidas's association in the speaker's imagination with

the decapitated Orpheus, a sylvan god, blends with other scenes of dismemberment throughout the poem. There is the pathetic fallacy beginning in line 37 in which there is mention of the rose attacked by canker, the flowers attacked by frost. "Such, *Lycidas,* thy loss to Shepherd's ear." The line is purposely delayed by Milton in order to mix visual imagery of the blasted flowers with the observation that without Lycidas to inhabit the pastoral landscape there is nothing to expect but echoes. "And all their echoes mourn." The flowers themselves are implicated in a *thanatopraxie,* an echoing of voice that is cut off when "Comes the blind *Fury* with th'abhorred shears, / And slits the thin-spun life." Is it not better, the poet ironically says, "To sport with *Amaryllis* in the shade, / Or with the tangles of *Neaera's* hair?" That is, would it not be better, since one is surely going to be castrated by woman, the blind Fury, to at least submit to a pleasurable castration associated with flowers, bowers, copses, and the like? To become feminized? Indeed, Edward Le Comte in *Milton and Sex* suggests that Neaera's hair is nothing less than a reference to what in *Glas* is called *la toison,* the fleece which is woman's pubic hair, that veil for the castrated genitals.[14]

It is more than Phoebus can stand. Life is cut off, but not the praise, he admonishes. Fame is no plant that grows on mortal soil, but is separated from the material and its biological cycles of reproduction, its physical repetitions. Fame is the plant that, like the unripe berries and leaves at the beginning of the poem, is cut off, severed, and it is this plant the shepherd may believe he is cutting when he comes "yet once more" to the laurels, myrtles, and berries harsh and crude; for, to wrest from them their poetic authority or power is at once to procure for oneself a certain "fame." Again, before the pilot of the Galilean lake is introduced, we see Camus pass by, his "Bonnet sedge, / Inwrought with figures dim, and on the edge / Like to that sanguine flower inscrib'd with woe." The bonnet, of course, is itself made of water plants, sedge, and seaweed and symbolizes the point at which both the water and flower imagery come together, at which the imagery of the shipwreck and the bloodied flower cut down in its prime are to be considered as a single unit. "'Ah! Who hath reft' (quoth he) 'my dearest pledge?'" That is, who has robbed the one entrusted to me? The word "reft" is ambiguous, because it means stolen, severed, cut off, suddenly taken away. The hieroglyph of the flower "inscrib'd" with woe is a hieroglyph that reflects the loss of the gentle Lycidas and is very much implicated in this question of Lycidas's being robbed or stolen, taken from the charge of the river Camus. It is as if Lycidas himself were that flower which is worn on the weedy bonnet of the river god, a flower that is sanguine, cut, watery, a flower that is fallen, yet in a very positive sense raised again from the depths.

That such a flower can be inscribed on the bonnet of Camus may seem odd until one recognizes that "sedge" was used by the Egyptians to make paper (sedge as papyrus). Thus the image of the inscribed flower marks not only the point where water and flower imagery meet and cross but also the point at which these images are implicated with a notion of textuality, of the white sheet upon which images or hieroglyphs are written. One can push the image of sedge even further to include the notion of an inscribed flower that is caught up in the thematic of dissemination. Sedge is wind-pollinated, its light reproductive material carried away by the wind, strewn on the water, cast into the elements. Here the problematic of cutting, death, and robbery is suddenly associated with dissemination in terms of a lawless process of reproduction that knows no proper bounds. For us, dissemination is a loaded word, of course, that defines a Derridean conception of textuality as *écriture*, as a writing that is always subject to radical breaks, to deviant transgressions, to thefts of all sorts. What is interesting is, not that Milton may have intentionally pointed to such a theory of writing in the image of Camus's sedge bonnet (and is there any doubt, if one looked long enough at classical sources, that such a theory could be found?), but that such a theory of writing as dissemination suggests itself so strongly at this point.

Following this brief walk-on by Camus, there is the well-known ecclesiastical detour in which the imagery of shearing, of a sort of two-handed guillotine which stands ready to smite once, and smite no more, presents itself. And it is only after this dread prophecy of violent decapitation, of death by sword or ax, that the famous flower catalog begins. "That the intended effect of this passage," Renato Poggioli writes, "is to relax the tension produced by St. Peter's speech is proved by the very length of the flower catalogue."[15] Certainly the passage puts us at ease, but only in the military sense in which an "at-ease" is always an anxious state of expectation, of waiting for the next command.

Surely the flower catalog, though not as obviously forbidding as the two-handed engine that sounds the death knell for Charles I and prophesies the decapitation of the monarchy, the splitting or dissemination of concentrated power, does, nevertheless, carry out a praxis of death that is foreshadowed in the passages we have already considered. The flower catalog is, in fact, another confrontation with the repetition automatism that opens the poem, for the shepherd comes "yet once more" to pluck nature's most potent bloom. To strew the flowers on the laureate hearse is to reenact that scene in which the shepherd shatters the leaves and rudely pulls off unripe fruit; it is to try to forget the false starts of the previous passages, especially the passage concerning the two-handed engine, and start once again. Yet, for all that, the flower catalog is really a repetition or *Aufhebung* of all previous passages, of even the message of the "dread voice" voicing *le glas*, the knell of death. But why must it repeat? Because something like Derrida's "Ce que je voulais écrire, c'est POTENCE du texte" is never far from the poet's intention.

Following Freud's short note on the Medusa's head, we might well argue that the multiplication of cut flowers signifies a traumatic return to the beginning of the poem, that the multiplication of flowers signifies a desperate attempt to ward off castration.[16] We are back to the "tangles of *Neaera's* hair" in the form of flowers which function much in the same way as the serpents on the head of Medusa (that *toison*, or tangle). They function as representations of the phallus which have to be multiplied in order to dispel the fear that the phallus (symbolically potency, authority, and truth) can be cut or lost. In themselves, Freud argues, such multiplications signify the overcoming of castration by way of an imaginary or fantastic mechanism of compensation. Jacques Lacan would add that such multiplication also signifies the working of a repetition automaton that is directed at once along the rails of pleasure and death, rails intimately acquainted with the castration complex.

It is evident here that the flower catalog, then, is but another Oedipal scene and can be largely explained in terms we have already established earlier in our discussion of the opening scene of *Lycidas*. What we need only stress is the fact that the flower catalog is, not an interlude that puts us at ease, but a traumatic displacement that repeats the castration complex and its accompanying anxiety. To the degree that the flower catalog returns us to previous mise en scènes in the poem, it becomes but a layer in a palimpsest, a pretty pastoral surface, an appealing metaphorical scene that is written over other texts, perhaps in the hope of repressing their force. To mourn for Lycidas—to scatter the pretty flowers on his hearse, to perform the proper burial rite—is in essence to ward off the fear of death, to repress the truth of castration. It is to recognize the loss of potency, to pay to Lycidas one's symbolic debt and in the process recuperate and restore that which has been given up within oneself. In this sense, the scene of cutting becomes a "POTENCE du texte," a strength founded upon the gallows.

III

"Le *coup* partage la semence en la projetant. Elle inscrit la différence dans la vie." ("The shot / throw / blow [*le coup*] parts the seed as it projects it. It inscribes difference in the heart of life.") In *La dissémination* dehiscence occurs by way of the blow, an action which for Derrida parallels the initiation of writing as the effect of a blow by means of which semes are dispersed on the page. In *Glas:* "La fleur phallique est coupable. Elle se coupe, se châtre, se guillotine, se décolle." ("The phallic flower is guilty. It cuts itself, castrates itself, guillotines itself, disengages itself.")[17] And it is this flower which mourns as wreath on the coffins of the dead, which is cut only to be bound into not only a funereal tribute but also into a book.

In Milton's *Lycidas*, too, the throat has to be cut in order for words to follow. The seme as seed and as word must first receive the blow. The flowers in *Lycidas*'s catalog which follows the dread voice pronouncing the blow or death sentence are of a linguistic or textual order, and they are, like Genet's flowers of which Derrida speaks in *Glas*, "cut" and "strewn" on the laureate hearse. It is this praxis of death that at once commemorates the dead Lycidas while giving rise to a potent text, to a poetic monument or *thanatopraxie* that is the very life of the text. Indeed, the flowers Milton has gathered in the catalog, like Genet's, are already cut out of previous texts, taken from the body of Renaissance symbolism that is itself based upon scattered religious and folk traditions, literary conventions, and magic treatises. From the outset, the Sicilian vales are already "cut" and "grafted" into *Lycidas*, an errant means of propagation which, as in Genet, makes undecidable the difference between cutting and binding, scattering and gathering, falling and rising.

Indeed, Milton's flower catalog is a classical garden sown into the text of *Lycidas*. And this comes as no surprise, for it is actually but a repetition. Just as the flower catalog repeats the complex of castration, it repeats the identification between flower or fruit and text which was made at the very outset of the poem (berry = poetic achievement) and further on in terms of Camus's bonnet. The pathetic fallacy also serves to remind us that flowers and words, and nature and the poet's voice are intimately identified with one another. When the voice passes away, the flowers fade too.

Once we recognize the identification of flowers and discourse, we begin to see that a rhetoric of flowers is operating in *Lycidas*; and it is of some import to probe the kind of rhetoric the flowers constitute. Do they, as the pathetic fallacy suggests, constitute a rhetoric founded upon the presence of the living voice? That is, do they constitute a living text that is suddenly given the death blow with the passing of their animating spirit, Lycidas? Or do the flowers suggest a kind of rhetoric or notion of textuality that subverts such a metaphysical and classical ideology of the text? The question is not a trivial one, for I think it is clear at this point that the leaves and berries at the beginning of the poem, like the flowers in the flower catalog, are implicated with the problematic of poetic discourse in terms of the Oedipal scene examined earlier. What I will argue is that the flower catalog is on the order of what Derrida cites in Hegel's *Phenomenology of Spirit* as the "religion des fleurs," that religion of flowers which engages,

un mouvement évanouissant, l'effluve flottant au-dessus d'une procession, la marche de l'innocence à la culpabilité.[18]

("a movement dying away, the effluvium floating above a procession, the motion from innocence to culpability.")

The religion or rhetoric of flowers is always dialectically engaged with the animal in Hegel; it is what precedes animal sacrifice. And in *Lycidas* these flowers suggest not simply the pathetic fallacy but the joyful exuberance of the poet-son figure at having lived to see his spiritual father die. In other words, where there is tragedy and loss, there is sadism too. Moreover, these flowers are in themselves images of cutting and falling, symbols of death which represent the *thanatopraxie* enjoyed by the mourning shepherd; and not only that, but the flowers manifest themselves as poetic discourse. Thus not only does the religion or rhetoric of flowers commemorate the loss of Lycidas, but it is the very stuff out of which the poem is made, the very material signifiers by way of which the shepherd accedes to potency, the "POTENCE du texte." In summary one can say, then, that by means of the flowers, castration, sacrifice, and death can be looked upon as nothing less than discourse itself, or, if one allows me to say so, *écriture*.

On a functional level as on a thematic level, the flower catalog, or *écriture des fleurs,* operates according to the economics of castration, or more specifically, to the *anthérection* referred to earlier. The flower catalog is not unique in this sense, for as Derrida has shown, *écriture* depends upon the *anthérection* or some kindred term that signifies a function similar to the *anthérection*. In *De la grammatologie* many such kindred terms are used, but the one I want to fix on is called "spacing." In defining *écriture,* a notion of writing opposed to the metaphysics of living speech, Derrida writes:

L'écriture phonétique *n'existe pas:* aucune pratique n'est jamais purement fidèle à son principe. Avant même de parler, comme nous le ferons plus loin, d'une infidélité radicale et a priori nécessaire, on peut déjà en remarquer les phénomènes massifs dans l'écriture mathématique ou dans la ponctuation, dans *l'espacement* en général, qu'il est difficile de considérer comme de simples accessoires de l'écriture. Qu'une parole dite vive puisse se prêter à l'espacement dans sa propre écriture, voilà qui la met originairement en rapport avec sa propre mort.

("Phonetic writing *does not exist;* no practice is ever totally faithful to its principle. Even before speaking, as I shall do further on, of a radical and a priori necessary infidelity, one can already remark its massive phenomena in mathematical script or in punctuation, in *spacing* in general, which it is difficult to consider as simple accessories of writing. That a speech supposedly alive can lend itself to spacing in its own writing is what relates it originarily to its own death.")[19]

Écriture is determined by spacing, which Derrida already conceptualizes in terms of death. Spacing in Derrida's later work becomes synonymous with castration as well and demands an antimetaphysical slant upon discourse, an iconoclastic slant opposing the notion that all words are discourses inherently indebted to a real father figure, an originating being, whose voice we can only echo, usurp, or parody. For Derrida, originals are not responsible for images or traces of themselves; it is the images or traces, rather, that constitute the illusion of originals, without which such images or traces cannot signify, cannot perform a representational function.

Derrida draws from Freud here, because he is relying upon the Freudian notion of the memory screen, the idea that discourse may be nothing but a phantasm that substitutes itself for an origin or originating experience that, in fact, has never taken place. If memory screens represent or remember, they do so in spite of the fact that they recall or reconstitute something that has never existed. In Derridean terms, they are traces which produce or elicit *arché-traces*.

There is a sense in which we could say that the entire poem of *Lycidas* is a memory screen. Milton, we recall, was never intimately acquainted with Edward King, the Lycidas mourned in the poem, and there is even some suspicion on the part of critics that Milton may have felt antagonistic to King.[20] Milton and King were not, at any rate, the best of friends, perhaps not even very good friends. Yet the poem *Lycidas* would have us believe otherwise. It would have us believe that Milton is drawing sustenance from an originating voice, from an intimate friend, when in fact such an originating voice was never properly there in Milton's consciousness. Still, that voice is exactly what the text desires, needs in order to come into its own.

And how is that voice, that symbolic father, that *arché-trace* brought into our view? Through the initial rite of berry-picking and leaf-plucking, but even more strongly through the catalog of flowers, which is the first scene to directly come into contact with the drowned man's physical presence in terms of the laureate hearse.[21] And yet this direct contact is only indirect in the extreme, for the hearse is empty. There is no body, only the textual illusion, created with the aid of the flowers, that the shepherd is attending the funeral of Lycidas, strewing his bier with flowers. In this sense the catalog is only a fantasy determined by a presence (of the corpse) that, in fact, does not exist, but is demanded by the very nature of the elegiac catalog of flowers. The catalog clearly does not supplement or decorate a hearse containing the deceased body of the poet, Lycidas, but functions like a memory screen in that it is a discourse that constitutes the illusion of an originator or originating condition of which the screen appears to be the effect.

The catalog, or *écriture des fleurs*, that memory screen I have described in *Lycidas*, is very close to Derrida's description of the "crypt" (writing / tomb) in his preface to *Cryptonomie: le verbier de l'homme aux loups*, by Nicolas Abraham and Maria Torok. It is an important connection, because Milton's pastoral catalog of flowers is founded upon the crypt, the laureate hearse that is enclosing a body even though it is empty. In Milton as in Derrida the crypt is synonymous with discourse. "So may some gentle Muse / With lucky words favor my destin'd Urn," the shepherd-poet says, making a strong identification between himself and the drowned Lycidas. Later, this urn emerges as the laureate hearse, a discursive crypt which has but one major purpose, to inter the corpse as "mort-vivant" ("the living-dead").

L'habitant d'une crypte est toujours un mort-vivant, un mort qu'on veut bien garder en vie, mais comme mort, qu'on veut garder jusque dans sa mort à condition de le garder, c'est-à-dire en soi, intact, sauf donc vivant.

(The inhabitant of a crypt is always a living dead, dead entity we are perfectly willing to keep alive, but as dead, one we are willing to keep, as long as we keep it, within us, intact in any way save as living.)[22]

For Derrida the crypt is a psychological or unconscious writing, a process of fantasy, of memory screens, whose purpose is to inter the father in a liminal vault or space in order to work out the Oedipal need to slay the father while at the same time recognizing his authority. The crypt is a liminal vault, because it serves to make of the father a "mort-vivant," a figure at once potent and impotent, alive and dead, present and absent. Like the economy of castration, the economy of the crypt plays havoc with the partition between binary oppositions like being-nonbeing and does so because the guardian of the crypt (in Derrida the wolf-man, in Milton the shepherd) has to dispel the anxiety that he can be threatened by a living father without at the same time having to suffer the anxiety that he is responsible for slaying the father. What is more likely in *Lycidas* is that he will have to suffer the anxiety of knowing the father is really dead, that death is possible for not only the most potent figures but the shepherd as well.

The purpose of the crypt, like the purpose of the memory screen, is to deconstruct the Oedipal complex of fears, to ensure the father's nonbeing while at the same time refusing to sacrifice his life and admit to the threat of death. Such deconstruction can occur only through the composition of an *écriture*, crypt, or screen subverting the very metaphysical distinctions upon which Oedipal anxieties are founded.

And this is the purpose of the flower catalog: to function as an *écriture des fleurs* which by way of an economy of castration deconstructs the presence of the precursor and thus problematizes the difference between living and dying, legator and legatee. Surely, if flowers metaphorically stand in as poetic discourse—here the discourse of mourning—and if they make up the crypt whose body they must wrap themselves around as well as braid out of themselves, the flowers make indistinguishable the difference between that which ornaments and that which is honored. The poet precursor who is the occasion and origin for the poem is merely the wrapping or floral scripture in which he is treasured up or mummified. The crypt is, in other words, the script. And beneath or inside the script is only a hollow or space (*la différance*) which constitutes and is constituted by a rhetoric of flowers.

It is interesting that in *Lycidas* the shepherd dismisses the flower catalog as false surmise, a pretty fantasy. It too is entombed and repressed. Derrida notices in "Fors" that the crypt is always catastrophic; the subject will inevitably attempt to neutralize this catastrophe by denying its place in his thoughts. However, "en tentant de le détruire, voilà le catastrophique même, il ne peut plus que le consolider" ("in trying to destroy it [the crypt as monument]—and this is what is so catastrophic—he can only consolidate it").[23] In *Lycidas*, this consolidation of the monument or crypt occurs in the scene in which we are directly confronted with Lycidas's shipwreck, the scene of the loss of the perfidious bark, of the fall, of cutting, death, and castration. It is here the shepherd admits to the absence of the poet's body, to the tearing apart, or *sparagmos*, in the Irish Sea that Lycidas's body undergoes, to the fact that there was nothing in the laureate hearse. And yet, at the same time, this passage concerning the shipwreck reconstitutes the body by insisting that the chaotic sea is itself a kind of crypt, a watery tomb in which the body is interred. "Voilà le catastrophique même, il ne peut plus que le consolider."

It is only after this truly terrifying moment that reconciliation finally seems to appear. And here again one encounters pastoral imagery, for a heavenly landscape is revealed. Here we notice "other groves and other streams along." It is an Edenic scene in which one washes with pure nectars, hears songs beyond human expression. But it is at once clear that this pastoral landscape, the landscape of an afterlife, situates the fallen Lycidas between water and land, for Lycidas's station in this afterlife is that of residing as a guiding spirit. "Henceforth thou art the Genius of the shore, / In thy large recompense, and shalt be good / To all that wander in that perilous flood." Lycidas stands, finally, between water and land, flower and sea.

He resides on that margin between pastoral ease and perilous flood as he has resided throughout the poem, for the ribbon upon which Lycidas stands is, after all, nothing but that edge separating life from death, presence from absence, order from chaos, an edge that at once marks their difference at the same time that it affirms their identity. That Lycidas is here on the margin and at the same time located in "other groves" in a pastoral afterworld whose streams and trees are cut off from our own only makes this liminality stronger, for we realize that the margin separates not only the horizontal contiguity of vales from seas but the vertical contiguity of heaven from earth. Lycidas is to be considered by us, not as a simple memory or a spirit (one could say, presence), but as himself that truth of castration that forms the margin, or *coupure*, between presence and absence, loss and return, a truth that can only be fetishized as test, hero, or spirit, but never reclaimed, never revealed beneath this endless number of disguises. Indeed, Lycidas's image of genius of the shore is but one of these fetishized moments; it is not, as one might think, the answer or resolution to the shepherd's self-conscious yearning for some final vision that will put an end to the disturbance over loss. That the shepherd must go "to fresh Woods, and Pastures new" is enough of an indication that he has not been able to overcome or exit from the problematic of loss, fall, and cutting off. It is, to follow through a negative reading, but the prelude to further twists of that chain Lacan calls the repetition automatism. And again, it is to the imagery of the pastoral landscape to which we return once more.

Lastly, it must be noted that it is as an "uncouth" swain that the shepherd-poet advances to fresh woods and pastures new, which is to say, that it is as a humble poet, but also as an uncertain, an unseemly, an estranged, or an unaccustomed man that the shepherd-poet moves out of our range. The word *uncouth* has other meanings as well: "solitary," "desolate," "rugged," "unpleasant," "unattractive," "awkward," "at a loss," but also "marvelous." What I am suggesting, of course, is that even at the end of *Lycidas* one is experiencing a repetition of the beginning, in which the shepherd appears at a loss, uncertain, awkward, and yet, for all that, marvelous. The word *uncouth* is itself antherected, is itself a sign for cutting that doubles as a sign for the poet's power, his uniqueness, his superiority. Certainly, to be "uncouth" in Milton's scheme of things is to be at once punished and blessed, to manifest the "uncertainty" that the word *uncouth* itself designated in Milton's day.

We end pretty much where we began, then, on a liminal site where a gap serves to keep apart and confuse, distance and identify, empower and wrest power. It is an anxious gap, or maybe it would be better, as Lacan might suggest, to call it a knot whose rope is nothing less than the economy of the castration anxiety, the *écriture* which in *Lycidas* is identical to its text, and as Derrida might add, its crypt.

Devant toutes les plaies d'Égypte, on imagine les docteurs hocher la tête et psalmodier: castration, fétichisme, castration de la mère, fétichisme, castration, castration je vous dis, encore castration.

("Before all the plagues or wounds of Egypt, one imagines the doctors nodding their heads and chanting: castration, fetishism, castration of the mother, fetishism, castration, castration I tell you, again castration.")

Jacques Derrida, *Glas*

CHAPTER 5

Samson Eikonoklastes

I

It is while appealing to God's mercy for a restitution of Samson's worth and dignity that the chorus of *Samson Agonistes* notices Dalila approaching. Abruptly, its attention focuses upon her entrance:

> But who is this, what thing of Sea or Land?
> Female of sex it seems,
> That so bedeckt, ornate, and gay,
> Comes this way sailing
> Like a stately Ship
> Of *Tarsus*, bound for th' Isles
> Of *Javan* or *Gadire*
> With all her bravery on, and tackle trim,
> Sails fill'd, and streamers waving,
> Courted by all the winds that hold them play,
> An Amber scent of odorous perfume
> Her harbinger, a damsel train behind;
> Some rich *Philistian* Matron she may seem,
> And now at nearer view, no other certain
> Than *Dalila* thy wife. [Ll. 710–24]

These lines are very reminiscent of Nietzsche's assertion in *The Gay Science:* "The magic and the most powerful effect of woman is, in philosophical language, action at a distance, *actio in distans*; but this requires first of all and above all—distance."[1] Throughout Milton's passage on Dalila, woman is kept very much at a distance; she is perceived as an object, ornate and gay, gliding over a surface much like a ship at sea.

From the start, the chorus perceives woman from a distance and is quick to assume that she has an amphibious nature, for it asks "what thing of Sea or Land" is approaching this way? Not unlike the god Dagon, who is at once half man and half fish, Dalila is accused of having a polluted nature, a mixed essence, and one would not be inaccurate in paraphrasing the chorus's question to read, "What kind of monster is headed this way?" For the chorus, the unfocused image of the distant vessel signifies a confused or ambivalent object whose exact nature cannot be clearly delineated, but more importantly within the larger context of the play, she signifies a vision of woman as monster, as a kind of Medusa whose aspect is at once alluring but terrifying and dangerous at the same time. As the image of the vessel sharpens, the chorus perceives it coming like a stately ship followed by a train of smaller vessels, her attendants. What first appeared as a monstrosity vanishes into the seductive show of billowing sails and flying streamers, into the image of a fine galley ship richly decked. Yet it is still a thing of land or sea and amphibian, and the reader must never lose sight that this mixed creature is not simply dropped from view but conserved in the image of the temptress, Dalila, as an alluring thing of beauty whose gliding over the surface of the waves hypnotizes at the same time that it calls attention to itself as a conspicuous monstrosity.

Nietzsche in *The Gay Science* comes very close to describing woman's attraction and repulsion from a similar standpoint when he writes:

Here I stand in the flaming surf whose white tongues are licking at my feet; from all sides I hear howling, threats, screaming, roaring coming at me, while the old earth-shaker sings his aria in the lowest depths, deep as a bellowing bull, while pounding such an earth-shaking beat that the hearts of even these weather-beaten rocky monsters are trembling in their bodies. Then, suddenly, as if born out of nothing, there appears before the gate of this hellish labyrinth, only a few fathoms away—a large sailboat, gliding along as silently as a ghost. Oh, what ghostly beauty! How magically it touches me! Has all the calm and taciturnity of the world embarked on it? Does my happiness itself sit in this quiet place—my happier ego, my second, departed self? Not to be dead and yet no longer alive? A spiritlike intermediate being: quietly observing, gliding, floating? As the boat that with its white sails moves like an immense butterfly over the dark sea. Yes! To move *over* existence! That's it! That would be something!

It seems as if the noise here had led me into fantasies. All great noise leads us to move happiness into some quiet distance. When a man stands in the midst of his own noise, in the midst of his own surf of plans and projects, then he is apt also to see quiet, magical beings gliding past him and to long for their happiness and seclusion: *women*. He almost thinks that his better self dwells there among the women, and that in these quiet regions even the loudest surf turns into deathly quiet, and life itself into a dream about life. Yet! Yet! Noble enthusiast, even on the most beautiful sailboat there is a lot of noise, and unfortunately much small and petty noise.[2]

In Nietzsche's dreamlike vision, or revelation, woman is seen as a "spiritlike intermediate being" or "ghostly beauty" and as such is situated in a position between life and death, spirit and matter, truth and falsehood. Reminiscent of the undecidability expressed by the chorus in *Samson Agonistes* at the beginning of the passage above, Nietzsche's remarks on woman here in section 60 of *The Gay Science* present her as something that is at once familiar and foreign, distant and near. She is, according to Nietzsche, "my happier ego, my second, departed self" and at the same time a mysterious alien sailboat that is "born out of nothing." Attractive, the feminine as ghost ship "has all the calm and taciturnity of the world embarked on it" and yet contains "much small and petty noise," which to Nietzsche is repulsive. Like the chorus's description of Dalila in *Samson Agonistes*, Nietzsche's observations on woman present her as at once seductive and traumatic, a haven for man's disquietude and a vessel that appears like a transport before the gate of his hellish labyrinth in the way the ferryman Charon appears on this side of the river Styx. Like Dalila, the woman Nietzsche describes is a type of Medusa, an emasculating woman allied with the sea, whose aspect is at once terrifying and seductive, a monster, since her nature is intermediate, or amphibious in Sir Thomas Browne's sense of the word.

One of Nietzsche's most striking observations in the passage from *The Gay Science* is that woman at once glides *over* existence as a ship glides over the sea only because her prow cuts so deeply into human affairs, into the pettiness, the matter of existence as symbolized by the oceans.[3] In the passage from Milton's *Samson Agonistes*, Dalila is also seen as buoyed up not only by the waters but by the winds that fill her sails. Yet the image of woman is not simply that of one who floats or sails over existence but also of one who is deeply involved in human affairs, in mercantile enterprise. She is, we recall, "like a stately Ship of Tarsus, bound for th' Isles" to do commerce, to traffic in goods, including slaves, of whom Samson can be seen as one. Like the Nietzschean ghost ship that appears before the hellish labyrinth as a transport to that land, Dalila in *Samson Agonistes* suddenly appears out of nowhere before Samson at once as a possible haven for his disquietude, a home "In leisure and domestic ease, / Exempt from many a care and chance," and as a porter to female snares, gins, and toils, to a labyrinth of misery and thralldom (ll. 917–18). Thus Samson: "This Gaol I count the house of Liberty / To thine whose doors my feet shall never enter" (949–50). It is clear that Samson perceives Dalila as materialistic, deviant, and unfaithful. Yet, in his speeches, Dalila appears more than immersed in existence, for she has strange arts that can touch man magically, as Nietzsche would say. She is human, but not all too human. That is to say, Dalila is a sorceress, a miraculous being, even in Samson's most bitter speeches, and when Samson insists, "Thy fair enchanted cup, and warbling charms / No more on me have power, their force is null'd," one wonders whether he is acknowledging by his very denial that she does possess in some sense these strange magical powers. Certainly, the chorus's first description of Dalila can be seen in retrospect to do nothing but heighten this sense of the miraculous, the enchantress in Dalila, as she sails on stage with tackle trim, sails billowing in the wind.

Although in Nietzsche's text the relationship between the miraculous quietude of woman and her ordinary, "petty noise" is stressed overtly, in the chorus's remarks about Dalila as she enters the stage the sense of the miraculous is not broken by the suggestion that she is really a garrulous fishwife of sorts. Besides, Dalila is already mentioned before she actually enters the stage, and her "petty noise" already has been thoroughly upbraided by Samson who has, as we know, succumbed to it:

> When must'ring all her wiles,
> With blandisht parleys, feminine assaults,
> Tongue batteries, she surceas'd not day nor night
> To storm me over-watch't, and wearied out.
> At times when men seek most repose and rest,
> I yielded, and unlock'd her all my heart.
> [Ll. 402–7]

Certainly the passage in which Dalila is described to us as a sailing vessel is meant to counterpoint this description of her by Samson, if for no other reason than that her silence in the chorus's description appears eerie when contrasted to Samson's portrait of her as an army of words, a barrage of "tongue batteries," as a "storm" whose fury does not end. What we see as a stately ship whose tackle trim, or control, maneuvers her in a silent, calm, orderly fashion is, Samson has already warned, really a fury of petty words. Our impression of her in the formal description of her entrance as a vessel, therefore, is "uncanny" in the Freudian sense of the term, as we shall elaborate shortly, for she appears curiously removed, distanced, unfamiliar, and yet familiar, quite in character, her ostentatious manner streaming in the breeze, her equipage "bedeckt, ornate and gay," her "damsel train behind."[4] Such are the signs, though not verbal, of a feminine pettiness that betrays the mysterious silence of her arrival, an arrival that appeals to us at the same time that it offends us. We have, of course, already seen to what degree such attraction-repulsion operates in the passage quoted from Nietzsche above.

The comparison of the passage of the chorus's describing Dalila's entrance in *Samson Agonistes* with Nietzsche's passage from *The Gay Science* is most helpful in showing how in certain texts woman is perceived in the Freudian sense of the "uncanny," a term Freud uses to signify the psychological economy of uncertainty, of undecidability. For Freud, the "uncanny," or "unheimlich," is an ambivalent interplay of attraction and repulsion, of that which is familiar and that which is foreign. Freud attributes the experience of uncanniness to the "return of the repressed," and goes on to comment that the uncanny can come only from the circumstance of the appearance of a double which in an early mental stage was benign enough, but in later mental stages becomes something of a terror. Nietzsche, we recall, names woman "my happier ego" in terror. He meets a familiar aspect of himself, really, in a displaced form which is at once identical with and different from himself. To put it more strongly, Nietzsche has an encounter in section 60 of *The Gay Science* with the "return of the repressed," with a recognition of something that he refuses to recognize but cannot ignore. It is this confrontation with the repressed that creates what Freud would consider the effects of the uncanny, the fact that Nietzsche sees woman as at once angelic (as butterfly, as gliding spirit) and traumatic (as ghost, as an empty ship before the hellish labyrinth), as floating over existence and yet immersed within it.

In *Samson Agonistes*, Dalila creates the effects of uncanniness because she too is a kind of double: she is Samson's other half, his wife. What makes her entrance eerie is that she is the intimate partner who is radically estranged, who appears as if in a dream of the one who represses. We note, of course, that Samson cannot see Dalila even when she returns, and it is the chorus who mediates the scene for him. That this mediation, which we have quoted above, is itself uncanny should not surprise us, since it is precisely the process of the subject's (Samson's) forced recognition of that which he refuses to recognize or cannot see. Thus, we confront the uncanny face to face; we see a creature whose attributes are contradictory, uncertain. For, if Dalila is pictured as a silent vessel, she is condemned as a petty noise. If she sails over existence, she is, at the same time, trafficking in the affairs of men. If she is a creature of the sea, she is also a creature of the land. If she is man's second half, she is also an unfamiliar creature that emerges out of nowhere. This list can be expanded. In all of these instances woman's un-Heimlichkeit is stressed; and the hyphen that separates the word is most important, for it is what Nietzsche would perceive as a factor of distance, the space that comes in between the oppositions and serves to confuse and separate them, at once.

We have already seen how Eve in *Paradise Lost* represents such distance as undecidability, and my intention is not to elaborate on Dalila in the same way. However, we must note the importance of this space, for this space, or distance, makes Dalila representative of the uncanny. It is particularly important to realize that in Freud and in both the Nietzsche and Milton texts, the uncanny is also involved in the psychological economy of the castration complex and that the space, or distance, we have just mentioned is characteristic of this most radical form of cutting. I will elaborate upon this theme of castration at a later time in this chapter, but I do wish for the time being to adumbrate the connection of undecidability, uncertainty, distance, space, and the uncanny with the appearance of the emasculating female figure (Dalila, Nietzschean woman) and the thematic of castration, that is, Samson's sheared locks, his blindness, his loss of strength, which are all displacements for castration, according to Freudian lines of thinking; and Nietzsche's fear of the petty noise, of the cutting of the philosopher from his philosophy.[5]

Before we talk about castration itself, we should notice the extent to which Dalila in *Samson Agonistes* acts from a distance in the Nietzschean sense and thereby reinforces the connection between the uncanny and the distance, or space, that marks this most uncertain or doubtful of terms. Especially when Dalila begins speaking to Samson, she is strikingly aloof. She begins:

> With doubtful feet and wavering resolution
> I came, still dreading thy displeasure, *Samson*,
> Which to have merited, without excuse,
> I cannot but acknowledge. [Ll. 732–35]

The speech is serpentine, wavering, elaborate, and also doubtful, uncertain. Her "wavering resolution" and her doubtfulness place her at an emotional remove that allows her to fabricate intricate sentences whose syntax itself is wavering or undulating:

> But conjugal affection,
> Prevailing over fear and timorous doubt,
> Hath led me on desirous to behold
> Once more thy face, and know of thy estate.
> If aught in my ability may serve
> To light'n what thou suffer'st, and appease
> Thy mind with what amends is in my power,
> Though late, yet in some part to recompense
> My rash but more unfortunate misdeed.
> [Ll. 739–47]

Samson's reply, "Out, out Hyaena; these are thy wonted arts," is his reaction to Dalila's distance and her uncanniness, and the image of the hyena is particularly apt, because it signifies during the Renaissance an androgynous animal.[6] It is, in short, a monster whose nature is mixed and in this way reinforces the reference to Dagon which is made earlier when the chorus asks whether Dalila is a thing of land or sea, and carried through on the thematic of uncertainty.

The thematic of uncertainty and distance, indeed, the uncanny itself, is even further elaborated in terms of voice by means of the hyena image. Dalila, apparently, can only counterfeit the human voice, can only sound familiar, while in fact she has a voice which is very unfamiliar, since it is really an alien, animal sound. According to Samson, the voice of the hyena is only a ruse, a seductive double-talk that is treacherous. Like the true voices of animals, the true voice of woman is alien to human discourse, to a speech that can carry within its words qualities like truth, goodness, and holiness. The speech of the female as hyena is but a noise, and a petty noise at that, as Samson stresses elsewhere. What is disturbing is that this petty noise is so easily confused with real speech, or all too human speech, that it can so easily seduce man and cut him off from the sacred, from his potency.

That is to say, the petty noise of woman as hyena in *Samson Agonistes* is not only itself the perfect representation for the uncanny, for distance, for uncertainty, but is the means whereby woman castrates the Hebraic hero. It is a symbolic or displaced castration, to be sure, but it results in the literal separation of Samson from the Father, God, as well as from the holy language of God, and results in Samson's blinding too, which in "The Uncanny" Freud would interpret as the most classical form of displacement for castration. What will concern me most, however, is Samson's estrangement from a masculine discourse and his consequent borrowing of what can only be called a feminine discourse. That is, by marrying Dalila and submitting to her seductive tongue, Samson finds himself aboard that eerie sailing vessel which the chorus sights, a vessel that like Nietzsche's ghost ship represents an *actio in distans*, a feminine discourse, a speech for the castrated.

In Nietzsche too it is admitted that the voice of the philosopher is not immune to a feminine discourse, and, in fact, Nietzsche often expresses himself with precisely such a feminine style. According to Nietzsche, the philosophical text expresses, like the female, a petty noise that is by no means coherent, of one piece. Rather, it is a fragmented text that reveals its own scars or sounds deep in its signifying structure or syntax. To look upon such a text is, for the reader, to witness a series of ghostly marks from which the truth is effaced, a writing removed from the true voice of the Father, God, a text that is exterior to any signified, any presence. At the same time that such a text moves over existence in such a way, it is immersed in petty prejudices and absurd opinions made by a philosopher who knows nothing of the truth, who never makes contact with any Muse. In *Ecce Homo*, Nietzsche talks about styles in the section "Why I Write Such Excellent Books" and makes a very significant reference to the passage quoted above from *The Gay Science* when he asks to whom he addresses himself. Answer:

> To you, the bold searchers, researchers, and whoever embarks with cunning sails on terrible seas.[7]

Throughout the sections that belong to "Why I Write Such Excellent Books," the matter of stylistics is intertwined with a discussion of the feminine, and Nietzsche's reference to the image of the sailing ship that embarks upon terrible seas is an allusion by way of *The Gay Science* to the fact that Nietzsche considers his style, or his text, to be a thing of ghostly beauty, a sublime style that at once sails over existence at the same time that its prow cuts deep into its matter:

> Before me, it was not known what could be done with the German language—what could be done with language in general. The art of the *great* rhythm, the *great* style of long periods to express a tremendous up and down of sublime, of superhuman passion, was discovered only by me.[8]

Nietzsche's sublime depends upon the sexual, on passion, and as Nietzsche indicates in *Ecce Homo*, on the difference and hostility between the sexes, the "battle of the sexes," as he calls it. Only by immersing itself in passion, by sailing the vessel that is woman, can style become superhumanly sublime. Yet we must always be aware that such a sublime style comes at a very heavy price, for the feminine which Nietzsche defines in *Ecce Homo* as distance, annihilation, danger, revenge, wickedness, and cunning is a violence that mutilates the text. That Nietzsche's comments about woman and style occur in *Ecce Homo* is especially interesting in light of the fact that it is this text, more than any of Nietzsche's others, that has undergone *sparagmos*, a violence at the hands of feminine furies, of the feminine sailboat whose inclination is to glide into treacherous waters, hellish labyrinths.

For Nietzsche the sublime style is at once a style that raises itself to superhuman heights only because it submits to violence (castration?) by the female and thereby finds itself cut off from the linguistic sources or powers that are traditionally considered masculine in our culture: God, truth, and presence. And in *Samson Agonistes* the hero undergoes a similar impairment of his voice or speech; it is upon this impairment that his sublimity depends. It is, finally, by means of what I will term, after Gilles Deleuze, a *langue mineure* rather than a *langue majeure* that Samson triumphs, that he recuperates his strength.[9] However, before we consider that impaired or castrated discourse in detail, we must outline more specifically what we mean by a feminine discourse, a *langue mineure,* at least within a Miltonic perspective.

II

If contemporary critics like Jacques Derrida and Bernard Pautrat have determined that Nietzsche's style is an *écriture,* which is to say, a style that is feminine, cut off from the father, the logos, the signified, and the symbolic phallus, a style that is decentered, mutilated, fragmented, Milton in his day ascribes many of the same attributes to feminine discourse, and thereby shows attitudes he inherits from a culture that has always condemned the speech of woman as an antilogos, a hysteria, or simply a cacophony.[10] Indeed, in the numerous seventeenth-century handbooks concerning the proper conduct of women, there is usually the admonition that a woman should, if at all possible, be as quiet as she can, an admonition Ben Jonson takes up satirically in *Epicoene; or, The Silent Woman* when he ironically implies that the only means to realize the ideal of a silent woman is to hire a man who will play the part. Since any wit should immediately recognize that a silent woman is a contradiction in terms, we should not spare (from a Jonsonian perspective) any sympathy for one who would accept such a ruse at face value, as the character Morose does in this play. Woman, the play submits, is unable to spare man her incessant, irritating chatter, and this, like labor, is an evil that man will simply have to accept.

However plentiful the criticism and censorship of feminine discourse was in secular circles during Milton's time, the major criticism and censorship stems from a theological or religious perspective that is largely Hebraic in origin. Julia Kristeva in *Des chinoises* addresses herself to this sexist criticism by the Hebrews when she advances the idea that in a monotheistic society truth can only be communicated from father to son, God to man, male to male.[11] Woman, especially in Hebraic culture, is not included in this transaction of truth, is not given signs that bear spiritual power, for she is by her very ontological status cut off from religious and cultural life, since she is considered to belong inherently to the natural order of biological reproduction, an order that is decidedly unclean, impure. Because woman is viewed in terms of natural modes of production rather than cultural ones, it should not come as any surprise that in relation to her language, which for man is cultural as well as religious, woman is inherently closer to the realms of nature, that is, animals, than to culture. And therefore, if by chance the female discourse sounds like man's reasoned speech, it must be considered suspect, considered a transgression, a counterfeit whose danger must be checked by the guardians of true culture, the males. Although Kristeva does not elaborate, she implies that the *Genesis* story of Adam and Eve is mainly a story about Adam's failure to recognize that not only is animal or serpent discourse to be distrusted but woman's discourse is similarly a dangerous and deviant form of speech whose counterfeiting must be silenced or restricted. Adam's undoing is the fact that he is seduced by such an ontologically inferior discourse, a feminine discourse that belongs to the natural order of serpents rather than to the cultural order of man.[12]

Milton recognizes this implication in the *Genesis* story, one could argue, when he excludes Eve in *Paradise Lost* from the conversation between Adam and the archangel Raphael. For Eve to participate in these dialogues would be perverse, for it would violate the premise that woman's discourse is essentially different in kind from man's discourse, that it is at best a counterfeit that must be checked, restricted, and limited. That Eve should be convinced by Satan's arguments is never attributed to the fact that Eve was never formally educated in argumentation and disputation, as Adam is to some degree, but that her speech is to a great extent homologous with a more natural or animal discourse. In book 9 both serpent and woman are committing the same sin before the Fall, which is participating with one another in a false, or counterfeit, discourse. Not only does the serpent speak in such a way that he overleaps his natural station in the great chain of being, but woman, similarly, transgresses against the masculine, and cultural, order by responding and replying to the serpent's arguments. Her right action would have been to keep silent, to ignore and remove herself from engaging in disputation with the serpent. By succumbing to the temptation to respond to Satan, Eve parodies Adam's dialogues with Raphael and usurps the husband's place; she allows her untutored, more natural, instinctual discourse to take the place of Adam's rational discourse and at precisely that time when Adam's powers of discourse are needed most to defend the prelapsarian couple's innocence from corruption.

It is, of course, difficult to guess whether Satan would have been able to deceive Adam, had Adam been in Eve's place, but there are suggestions in *Paradise Lost* that Adam would have withstood the temptation. First of all, Satan chooses to seduce Eve because he is aware of Adam's rhetorical proficiency. More importantly, when Adam meets Eve after she has plucked and eaten of the forbidden fruit, he is not for one moment deceived by her. The seduction of Eve's lowly discourse does not convince Adam to eat. Rather, Adam eats of the apple knowing full well what it is he is doing. He eats, not because Eve tempts him with words, but out of loyalty to her. Here Milton's reading of *Genesis* differs drastically from Kristeva's, yet without changing the binary oppositions, male-female, nature-culture, which Kristeva isolates as key.

In *Samson Agonistes,* Samson is only too aware of the difference between a *langue majeure* and a *langue mineure,* a primary and a secondary language, which corresponds to the discourse of men and the chatter of women:

> As I deserve, pay on my punishment;
> And expiate, if possible, my crime,
> Shameful *garrulity.* To have reveal'd
> Secrets of men, the secrets of a friend,
> How heinous. [Ll. 489–93]

What Samson laments is not merely that he has revealed the secrets of men, the code of the superior discourse, to the one who must be subject to it, to the one from whom the power (the secret) of language must be hidden or kept in reserve, but that in doing so he has himself been reduced to garrulity, which is to say, to a womanish discourse or inferior language. The result of Samson's crime is self-castration, a radical separation from the "secrets of men" (that is, the power of men, the masculine) and an identification with the publishings of the female: an inferior discourse which keeps nothing in reserve, nothing secret, but which reveals everything. Dalila informs us of this when she says:

> It was a weakness
> In me, but incident to all our sex,

> Curiosity, inquisitive, importune
> Of secrets, then with like infirmity
> To publish them, both common female faults.
> [Ll. 773-77]

And Samson, much earlier, uses the term *publish* in a similar context when he describes betraying the "secrets of men" to woman:

> But I
> God's counsel have not kept, his holy secret
> Presumptuously have publish'd, impiously,
> Weakly at least, and shamefully: A sin
> That Gentiles in thir Parables condemn
> To thir abyss and horrid pains confin'd.
> [Ll. 496-501]

These are the only uses of the word *publish* in *Samson Agonistes*, and their context suggests a marked difference between two kinds of discourses, one a feminine discourse that is inferior and that publishes everything, that reveals all secrets openly like a text or pamphlet that is widely circulated, the other a secretive, masculine discourse that is superior and is communicated by means of word of mouth in a clandestine manner. It is Manoa who tells us that the "secret" of Samson's gift is first revealed by an angel who does not, we note, publish the truth, or "secret," for all to see, but who quietly ordains Samson a select man. This contrast between feminine publishing and masculine speaking is further reinforced when Samson in yet another passage uses the term "author" to underscore in what way he has revealed the secret to woman. Thus:

> Sole Author I, sole cause: if aught seem vile,
> As vile hath been my folly, who have profan'd
> The mystery of God giv'n me under pledge
> Of vow, and have betray'd it to a woman.
> [Ll. 376-79]

It is through the use of the word "Author" that Samson lets us know the extent to which he realizes he has lost access to the superior discourse of men and has now taken on the identity of one who publishes, of woman. In the passage above, Samson becomes an author, or speaker, of an inferior discourse because he has authored the profanation of the mystery of God. He has broken the "pledge / Of vow," has betrayed or submitted the verbal bond between man and God to an unholy, Philistine woman. His discourse, as I will argue later, has been castrated by woman, his vow broken through her.

What we must emphasize is that the discourse of woman, like the written text, is an imitation, or copying down, of another discourse, the superior discourse, and this imitation, or counterfeiting, is very pronounced in *Samson Agonistes*. For example, the equation of Dalila with the hyena, which we have already mentioned, makes clear that feminine discourse is of the animal order and that its mimicking of the human voice carries all the perversity of the mimicking serpent in the Garden of Eden. It is a discourse that transgresses by trespassing on the true discourse of the male, by reproducing what is supposedly real. Dalila is a monster to Samson because she wishes to usurp the place of his speech with her inhuman voice, her petty noise, and therefore he accuses her of arguing with "wonted arts" and "circling wiles." Samson recognizes that Dalila's arguments are not reasoned or true arguments, but merely bestial seductions, temptations aimed at man's animalistic desire for creature comforts, seductions that confuse superior and inferior discourse in order to achieve their aim.

The seduction, of course, works, and Samson is betrayed by Dalila's imitative voice, for Samson cannot distinguish between the original and its copy before he falls prey to the consequences that follow his submission to her. The confusion between an inferior and superior discourse is elaborated by Dalila, who talks to Samson of two laws in conflict: the "Universal law of God" and "love's Law." Like Eve, who in *Paradise Lost* realizes that she must "add what wants / In

Female sex, the more to draw his love" and therefore tries to become more equal to Adam by attempting to appropriate his discourse when she eats of the fruit of the tree of knowledge, Dalila tries to erase the difference between male and female orders, which she sees as an obstacle to a perfect union between man and wife, by knowing Samson's secret, the "secrets of men." But whereas Eve attempts to accede to wisdom in order to become more equal with man, to appropriate his language so falsely offered by Satan, Dalila opts for making Samson less unequal by divesting him of his strength, his link with the "secrets of men." It is her desire, in other words, to transform the inferior language of woman into the superior language of men, the law of the Father into the law of Love, or again, masculine into feminine:

> I knew that liberty
> Would draw thee forth to perilous enterprises,
> While I at home sat full of cares and fears
> Wailing thy absence in my widow'd bed;
> Here I should still enjoy thee day and night
> Mine and Love's prisoner, not the *Philistines*',
> Whole to myself, unhazarded abroad,
> Fearless at home of partners in my love.
> These reasons in Love's law have pass'd for good,
> Though fond and reasonless to some perhaps:
> And Love hath oft, well meaning, wrought much woe,
> Yet always pity or pardon had obtain'd.
> [Ll. 803–14]

Here, Dalila's statement, "pass'd for good," suggests that like the voice of the hyena or the writing of an author, "Love's law" is a counterfeit, a mimicking, an inferior code that is supposed to pass for one that is superior. This inferior law is the law of the female's desire for complete dominance over the male; it should be pardoned, according to Dalila, and it expresses itself in terms of the language of seduction, an irrational ("reasonless") and unholy discourse that, as we mentioned, marks the style of all Dalila's passages.

What is most troublesome about the counterfeit discourse

of Dalila is that, if it is a discourse that publishes or reveals the secrets of men, it is, at the same time, secretive in its own way. The very fact that such a discourse can only counterfeit or mimic means that it has no real essence of its own, no signified, and that it is, for all its ability to pass for good, an inferior means of communication that cannot be known or fathomed. It is a speech that is cut off from truth. No matter how much it explains or reveals itself, such a discourse will always be "reasonless to some," will remain a mystery, for it lacks the divine presence and only behaves as if it had one. Thus Dalila's words are "baited" or "honied" words, her voice "enchanting."

Dalila's inferior language has many prototypes, of course, and Milton certainly was very familiar with them. The voices of the Sirens and Circe in Homer, the voice of Echo in Ovid, and the voice of Cassandra in Aeschylus are but a few examples taken from antiquity of a feminine discourse that is seductive, irrational, and dangerous. In *Samson Agonistes*, Milton makes specific reference to Circe, and we should recall that in Homer's *Odyssey* it is her voice that is bewitching Odysseus's crew, long before they drink her potions:[13]

> In the entrance way they stayed
> to listen there: inside her quiet house
> they heard the goddess Kirkê.
>   Low she sang
> in her beguiling voice, while on her loom
> she wove ambrosial fabric sheer and bright.[14]

Once she has snared the men, they lose their human voices and make animal sounds:

> So, squealing, in they went. And Kirkê tossed them
> acorns, mast, and cornel berries—fodder
> for hogs who rut and slumber on the earth.[15]

That Circe's transformation of men into swine is a form of castration is clearly pointed out by Hermes to Odysseus when he tells the commander that Circe is a castrating lover:

> And she will cower and yield her bed—
> a pleasure you must not decline,
> so may her lust and fear bestead
> you and your friends, and break her spell;
> but make her swear by heaven and hell
> no witches' tricks, or else, your harness shed,
> you'll be unmanned by her as well.[16]

And later Odysseus says to Circe,

> Now it is I myself you hold, enticing
> into your chamber, to your dangerous bed,
> to take my manhood when you have me stripped.[17]

The connection between woman, her voice or song, and her desire to unman the male is clearly suggested by Homer in book 10 of the *Odyssey*, then, and it impinges strongly upon the references made by Samson that Dalila is a Circe figure, a singer who desires to unman the hero.[18]

Nowhere is the identification of Dalila as a castrating female more strongly made than in Samson's retelling of his fall into the "lascivious lap" of Dalila.

> Then swoll'n with pride into the snare I fell
> Of fair fallacious looks, venereal trains,
> Soft'n'd with pleasure and voluptuous life;
> At length to lay my head and hallow'd pledge
> Of all my strength in the lascivious lap
> Of a deceitful Concubine who shore me
> Like a tame Wether, all my precious fleece,
> Then turn'd me out ridiculous, despoil'd,
> Shav'n, and disarm'd among my enemies.
> [Ll. 532–40]

Like Circe and the apocryphal Judith, Dalila promises sexual fulfillment, but performs castration instead. In the passage just quoted, there is an obvious metaphorical confusion between sexual intercourse with a wife and castration at the hands of a deceitful concubine. Clearly, the lines, "to lay my head and hallow'd pledge / Of all my strength in the lascivious lap / Of a deceitful Concubine" carry a double meaning in the sense that the words "head" and "lap" have slang meanings current in Milton's time that allow one to read the lines as referring to sexual intercourse, while at the same time the lines refer to the manner in which Dalila cuts off Samson's hair, in which she symbolically castrates him by cutting off that which contains his potency or strength. Like Circe, Dalila turns out the male, after the dismemberment of manhood, as a "ridiculous" and "despoil'd" creature, and that is the state in which we first encounter Samson and in which he tells us of his terrible fall from power.

The scene that Samson recounts above is most important, because it describes what Bernard Pautrat views, after his reading of Freud, the "scène Médusé." Sigmund Freud's note on the Medusa, entitled "Medusa's Head," is of major interest to French scholars because it amplifies in terms of the phantasm the significance of the "castration complex" which, from the French perspective (Lacan, Jean Laplanche, J.-B. Pontalis, André Green, Derrida) has important bearings upon the problematic of the origin of signification. Freud begins with the formula (an extension based on the formula *blindness = castration*, which appears in "The Uncanny") "to decapitate—to castrate. The terror of seeing Medusa is thus a terror of castration that is linked to the sight of something."[19] Freud then proceeds to demonstrate how this terror is emblematically displaced in terms of the mythological and phantasmic head of the Medusa, a head that, like a coin or token, stands for something—in this case, the female's genitals. Freud maintained in earlier studies (such as the case of the wolf-man) that for man the female's genitals suggest the threat of castration, because the phallus (the symbolic penis) is missing, and he hypothesizes that the head of the Medusa is nothing other than an emblematic displacement that is both a repression of the terrifying truth (that castration exists) and an expression of this truth in terms of a more acceptable metaphor, the Medusa's head that contains a proliferation of phallus symbols in order to assuage the fear of castration while preserving the element of terror that accompanies the castration fear. The French Freudians following Jacques Lacan have preserved the view that the truth being displaced is not a transcendental signified: that which is not a reified concept, ideal, presence, absolute. Indeed, for Lacanians the truth cannot be signified but only construed as cutting, spacing, difference, and distance, since discourse is itself punctuated by the Oedipus complex. Lacan suggests that such punctuation occurs by way of castration anxiety and that it is not only a consequence of the Oedipal father, but of the mother as well, since she marks the locus of a lack which she not only physically embodies but which she transfers onto her child. The mother signifies for the child the terrifying recognition that the child cannot fulfill mother's sexual demand and in doing so establishes the father in what the child once saw as its rightful place. This recognition of lack facilitates the child to make demands (discourse), to construct a language of desire which is painfully aware of a narcissistic ego threatened both by an awareness of its own inadequacy as well as the inadequacy of a world to provide it with what it wants. What fills the void is the demand, then, which is itself maternal to the degree that it is itself a castrated speaking body, a body of words whose very utterance is a sign that lack exists.[20]

In *Samson Agonistes* the pre-Oedipal faith in a language of presence must give way to a more Oedipalized or feminized discourse in whose very utterance there is a saturation of lack. Samson must accept a lower and seemingly inferior discourse which is produced or conferred on him by means of a *scène Méduse*. The Medusa is Dalila, of course, since she represents castration in terms of the "lascivious lap" that is both appealing and terrifying. Like the Medusa, Dalila is a "specious Monster" who snares men in an entanglement of "venereal trains." If Medusa is pictured with serpents for hair, an icon that represents the displaced presence of the phallus as well as its absence or amputation, Dalila is associated with the "bosom snake" and the "manifest serpent," and, too, with "hair," the potent hair of the lover she amputates from his strength. What both Medusa and Dalila have most in common is not simply that they are castrating women but that they themselves are castrates, what Germaine Greer has called the "female eunuch," and it is this truth more than anything else that ensures castration will take place, for reasons Freud has made apparent.[21]

One can argue that in Milton's drama there is enough thematic and stylistic evidence to prove that Samson does, in fact, adopt a feminine discourse, an inferior speech, and that this speech is closely associated with the *scène Médusant* in which Samson is symbolically castrated. Now I am not going to argue that Milton exemplifies a strictly French Freudian position, but simply that such a contemporary position is useful in giving us access to certain aspects of *Samson Agonistes* that might otherwise be overlooked. What is interesting, certainly, is the extent to which *Samson Agonistes* does contain a *scène Médusant*, a scene closely related to the production of signification or, more precisely, a discourse that is founded upon the nontruth of the castration complex, of the female eunuch. It is with this discourse as it is adopted by Samson that we now turn in order to give the reader a detailed description of what such a discourse is like and to what degree Samson does actually use it.

III

The weight of the female eunuch's effect is felt heavily on the fallen hero, whose discourse has been lowered to that of the female castrate, to that of a Dalila. This is not to say that Samson speaks with the glib, seductive tongue of a temptress, but that his discourse is decidedly unheroic, unmanly, "effeminately vanquish't." Samson himself describes the extent of his metamorphosis when he says,

> Now blind, disheart'n'd, sham'd, dishonor'd, quell'd,
> To what can I be useful, wherein serve
> My Nation, and the work from Heav'n impos'd,
> But to sit idle on the household hearth,
> A burdenous drone; to visitants a gaze,
> Or pitied object, these redundant locks
> Robustious to no purpose clust'ring down,
> Vain monument of strength. [Ll. 564-71]

Like a woman, Samson is only fit to sit on the household hearth, he tells us. Like Dalila, he appears but a vain monument or spectacle (the image of the ship is relevant here), an object upon which one merely gazes. If Samson is shamed, dishonored, quelled, and blind, it is because he has himself become feminine, has become a symbolic castrate cut off from truth, from the secrets of men. The image of the redundant locks is very much a synecdoche for the image of woman, who like these locks is superfluous or redundant, but, more importantly, who is cut off from the sacred, from the masculine. It is because woman is outside, alienated from the masculine order of things, that she becomes an image of powerlessness on the one hand and deviant cunning on the other. Woman's prettiness is only a sign of her redundancy, her own excessiveness that remains outside the strictly necessary.

Again, in the passage above, the image of the drone is particularly important, because it refers to a passage in Hesiod's *Theogony* in which woman is compared to the drone:

And as in thatched hives bees feed the drones whose nature is to do mischief—by day and throughout the day until the sun goes down the bees are busy and lay the white combs, while the drones stay at home in the covered skeps and reap the toil of others into their own bellies—even so Zeus who thunders on high made women to be an evil to mortal men, with a nature to do evil.[22]

That Samson should consider himself a drone shows to what degree he has taken on the identity of the female as one who is unmanned, of the female as female eunuch, as not-man.

It could be argued, of course, that what Samson is doing in the passage on his effeminacy is nothing more than hurling insults upon himself and that his identification with the female is an indication of how deep his misogyny runs. However, if we move to the beginning of the play, we discover that already there Samson's discourse is betraying his "foul effeminacy." Not only the imagery but also the tentative and somewhat hysterical nature of the discourse indicate a kind of speech that resembles, not that of a masculine hero whose words are affirmative, rational, powerful, authoritative, but that of a more feminine character who like Dalila appears on stage "with doubtful feet and wavering resolution."

Of course, Samson is not the first seventeenth-century stage hero to display effeminate speech qualities. Shakespeare's Macbeth, we recall, is accused by his mannish wife of hysterical outbursts that are embarrassingly feminine, and Hamlet's moody fits of delirium are not so far removed from Ophelia's discourse in her mad scene. Although Samson is not tortured by phantasms like Macbeth, or prone to speak in riddles like Hamlet, his discourse is disturbingly self-reflexive, self-pitying, moody, and obsessed with images of death and suffering ("Myself my Sepulcher, a moving Grave / Buried"). Morever, it is a discourse burdened with the imagery of emasculation, as we have already noticed.

Just as the drone becomes a central image of importance in the passage in which Samson berates his "foul effeminacy," the image of the hornet becomes of interest in the opening monologue, for the flitting, or swarming, of thoughts implies that Samson is not in complete control of his reason and is subject to a distempered or hysterical mentality in which the imagination, like a plague of hornets, torments him:

> Ease to the body some, none to the mind
> From restless thoughts, that like a deadly swarm
> Of Hornets arm'd, no sooner found alone,
> But rush upon me thronging. [Ll. 18–21]

Indeed, he is plagued by his own memories, his doubts, his ignorance. "Why was my breeding order'd and prescrib'd / As of a person separate to God . . . ?" (ll. 30–31). In this opening monologue the thoughts are erratic, their expression stemming from passion, not reason. His thoughts glide swiftly in the opening lines from a consideration of the place Samson is "wont to sit" to his role as prisoner, to the breath of heaven "fresh blowing," to the recollection of Dagon's feast day. After the monologue, the chorus confirms our suspicion that Samson is deranged, subject to fits and melancholia:

> This, this is he; softly a while,
> Let us not break in upon him;
> O change beyond report, thought, or belief!
> See how he lies at random, carelessly diffus'd,
> With languish't head unpropt,
> As one past hope, abandon'd,
> And by himself given over;
> In slavish habit, ill-fitted weeds.
> [Ll. 115–22]

Like his own discourse, Samson is lying "at random." He is "carelessly diffus'd"; he is, like the hysteric, in disarray. But if the content, or message, of Samson's speeches betrays his effeminacy, so does his style, and nowhere is this more apparent than in Samson's use of the metaphor.

In *Milton's Grand Style*, Christopher Ricks charges that Milton's *Samson Agonistes* is seriously flawed because the metaphors given to Samson do not give rise to new meanings; they do not, he charges, "invigorate" the text. Instead, they abort or frustrate the poem by denying the proper consistency between vehicle and tenor that allows for a particularly rich comparison to develop in the reader's mind. What Ricks contends is that these metaphors are separable from their contexts, do not fuse vehicle and tenor, and therefore cannot ensure that the text is a "living tissue." Rather, these metaphors only testify to the fact that the text is a machine with interchangeable parts. Thus "the metaphor, which has been slotted in, can as easily be slotted out."[23] But even more serious than the use of interchangeable parts is Milton's tendency to let Samson actually mix metaphors that are incongruent. Such mixing is disappointing, Ricks charges, because it actually arrests the "thought" of the poem by denying the very connections a reader needs to transport himself from one line to the next. That is, the text is, according to Ricks, a tissue of fragments, of discontinuous pieces that suggests a failure on Milton's part to produce a "living" poem in which the current of "life" (meaning?) is, as in an organism, "efficiently" carried along.

Eugene McCarthy in "Metaphor and Plot in *Samson Agonistes*" argues against Ricks by showing, as we might argue, that the metaphors are mixed "because Samson is himself confused and unable to keep his mind fixed to the elaboration of one figure."[24] That is, in our terms, Samson has lost sight of what Kristeva in *Des chinoises* calls the "Speech" (*Parole*) of the "Name-of-the-Father," the rational, scientific, holy, and superior language of the male, and can only speak and think now in terms of an inferior language, a feminine language cut off from the law of the Father, divorced from reason, logos, and truth. Thus it is only fitting that when Samson speaks in *Samson Agonistes*, he transgresses the law of the superior speech, mixes metaphors, and in so doing breaks the standards that Ricks, who is a champion of the superior discourse, upholds.

From our perspective, what Ricks has identified in *Samson Agonistes* is not simply poetic failure (which is what he means by the subchapter heading "The Unsuccessful Metaphor") but, rather, a syntactic clue that identifies Samson's style as ruptured from the speech of the Father. Such a style reveals certain unexpected syntactical deviations or linkages that might easily be perceived as syntactical breakdowns, the mixed metaphors. "Thus Samson confounds loquacity with a shipwreck," Ricks writes, and his accusation appears sound enough, since "Samson is like a bad pilot only in the respect that he has carelessly shipwrecked—loquacity has nothing to do with it. Pilots don't shipwreck because they divulge secrets."[25] To Ricks the style is inexplicably flawed, and the sympathetic Miltonists, of whom Ricks considers himself one, can admit only that in *Samson Agonistes* Milton has seriously missed the mark of fabricating a grand style in which the text lives.

However, we have already seen that there is every indication in *Samson Agonistes* that Samson's style, when seen against the thematics of the poem, makes a very consistent counterpoint. Notably, the metaphor Ricks cites is most consistent at that point Ricks feels it is incomprehensible, the point at which loquacity and shipwrecking meet, for we have noticed that in the more elaborate metaphor in which Dalila is compared to a ship, the eeriness of her entrance is based on her silent floating over existence, her reticence, which in the metaphor Samson uses in the Ricks citation is elaborated in terms of the emasculated male:

> How could I once look up, or heave the head,
> Who like a foolish Pilot have shipwreck't
> My Vessel trusted to me from above,
> Gloriously rigg'd; and for a word, a tear,
> Fool, have divulg'd the secret gift of God
> To a deceitful Woman. [Ll. 197–202]

Samson uses the equations of man as pilot as ship not only because it describes the castrating effect of woman on man, the criminal act of Dalila's cutting of the hair and the resulting demise of the hero, but because Samson recognizes it as a feminine topos, as the chorus similarly does, and therefore most useful as a means to describe his own unmanned state.[26] It is significant that in Ricks's citation of this passage, the phrase "to a deceitful Woman" is deleted, a deletion which may indicate that he does not see the connection between shipping and the feminine here as in any way important. That Milton, perhaps, expected a reader to gloss the passage Ricks cites in terms of the lines we cited at the very beginning of this chapter in which the chorus describes Dalila's entrance is never considered by Ricks.

And this is an unfortunate oversight, for if one takes the trouble to compare the passage, one discovers that in the lines cited by Ricks one has a complex example of how the style reflects the thematic of the poem, how what Roman Jakobson would call code is bound with what he would call message.[27] That is to say, one can answer why the style or, preferably, the code is the way it is (fragmented, broken, inconsistent), for, in taking on a metaphorical string of associations, man = pilot = vessel = shipwreck = loquacious, Samson's discourse becomes identified with this particular feminine string of associations.[28] But in addition to this identification through the level of content, or message, the discourse becomes a simulacrum for the feminine in terms of its style or code: the syntax of the signifying chain in which unexpected deviations, or perverse relationships between words, lead to what appear to be syntactical breakdowns, linguistic dysfunctions. That the code and not merely the message should behave this way is, of course, not surprising, for haven't we already seen that the discourse of the female is by its very nature irrational, deranged, perverse?

We find in another passage from *Samson Agonistes* that Ricks cites a similar collaboration between the message and the code, a feminine collaboration that expresses a disruptive or destructive mode of linguistic productivity which mutilates, or wounds, the text in those very places where thought and meaning are most forcefully brought to so-called life: the metaphorical moment in which a vehicle designed to carry meaning is plotting its own death.

> How counterfeit a coin they are who friends
> Bear in their Superscription (of the most
> I would be understood); in prosperous days
> They swarm, but in adverse withdraw thir head.
> [Ll. 189–92]

Ricks claims that this passage is flawed because the image of the coin and the image of the swarm are incongruent and that the phrase "withdraw thir head" can only be dubiously applied to a swarm, "which moreover is unhelpfully apt to a coin, which has a head but cannot withdraw it."[29]

And certainly, Ricks is correct in considering the passage flawed or mutilated, the discourse disjointed and perverse, which is exactly what we should expect when the chorus warns us before Samson speaks that his mind is troubled, his wound festering. If the metaphor "dies," as Ricks would have it, it is because Samson lets the word "friends" (the metaphorical tenor) take on two analogous terms that clash with one another, that cancel each other out: "coin" and "swarm." Yet these two registers, "coin" and "swarm," are, even if one looks closer at the word "friends," more compatible than one might at first believe; for the word "friends" does not refer simply to the chorus but to Samson's wife as well. It is Dalila, of course, who dominates Samson's thoughts, and it is she who has sold him out for Philistine gold (ll. 958–59). To this friend Samson says, "Cherish thy hast'n'd widowhood with the gold / Of Matrimonial treason: so farewell." Dalila is the one who is most clearly identified in Samson's mind with gold coin as well as with hypocrisy and the counterfeit. The image of the coin with its false superscription (superficial writing) represents a hypocritical overlay of words that flit above the language of the just, the discourse of the Father, and this flitting of the superficial is, of course, allusively linked to the notion of the flitting of insects, the "swarming" of hornets encountered earlier in Samon's opening monologue.

It should come as no surprise to see the term *swarm* in

this complex metaphorical passage we are considering now, for the metaphorical tenor, "friends," when thought of in terms of the femine (Dalila), provides the way of access from numismatics to the feminine image of swarming, a way of access that is at the same time a partition, a means of blockage and of fragmentation. The metaphorical identification of "friends," which is itself already a complicated meeting of two terms (chorus, Dalila), with the image of coins and swarms begins to deconstruct in the phrase, "but in adverse withdraw thir head / Not to be found, though sought." The use of a synecdoche like "head" as a figure which represents both the "coin" and the "swarm" only shows how the violent yoking together of unlike images results in not only a binding together but a falling apart as well. Within each of the metaphors, *friend = coin* and *friends = swarm*, there is a feature that will terminate their significance, a feature that will violently disrupt the signifying chain, and this feature is the image of the head which sylleptically connects two fundamentally dissimilar registers. Such a sylleptic feature assures our being able to cross from one register to another (*friend = coin* to *friend = swarm*) while at the same time ensuring we do not confuse the two.

In the complex of metaphors we are considering, however, the sylleptic crossing does not simply mark the identity and difference of two registers simultaneously but creates a Batesonian double bind in which not only are two elements kept in proximity but are just so kept in order that they will cancel each other out. To push the figure of the metaphor to this extent, in which two dissimilar images with a common property, the synecdoche of the head, are placed into a proximity that neither can sustain logically is seriously to injure or dis-figure the text. It is to wound the text in those very places where the modes of imaginative production (Freud's condensation and displacement) are most conscious and most powerfully expressed. For Ricks this means that Milton is slaying, with what Eliot called the "original acts of lawlessness," the living metaphor whose task, the critic feels, is to exfoliate in luxurious analogies whose differences may collide without necessarily negating anything, without destroying the task of the "figure" which is always to amplify, to add.

IV

It should be possible at this point to see not only that Samson's discourse refers semantically to his effeminacy and his exiled condition but that his use of figures syntactically works to bring about a fragmented style, a mutilated discourse, a dead text. To this extent Samson's style is not far from Nietzsche's style in *Ecce Homo* (and the irony in Nietzsche's title should not escape us), which is similarly confused or bound up with the feminine, a style which depends upon the passion for woman, upon the battle of the sexes, upon the *Distanz*, the cutting off that woman effects. ("The perfect woman tears to pieces when she loves.")[30] Like the broken style Ricks finds in *Samson Agonistes*, Nietzsche's style in *Ecce Homo* is similarly splintered, broken, fragmented. It is a style freighted with all the pettiness Nietzsche ascribes to woman, a pettiness we see reflected in terms of misogyny, racism, pride, a pettiness Samson also expresses in *Samson Agonistes*. Such is the Miltonic and Nietzschean sublime, whose basis is the base and the loquacious.

Jacques Derrida has analyzed this style in terms of *écriture*, and by that he is referring to a script that is propelled by an "aphoristic force," as he calls it in *De la grammatologie*. In "La question du style" as well as in *Glas*, Derrida elaborates the conception of *écriture* in terms of what can only be called a radical theory of the sublime, a theory that accounts for a sublime style whose base is nothing less than a style composed of everything a critic like Ricks would consider detestable, or at least very unsublime, both in terms of stylistic construction and nobility. Hence, for Derrida the styles of Hegel, Nietzsche, and Genet, styles that are all rooted in the most perverse tendencies (that is, anti-Semitism, homosexuality, masochism, misogyny) are as elevated as, if not more elevated than, what has been considered in the West as the most sublime of all styles, the discourse of presence, since these *anthérections*, as Derrida terms *écriture* in *Glas*, are not deluded by the metaphysics of presence or truth, but are aided by the *blessures* of the text, the wounds, the mutilations, the perversions to which a text or style is subject.[31]

Certainly, a good case can be made for the argument that Milton's *Samson Agonistes* is another of these sublime texts. Any reader can ascertain for himself the kinship in tone between Samson's misogyny, his disgust for the unchosen races, and the prejudices against women and race one encounters in Nietzsche, for example, or Hegel or Genet. But more importantly, one can discern the extent to which an *écriture* of the sublime is predicated upon the thematic of castration, of an anxiety about women. However, if such an anxiety is as negative and traumatic as it appears to be in Milton, Hegel, Nietzsche, and Genet, it is also more positive and less threatening to the writers in question than one might at first suppose, because, as Derrida has tried to show in both "La question du style" and *Glas*, the castration complex is not simply a psychoanalytical analogue to the religious conception of the Fall, of a radical separation from paradise, figuratively represented in psychoanalysis by woman, but is a suspended relation, a breach that is not a breach, a gap that suspends the either-or logic of separation-union. In fact, it is the castration complex that provides the writer with an access to paradise, to woman, to potency, to the style or stylus.

It is in this context that the Derridean conception of the *antérection* becomes most significant for our discussion, since the *anthérection* is a term meant to describe the castration complex as a radical separation that is necessary in order for one to achieve unseparatedness. In *Glas*, we find that the prisoner, Genet, is radically cut off from woman, society, and life; yet it is precisely this castrated state that gives Genet his *potence* as lover, writer, and cultural, or social, figure. "Fonction du bagne: c'est le lieu de ce que nous appellerons désormais l'*anthérection*." ("Function of the penal colony: the place of that which we will henceforth call the *anthérection*.")[32] In "La question du style," the *anthèrection* is developed in terms of the umbrella that Nietzsche forgets. "On sait, ou l'on croit savoir, quelle est la figure symbolique du parapluie: . . . phallus pudiquement replié dans ses voiles, organe à la fois agressif et apotropaïque, menaçant et / ou menacé." ("The umbrella's symbolic figure is well known, or supposedly so: . . . a phallus which is modestly enfolded in its veils, an organ which is at once aggressive and apotropaic, threatening and / or threatened.")[33] Nietzsche's forgetting of the umbrella is indicative of his denial of the *anthérection* and the consequent retirement from philosophy, from *écriture*. As long as Nietzsche could recognize the *anthérection* (the castration complex, the primal scene, the difference between male and female), he had access to the sublime, to his stylus, which in Derrida is nothing other than the metaphorical "organe à la fois agressif et apotropaïque."

It is a colossal writing that Nietzsche inscribes, a writing supported by the classical columns of all the greatest philosophical texts, and yet it is a writing whose purpose is to break those sublime supports to pieces. Nietzsche's project is to compose a writing that dares to shatter the classical supports in the hope that it will endure the collapse of metaphysics, the death of God. And this wager, as we have pointed out, is based precisely on Nietzsche's strategic reliance on what Derrida calls the *anthérection*. In itself, this constitutes a *thanatopraxie* of writing, a conversion of the *classique* to the *galactique*, of *classe* to *glas*. And in *Samson Agonistes* we have witnessed very much the same thing. For in Milton's play, the castration at the hands of Dalila is not only a prerequisite for repetitions of radical separation that

Samson must endure, such as his blinding, his imprisonment, and his alienation from the holy but also constitutes a way of access to the great display of power Samson achieves at the end of the drama when he breaks the columns and thereby symbolically castrates the temple of the heathen Philistines. It is in this breaking of the Philistines' phallic supports that the thematic of castration is now to be considered in terms of the radical separation of death, for both the Philistines and Samson, as well as in terms of unseparatedness, for it is beneath the ruins of the temple that both Philistine and Hebrew are buried. In this most violent scene, which, incidentally, we do not see occur, a scene which is repressed by the author (the primal scene, the scene in which castration is revealed?), the *anthérection* is most evidently manifest, symbolized by the columns themselves. Like Nietzsche, Samson is an iconoclast whose project is to destroy the fetish of the vulgar Philistines, to ruin the house of metaphysics. But like Nietzsche, Samson only endures the debacle with his reputation, his Hebraic style, which is symbolized in the noise of the crashing temple, a crashing that is classical, but which also sounds "le glas." Again we are brought to consider Milton in terms of *thanatopraxie*, in terms of a praxis of death which recognizes the fact that something always endures, which takes into account the remnant, "le reste."

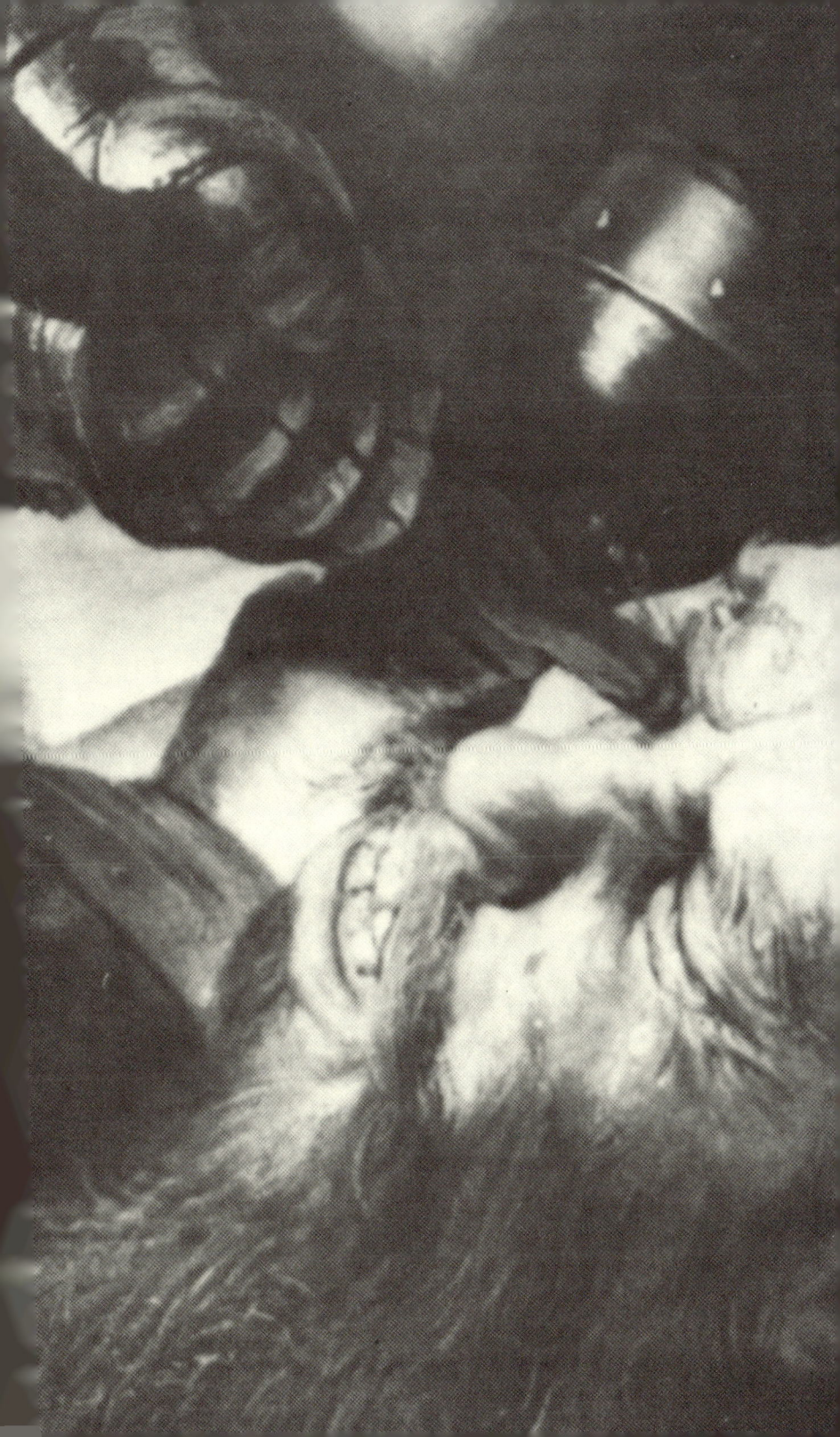

Mais la langue, comme performance de tout langage, n'est ni réactionnaire, ni progressiste; elle est tout simplement: fasciste; car le fascisme, ce n'est pas d'empêcher de dire, c'est d'obliger à dire.

("But language—the performance of a language system—is neither reactionary nor progressive, it is quite simply fascist; for fascism does not prevent speech, it compels speech.")

Roland Barthes, Leçon,
translated by Richard Howard

Ce qu'ils nous apprennet, c'est qu'un fascisme réussi ce n'est pas seulement Léviathan en guerre contre le Peuple, mais le Peuple lui-même en guerre contre Léviathan.

("They teach us that a successful fascism is not only Leviathan at war with the People, but the People itself at war with Leviathan.")

Bernard-Henri Lévy,
Le testament de Dieu,
translated by George Holoch

Revolution
Constitution
Bump it—Just sing.

Teena Marie,
"Revolution"

CHAPTER 6

Milton and the State

We know what kind of state it is that Milton and his countrymen inherited in the early seventeenth century: a state whose aristocracy had not yet heard the passing bell, the death knell for absolutism and its simulacra. Even if Thomas Hobbes legitimized sovereignty and monarchy on the grounds that the Leviathan inevitably rests upon hierarchy and dictatorship—that might, however benevolent and representational, or harsh and repellent, meant civil right, since order was always to be preferred to chaos—there were those who rejected such political apologies for tyranny, what amounted to an idolatry of princes. And one of those people was John Milton, Englishman. Already in *Lycidas* an ax is falling; the clock of history is chiming. A king must submit to decapitation in the *thanatopraxie* of revolution, the revolution of the bourgeoisie.

Was this "barbarism with a human face," this revolution against Charles I, what a Royalist would have perceived as the end of legitimate sovereignty, as a well-established power structure which any state necessarily requires for the sake of order, justice, culture, peace of mind? Was this what a Nouveau Philosophe like Bernard-Henri Lévy might perceive as the prefiguration of National Socialism in the West, the introduction in the 1650s of a maniacal dictatorship baptized in the blood of a monarch and committed thereafter to harsh and militaristic practices of purification, a *thanatopraxie* which led to mass murder in Ireland and wild visions of mass deportation? Or was this the founding of a state which put an end to metaphysical politics, to an absolutist and logocentric system rooted in a tyrannical and vicious divine right? The founding of an iconoclasm that put all fetishes to the sword, that emphasized the social contract between men and leaders and the right to bear arms against oppression, against what John Knox a century earlier had called "idolatry" and the "condemnation of true religion"? That emphasized the need for a determination of power relations, of what G. W. F. Hegel would have seen as a needed division between what he would have called civil society (or "die bürgerliche Gesellschaft") and the state (or "Staat"), a division which as Derrida shows in *Glas* is always already deconstructing itself as it builds itself up?

We must then determine Milton's political direction, inquire into the articulation of his political attitudes, and ascertain what political thoughts this secretary of foreign tongues held on the eve of the rise of a modern state, a rise which anticipates Rousseau and the French Revolution by over one hundred years. Such a rise foreshadows so much in Hegel by inscribing a Hegelian political thought, as it were, before the birth of German romanticism. And this rise looks forward as well to so much state barbarism in the twentieth century which is predicated, to recall Georg Lukács in *The Destruction of Reason* and Jürgen Habermas in *Theory and Practice,* upon the irrationalization or instrumentalization of reason, the implementation of ahistorical and culturally disruptive relations which serve capital and the modes of production at the price of fracturing social consciousness.[1] Certainly Milton is far removed from what Habermas calls the technocratic mentality with its decisionistic rationales and performance principles, though we can see in Milton and his revolutionary contemporaries a tendency in that direction, for those of the middle class who moved with Cromwell in the 1650s did so in the name of greater economic efficiency and stepped-up performance of industry, trade, commerce, and investment: in terms of the accumulation of capital and material expansion. As Joyce

Oldham Appleby points out in *Economic Thought and Ideology in Seventeenth-Century England*, the financial experts of the 1620s are no longer courtiers to the king, but men like Edward Misselden and Thomas Mun, who "did not debate the wisdom of sovereign power; they denied its efficacy." And "thus the challenge that the experts on trade laid down to authority was not political but scientific."[2] Jürgen Habermas argues that it is just this shift, or break between the political and the scientific, which institutes a technocratic rationalism that advances the principles of success and performance in economic terms, leaving behind the more political question of human values and the status of the individual with respect to the society in which he lives. It is in this context that we must interpret Appleby's statement:

Despite the unchallenged assumption that the English government had the right and the responsibility to regulate economic activities in the interest of the common good, the ambit of private initiative widened considerably during the middle decades of the seventeenth century. Circumstances—usually in the form of a political crisis—permitted men to pursue their private profit with little official interference. The only enduring policy decision in the economic domain came early in the century when, as Barry Supple has explained, "as far as official doctrine was concerned, all thoughts of unduly restraining the processes of industrialization had disappeared."[3]

Such development anticipates an instrumental reason stripped of dogmas which are both political as well as religious. For instrumental reason wishes to dominate by means of scientific method or, what amounts to the same thing, by way of the modes of industrial production. In dominating not only through technology but *as* technology, the legitimacy of precapitalist modes of domination expressed through the political and religious orders loses its veracity. We already see this in the *Areopagitica*, of course, in which Milton advances the positivistic view that the individual, and not the political or religious order, is fit to decide how to articulate the value of what he reads. Whereas the Church of England or the Roman Catholic church may once have had the privilege of determining human values and organizing the perspective from which one viewed a world in terms of a coherent ethical picture or great chain of being for middle-class man, such privilege goes the way of governmental interference with the ambit of private initiative in the economics of capital accumulation. Indeed, Milton was a capitalist who traded in ideas and as such may have been one of the first great modern intellectuals, a man who had no nostalgia for a metaphysics of knowledge resting on the religious and political edifices of late feudalism. Milton's interest is in a *thanatopraxie* of knowledge, an assimilation of ideas which did not center itself in dogma or mere skepticism, but which followed the path of an instrumentalization of thought, everywhere evident in the political tracts of the 1650s. It is an instrumentalization which I will take up later in terms of the death of the proper name and the expropriation of language.

In this chapter my intention will be, not to summarize Milton's political beliefs, but to uncover in the prose works a politically oriented figure whose imagination anticipates the rise of the modern states in which we now live. Such Miltonic adumbrations ambitiously predict so much darkness, such as the instrumentalization of reason, whose effect is to totalize relations from within technology or modes of production as well as to institutionalize a fracturing of social relations, what Habermas notes as the impossibility of a self-reflexivity to allow for the understanding of human interests and their relation to society as a whole. With the violent separation of church and state, of private from public man, epistemological reason is already put on the block, because the social subject undergoes a disidentification with the whole to which he is related, submits to the fracturing of his consciousness as it appears in a totality of human and natural relations.

Lucien Goldman in *Le dieu caché* addresses this detotalization, or fragmentation, in terms of Descartes, Pascal, and Racine:

> Hommes et choses devenaient de simples instruments, *objets* de pensée ou d'action de l'individu rationnel et raisonnable. Le résultat fut que les hommes, la nature physique et l'espace, abaissés au niveau d'objets, se comportaient comme tels: il restaient muets devant les grands problèmes de la vie humaine.
>
> Privé de l'*univers physique* et de la *communauté humaine*, ses seuls organes de communication avec l'homme, Dieu qui ne pouvait plus lui parler avait quitté le monde.[4]

("Men and things became simple instruments, objects of the thought or action of a rational and reasonable individual. The result was that men, physical nature and space, lowered to the level of objects, behaved as such: they remained mute before the great problems of human existence.

Deprived of a *physical universe* and of a *human community*, his only modes of communication with man, God left the world, for he could no longer speak to man.")

Not only Descartes and Corneille but Milton as well were only too willing to underwrite such a cultural breakup; in fact, Milton is the only of such figures militantly to propagandize for the "tragic" rupture Goldmann outlines in terms of the justification of armed violence, on what amounted to a callous takeover of the English monarchy and the repression of the lower classes.

The question is how we are to evaluate a political thinker who not only was a great writer of religious poetry, an extraordinarily brilliant classical scholar, fluent in ancient tongues even as a child, but who also writes tracts which look ahead to what in our day appears as the legitimation of storm troopers, death squads, and the other political apparatuses of terror, and all in the guise of an instrumentalized reason? It is a question I will leave in suspension, of course, one I will fill out in order to counter the Anglo-American reception of Milton as a great humanist in the democratic tradition, a line Douglas Bush takes in *"Paradise Lost" in Our Time* (1945) when he considers Milton a "poet-priest."

Bush's English hero of letters, emerging as he does during the war with Hitler, looks like the antithesis to National Socialism. But I will stress very much the opposite line of thought, for I stress, not Milton's resistance, but his complicity with the most repellent aspects of fascism, or totalitarian action. Recall, as an instance of this view, Milton's acid response to the learned Salmasius, who charges from the Continent that Cromwell's England is in no sense based on a popular revolt, but on a brutal, implacable military blackmail. As minister of propaganda, Milton refutes this charge, though one notices how quickly Milton's refutation only confirms Salmasius's worst suspicions:

> I say it was the people; for why should I not say that the act of the better, the sound part of the Parliament, in which resides the real power of the people, was the act of the people? If a majority in Parliament prefer enslavement and putting the commonwealth up for sale, is it not right for a minority to prevent it if they can and preserve their freedom? "The officers did it with their troops." We should then thank the officers for standing by the state, and for driving off that raging mob of London hirelings and hucksters which lately, like the vermin who followed Clodius, had laid siege to the house of Parliament itself. Are you for this reason to call the first and the peculiar duty of Parliament, which is to maintain above all else the freedom of the people by peace or war, "a military tyranny?"[5]

By denying that the revolution in England was by no means a popular one, Milton admits that "the people" can only act through violence and terror of a military apparat, that revolution is never the handiwork of a mob, but is the calculated seizure of power by the officers and their troops. "We should then thank the officers for standing by the state," Milton declares. In this view of the people of the streets, that raging mob of egalitarians (Levellers, Familists, Quakers, Diggers, and so forth) is by definition to be considered, not a "political entity with a legitimate will," but simply opportunists without direction or cause except self-interest. And what is the army but a large assembly of such similar people, such low factions organized into a fighting machine? These officers and troops we must thank, for they represent the kind of justifiable violence which arises from a new politically organized system of relations, one in which the proper name of a king no longer serves; or to quote Derrida's *Glas*, "Que signifie le glas du nom propre?" For Milton *le glas* signifies a political system wrested from a king and maintained, not in the name of any patriarch, but in the name of violent revolution and dramatic social change, in the name of a modern state, what amounts to the name of the people. And what that signifies we will see in due course.

At the moment we wish to ask what can be said about a political view which has so much in common with V. I. Lenin when he insists that the task of a revolutionary army is always to "proclaim insurrection: to give the masses the military leadership."[6] How do we square the humanist Milton with the Milton who has affinities with Lenin, a Milton who noticed that military leadership amounted to the rightful dictatorship of a particular class and extended to the political management of the people's entire affairs? Since Lenin says this so well, let us briefly cite him:

A revolutionary army and a revolutionary government are two sides of the same coin. They are two institutions equally necessary for the success of the uprising and for the consolidation of its results.[7]

This simply rearticulates Milton's refutation of Salmasius's charge concerning a military takeover in England. In Milton's prose too, the great historical questions can be solved only by violence through military action, by the political organization of violence rather than the political organization of the name: monarchy, nobility, genealogy—a metaphysics or cratylism of proper names. Thus we are asked to thank those instrumental officers who stand by the state, for indeed they are people whose proper names do not serve as the basis for a social organization. They are merely "the people" who are righteously carrying out revolution against what for both Milton and Lenin was tyrannical monarchy. So much, then, for the end of the subject in history, for man as proper name.

What must be admitted about Milton, political thinker? That he was peculiarly modern, however unattractive his views seem to us, for his politics anticipate aspects of the totalitarian states we have witnessed in our own time, states which are based upon extremely detotalizing premises, upon an antimetaphysics. In *One-Dimensional Man* and "Repressive Tolerance," Herbert Marcuse explores how modern capitalism with its detotalizing ideology manages to coopt and absolutize culture, reduces all capitalist peoples to a flattening or one-dimensionality (Jean Baudrillard would call it a "surface") that appears incongruous with the functioning of what we assume is a heterogeneous and free marketplace.[8] More recently the French New Philosophers have been arguing, albeit in a polemical and slick vein, that both communist and fascist absolutisms are not based upon rigid hierarchical structures, upon what we would call direct dictatorships, but are based upon a dissolution of power, a fragmentation of political formations, and, too, a definite program to eliminate transcendental superstructural supports, that is, metaphysical ideals and, above all, Christian religion. Though not contemporary with us, Milton does mark a political shift away from absolutist feudal orders and stands before the rise of new political configurations, the modern states; and not unlike Hegel, Milton holds views that often foreshadow just those aspects of the modern states which commentators like Hannah Arendt found most dehumanizing and brutal. It is this outlook which we will see is not so much a consequence of late capitalism or simply the rise of socialism(s) but more or less present in the seventeenth century and articulated according to deconstructive moves which one might not expect to find at so early a time in the history of what is generally speaking a modern historical period.

I

Like Marx, Engels, Lenin, and Mao Zedong, who had profound distrust of the people as a whole, Milton had little respect for the mass. In this we sight a particularly conservative, or classical, reservation, and in Milton it marks what must be faced as a reactionary view, one the communists of the nineteenth and twentieth centuries did not and, of course, could not overtly share. The famous *Defence of the People of England* was written in Latin, not English, and its prose style is utterly classical in its parodies and mimicries of every well-known Roman orator who had anything to say about politics. The *Defence* is nothing less than a highly scholarly and elitist tract, filled with the most minute details concerning religious and political precedent, and all tactically elaborated with the barbs provided by satirical oratory. One could say that Milton's tract was a defense not so much of the English as of the Roman people, an attempt to reinstate Roman politics, or republicanism, in seventeenth-century England and that it represents the most hopelessly out-of-date views imaginable for a man of Milton's time. Even Milton's proposition that one return to Roman law can be said to have been unoriginal and uninsightful, since European states in the fourteenth and fifteenth centuries had already begun to make legal revisions which made the crucial Roman distinction between *jus* and *lex*, civil law and state law.[9] Even if many educated Englishmen read Latin as a matter of course during the 1650s, we must note that a Marxist might scoff that Milton's *Defence* is somewhat farcical in its attempt to revive historical relations which have been canonized in the Latin literature of the great Roman orators, and that what Milton had read was merely political rhetoric and not even the real history of Roman political thought and action.

Let us first of all concede that such criticisms can be made of Milton, that we know how extremely reactionary his tracts are, how much they breathe the lifeblood of a classical age which lived in the mausoleum that was Milton's scholarly imagination. And let us remind Christopher Hill of this fact: that however much he wishes to place Milton at the historical forefront of seventeenth-century politics, that however much he may feel Milton had strong leanings and sympathies with Levellers, Familists, Ranters, Antinomians, Socinians, Quakers, and Diggers, Milton never actually wrote for them, never trusted them, and never fully participated in their revolution.[10] His party had died centuries before. It had fallen with Rome.

And yet we must not dismiss Hill's *Milton and the English Revolution*, because it reflects so much of Milton's divided spirit, a mind committed to the republicanism of Rome and to ideals of freedom and liberty, everywhere stressed in the *Areopagitica*, but a mind also harboring a darker fascination with dictatorial takeover, with what amounts to another absolutism much bleaker and calculating than the foppery of Charles I and the grand schemes of the Anglicans under Archbishop Laud. There is, on this other hand, this left hand of Milton's thinking, a *thanatopraxie* of politics which calls for the merciless decapitation of a king and of all subjects who support royalty. It is a sinister side to Milton's thinking which he justifies everywhere in terms of freedom, reason, liberty, conscience, and the pursuit of truth. Indeed, the French Revolution, when it came in the late eighteenth century, predicated its terror upon the same ideas, and this is repeated in Hegel and others who followed him in turn.

The terror in Milton is set forth in a rather chilling passage which carries forward the mentality of the *Einsatzgruppe*. This differs substantially from what one might call an inquisitorial barbarism based, ultimately, on a metaphysical fanaticism of the absolute. We recall that with inquisition there is still operative a theory of mercy: what is punished on earth may be saved in the hereafter. With the coming of what Bernard-Henri Lévy calls the new gravediggers, or death squads, mercy plays no role. Metaphysics has no part in the action. War and metaphysics are sundered. In the quotation that follows, someone is about to be killed, and this someone cries out for mercy, and to this Milton, poet and politician, replies:

Do not pay too much heed to that presence of mind so often manifested by the commonest criminals at their death; frequently desperation or a hardened heart gives, like a mask, an appearance of courage, as dullness does of peace. In death as in life, even the worst of men wish to seem good, fearless, innocent, or even holy, and, in the very hour of execution for their crimes, they will, for the last time, display as showily as possible their fraudulent pretence, and, like the most tasteless of writers and actors, strive madly for applause as the curtain falls.[11]

For Milton it is a matter of preventing history from turning into theater, for opening the curtains, not onto a stage, but onto a scaffold on which the practitioners of the popish and absolutist state are mercilessly executed without qualm, without guilt. However repulsive liquidation, as Milton and also Heinrich Himmler note, it must be carried out with courage and moral strength. And thus a leitmotif enters history: "Do not pay too much heed to that presence of mind. . . ."

Suddenly the modern totalitarian state has made its hideous entry. The Third Reich speaks *avant la lettre*. The death warrants of so many men, women, and children are sealed. "Do not pay too much heed . . ." ". . . like the most tasteless of writers or actors . . ." ". . . strive madly . . ." ". . . the curtain falls . . ." Let us recall, then, the words of B.-H. Lévy and André Glucksmann, whose so-called confusions of thought have made sense out of what is almost a century of the most highly advanced and controlled of technological crimes committed on massive political scales, what Lévy calls "la barbarie à visage humaine." It is a barbarism whose human face is predicated on a *thanatopraxie* of the state, a *thanatopraxie* which writes itself in the seventeenth century in unmetaphysical terms: "Do not pay too much heed to that presence of mind. . . ."

We must seriously consider Lévy, even if Michael Ryan and Gayatri C. Spivak find him so terribly facile, even if so many self-fashioned Marxists find him so naïve and reactionary.[12] For Lévy says something which is useful for an understanding of Milton's political orientation, to say nothing of the political orientations of so many well-known figures who will follow: Rousseau, Marx, Lenin, Hitler, Mao, Franco, Johnson, Ho Chi Minh, and others. Lévy notes that politics and religion are inextricably bound together and that when the state dispenses with religion, the state suddenly

> corresponds to nothing, is accountable for nothing, no longer has a counterpart or transcendental imperative: It is impossible to understand Hitlerism, for example, if we forget that one of its targets was precisely the beyond, as a recourse for the subject and a limit for the sovereign, the image of transcendence as a limit to the omnipotence and the murderous madness of power.[13]

Lévy is not that far from Hobbes, and he knows that. But he speaks from another vantage point, acknowledging that when one dispenses with religion, one also dispenses with politics, since the absence of the transcendental leads to a totalitarianism which is a form in which sovereignty is everywhere and nowhere, determinate and indeterminate, whole and fragmented. In short, the modern state is predicated upon a deconstruction of sovereignty, not merely a destruction of kingship.

The quotation taken from the *Defence* in which Milton speaks about killing an enemy in cold blood refers to no one else, specifically, than Charles I, who represents for Caroline England a transcendental signified, the image of transcendence, the beyond in terms of the here and now. What Milton wishes to justify is the iconoclastic removal of the transcendental imperative which results or remains, to recall Derrida's "Tombe, reste" from *Glas,* in a prince who is none other than Oliver Cromwell, a prince who even in refusing to be crowned king still has to take himself for sovereign and in doing so must realize that with him power is at once constituted and deconstituted. Maurice Blanchot and, again, Derrida would see this as the bourgeois *arrêt de mort*, the political suspension which ruptures or disseminates static formations. As Lévy argues, the moment such a suspension occurs, the state loses its hold on reference and corresponds to nothing, is accountable for nothing, save one thing: violence. The New Model Army is well known as that bloody agency of Protestant revenge, and yet even this transcendental drift is undermined by thinkers like Milton for whom it is important to separate religion and politics, to argue against a state church and a state religion.

Under the name of freedom, conscience, and liberty, Milton thinks there is everything to gain by loosening the state's metaphysical attachments to religious doctrine. According to Milton, the individual has the right to practice Christianity as his conscience dictates, for the authority of Scripture is revealed through natural reason, which has been granted by God. It is a step towards texts like *Paradise Lost* and the *Christian Doctrine* whose purpose is justifying God's ways to man. But if the appeal to conscience in religious terms suggests the humanization of man and the impulse towards profound speculation which is unimpeded by ideology and superstition, from a political perspective such a freeing and loosening of conscience does not so much signify access to the notion of a self-reflexive reasoning or hermeneutic of consciousness which knows how to interpret a technical world (as well as subjective experiences), as usher in a fragmentation of experiential and technical relations in the name of individual autonomy which opposes the absolutism of the feudal state. Marx and Engels put it this way in *The Communist Manifesto:*

> The bourgeoisie, wherever it has got the upper hand, has put an end to all feudal, patriarchal, idyllic relations. It has pitilessly torn asunder the motley feudal ties that bound man to his "natural superiors," and has left remaining no other bond between man and man than naked self-interest and callous "cash payment." It has drowned the most heavenly ecstasies of religious fervor, of chivalrous enthusiasm, of philistine sentimentalism, in the icy water

of egotistical calculation. It has resolved personal worth into exchange value, and in place of the numberless indefeasible chartered freedoms, has set up that single, unconscionable freedom—free trade. In one word, for exploitation, veiled by religious and political illusions, it has substituted naked, shameless, direct, brutal exploitation.[14]

Moreover, Marx and Engels are only too aware that the rise of the bourgeoisie is predicated, not upon the conservation of modes of production in an unaltered form, that "first condition of existence for all earlier industrial classes," but upon a constant "revolutionizing the instruments of production, and thereby the relations of production, and with them the whole relations of society." What characterizes the bourgeoisie is the "uninterrupted disturbance of all social conditions, everlasting uncertainty and agitation." That is to say, what characterizes the modern state of the bourgeoisie is a molecularization of power invested in the constant revolutionizing of the modes of production. On the other hand: "The bourgeoisie keeps more and more doing away with the scattered state of the population, of the means of production, and of property." That is, the bourgeoisie "has agglomerated population, centralized means of production, and has concentrated property in a few hands."[15] Thus with molecularization comes absolutism once more in terms of property and class relations, what Marx and Engels talk about in terms of centralization. The Miltonic quest for tolerance of free conscience at the price of feudal, patriarchal, and idyllic relations amounts to little more, from the perspective of the *Manifesto*, than the dehumanization or molecularization of the individual and his subjection to the unconscionable freedom of uninhibited trade.

And this issue of trade is exactly what Milton addresses in the *Areopagitica* when he says,

There is yet behind of what I purposed to lay open, the incredible loss and detriment that this plot of licensing puts us to. More than if some enemy at sea should stop up all our havens and ports and creeks, *it hinders and retards the importation of our richest merchandise, truth.*[16]

To prohibit conscience, then, is equivalent to placing a ban on free commerce, as if thought in Milton's view were always already exchange value by which we come to know something by way of something else. Thought as commerce molecularizes but also centralizes by way of raising the trading or appropriation-expropriation of thought above what Marx and Engels call the "ecstasies of religious fervor, chivalrous enthusiasm, and philistine sentimentalism." To go one step further, in Milton free-thinking leads to a shameless and brutal exploitation by what is nothing other than a bourgeois intelligentsia whose mode of intellectual production is knowingly modeled on capitalist economics, and it is to this intelligentsia that Milton will belong in terms of a governmental post during Cromwell's leadership: secretary of foreign tongues. In this sense, religious freedom is dialectically anchored within an economics of free trade in which consciousness as such turns into a mere reflection of productive modes and reconstitutes itself as merely a social relation characterized by "everlasting uncertainty and agitation," by the kind of revolution Milton himself supports.

Certainly the manifestos of the New Philosophers do not differ as much from the central tenets of the *Communist Manifesto* as we may be led to believe, but they do offer an important supplement which meditates on a much later manifestation of bourgeois revolution: fascism. As Lévy notes:

Fascism neither blocks, prevents, nor prohibits; on the contrary, it fosters power and pushes its tendencies to their extremes. It neither censors, silences, nor gags; on the contrary, it unleashes, it forces us to speak. Extravagant, lavishly spend-thrift, barbarism is not the *transfiguration* but the *exacerbation* of capital, power not *renouncing* but *preserving* in its work.[17]

Inherent in such passages is Michel Foucault's observation that the bourgeoisie has learned to repress, not by forbidding, but by encouraging, enlightening, lifting the prohibitions. In this way the state can begin to penetrate, or saturate, the forbidden with its ideological apparatuses of power. By means of the enlightened exploration of madness, sexuality, criminality, or simply human behavior, so much experience can be brought under the auspices of the state, flattened out on a single register, and subjected to the relation of knowledge-power which comprises state action or what Habermas calls "performance" affecting questions of hygiene, family care, correction or discipline, and science: what in the more advanced bourgeois states translates into the liquidation centers or gulags.

Again, these terrifying modern institutions rest on principles which are at least broached in texts like the *Areopagitica*.

> As therefore the state ["the state" as *Staat?*] of man now is, what wisdom can there be to choose, what continence to forbear without the knowledge of evil?

Of course, Milton is not arguing that we ought to practice evil; on the contrary, he thinks that man should do good. Yet in the *Areopagitica* Milton is turning against the idea of repressing evil. Rather, we must allow the clarity of enlightenment to shine upon evil's darkest recesses. Furthermore:

> It was from out the rind of one apple tasted, that the knowledge of good and evil, as two twins cleaving together, leaped forth into the world.

The reason is that

> the knowledge of good is so involved and interwoven with the knowledge of evil, and in so many cunning resemblances hardly to be discerned, that those confused seeds which were imposed on Psyche as an incessant labor to cull out and sort asunder, were not more intermixed.[18]

Certainly, "Psyche" refers to conscience, and, too, it seems that long before Derrida, Milton has been thematizing dissemination in terms of a certain undecidability with regard to morality. The problem is that the difference between good and evil concerns "la thanatopraxie, technique de la pompe funèbre aujourd'hui enseignée dans des instituts."[19] That is, the knowledge of good and evil, everywhere confused by their *différance,* is born with the *institution* of death which results when Adam and Eve eat of the apple. At this instance the gravediggers of history enter, the recognition of a confusion between good and evil is faced, the praxis of morality, forever suspended in a dialectics of knowing good by knowing evil (and the reverse), set up in office.

If I have taken extreme liberty with Milton's use of the word *state* in the phrase "state of man" above, it is to alert us to the coming of revolution in which good is to come about through the praxis of evil: regicide, violent appropriation of lands, the stripping of church icons, the merciless barbarisms committed on Irish soil, and so forth. Already in the *Areopagitica* we see this turn from the "state of man" to "man in the state," and all in terms of enlightenment and transcending superstition. We see Milton as poet and politician standing before the rise of the modern state not unlike a Faustian character who knows that in the beginning there was the deed and that this deed is morally undecidable, immensely questionable. It is a perception not lost in our own time by those bloody heroes of the state to whom we owe so much: the Stalinists, Maoists, National Socialists, imperialists, and others.

II

Without doubt, Bernard-Henri Lévy acknowledges proto-fascism in sixteenth and seventeenth-century Europe, for he knows that the Reformation, long before Nietzsche, knew about the death of God and embraced it willingly:

God is dead? This is hardly a surprise for anyone who has read Pascal, Meister Eckhart, and especially Luther, where the statement is explicitly set out. The news had been known, thoroughly known by everyone, in the air ever since the Middle Ages in the chapter on Calvary and the Resurrection of the most insignificant catechisms. The catastrophe is not a catastrophe provided one knows enough to interpret it in its classic and liturgical sense of recognition—beneath the corpse and the incarnation—of the form of the New God.[20]

If we consider Milton's acceptance of evil as something, and not nothing (as Augustine argued), a something by which good could only be known or foregrounded, one wonders to what degree Milton may have suspected the death of a Catholic God whose host was believed by the faithful to perform miracles. Certainly in a poem like "The Passion," Milton appears to be burying this old, feudal God, a burying which may be in some senses more radical than Nietzsche's proclamation in *The Gay Science* of God's passing. For while Nietzsche's madman announces the immensity of the crime of murdering God in a spirit of cataclysmic shock, in Milton this death is marked simply with silence. It is as if one day it was no longer possible to conceptualize a God in the way of so many generations before. The deity passes away even though there is no twilight of the idols, no rivalry with new gods. There is only the blank which the writer's pen has left. An old conception of God passes away into the wash of religious history, and what remains is but a fragment about sacrifice. This rupture or refusal to represent the Crucifixion appears again so many years later in Milton's better-known poetry, but we must recall, too, that it is noticed in more orthodox poems of the seventeenth century, of which John Donne's "Good Friday, 1613: Riding Westward" is a remarkable example.

In Donne's poem we remember that the speaker asks God to "restore" the image of the sacrifice, an image which man cannot look upon, comprehend, or represent. There is only the trauma of this even in the memory, an anxiety which accompanies the unrepresentable. "Who sees God's face, that is self-life, must die; / What a death were it then to see

Milton and the State 185

God die?" Suddenly the Crucifixion appears to the speaker as a revelation of a violence which no man can sustain without turning away, a violence which is impossible to contain in an image or conception. The emphasis does not fall upon redemption and restoration, upon a sacrifice which leads to the production of a harmonious community of Christian men and women who wait for the Last Judgment, but upon destruction and death. Woe to him who looks directly upon the death of God.

In "Good Friday" the religious community of men and the order of the sacred are so radically different that the likelihood of an interpenetration between these spheres is not great, for it is not in man's power to comprehend sacred events. What saves the speaker in the poem is nothing less than the trope of paradox which comforts the speaker by insisting that a movement away from God is really a movement towards him too. But in using such a paradox, is not the speaker substituting a trope for the unrepresentable Crucifixion? Does not the trope make religious representation possible on a meta-conceptual level, and in doing so does not a poetic figure stand in for God?

One could argue that in "Good Friday" there is a recognition that God is dead insofar as he can be represented to man, that the Crucifixion marks an aporia which rhetoric or figuration must supplement, and with such supplementation there is the abandonment of what Walter Benjamin viewed as a symbolic relation between signifier and signified for an allegorical one in which representation problematizes itself in terms of the recognition of death, of a jagged demarcation between the materiality of language and the spirituality of meaning, between representation and truth. For Donne, there is still logical argumentation, the employment of paradoxical relations by means of which one can explain with fallen perceptions a sacred truth. And yet is it not clear that even such an effort constitutes a skeptical view in which the concept of God as it was formulated in the Middle Ages has altered drastically, particularly since the emphasis upon the presence of God is now placed in a negative relation to man and is reconciled or neutralized only by poetic figuration, by clever argumentation which does not convince so much as represent a wish for a state of affairs that is clearly not the case?

Unlike Donne, Milton does not resort to tropes of faith like paradox, but allows the pen to stop short. "The Passion" cannot be completed, but remains as a fragment thematically compatible with the "Nativity Ode." This refusal to complete a poem about crucifixion concerns Milton's similar awareness of sacrifice as violence, as that upon which man cannot look. In Donne, Milton, and so many other Protestants, this recognition of crucifixion as more than just representation discloses a view the New Philosophers call deconstructive, particularly when considered by way of René Girard's controversial religious anthropology.

Since Girard's theories are well known, I will not explicate them at length, but wish to refer to his view in *Des choses cachées depuis la fondation du monde* that Christianity recognizes a fundamental truth about representation:[21] mimesis is a series of differential repetitions ungrounded in any absolute, but propped up on simulacra which are displacements of an illusory transcendental signified which is the object of human desire or what Lacan calls "demand." This view is consistent with Hegel's *Phenomenology of Spirit*, the general perception that history is a complex series of mediations profitably studied from the vantage point of religious anthropology. Where Girard differs from Hegel is in the belief that what Hegel calls spirit or mind [*Geist*] is consciousness developed in terms of mimetic desire, expressed by way of privileged mediators, which that desire must at once worship as a facilitator to expression and sacrifice as an obstruction to one's final aim. This interpretation of Hegel is already worked out by Alexandre Kojève in the *Introduction à la lecture de Hegel*, and we see there Girard's notions of mediation, desire, mimesis, violence, and cultural institutions more or less clearly in a preface that chants the triumph of the will. Kojève argues that "l'histoire humaine est l'histoire des Désirs désirés" ("the history of mankind is the history (or narrative) of desired Desires").²² And crucial to this history is the question of "le risque de la vie," or sacrifice, whose consequence is the separation of man from animal as well as the stabilizing of a human community or civilization as "conscience de soi." Such stabilizing is always the result of a "lutte à mort," or struggle to the finish, whose result is the proper recognition of differences between masters and slaves, of those most fit to survive. Kojève knows that men will not simply kill each other, for as Hegel wisely explains, the masters need the recognition of the slaves in order to be masters. Or, desire cannot be articulated without the presence of a mediator, cannot become real but by way of an other.

Girard's thinking is greatly indebted to this interpretation of Hegel, which establishes the view, everywhere apparent in the 1930s, that culture is based, not upon transcendent values, but upon a struggle of mimetic wills and their resolution in the development of a social hierarchy grounded by an arbitrary signifier, the mediator. Religion, of course, is for Girard the institutionalized social form of mimetic desire and displaces the struggle for supremacy by way of symbolic appropriation. For Lacan this amounts to the *symbolique*, or unconscious, with its law, while for Girard such appropriation is evident in the more tangible social institutions. Certainly this view differs drastically from Kojève's formulations, which assume Hegel rejected religion in favor of an absolute knowing or economy of dialectical operations. Kojève's interpretation is thus existential and also Marxist, for he stresses labor and social conflicts structured by the all important master-and-slave chapter of the *Phenomenology*.

Girard has been misinterpreted as privileging the "lutte à mort," or "risque," as an existential category or idealism upon which man builds his church. Rather, he privileges the Derridean perception that mimesis is unrecuperable as a presencing, though Girard does so by way of arguing that mimesis is always concerned with mediated desire whose economy necessarily reaches an aporia: it cannot easily reconcile or come to know a mediation at once necessary and obstructing, loved and hated. Sacrifice is the process by which this aporia is articulated in societies, and Christianity is significant to the extent that its sacrificial mechanisms recognize a mimetic desire which is antimetaphysical even while it attempts to posit a metaphysical alibi which will hide this truth. In *Des choses cachées* Girard works this point out in detail.

Whether one can accept the universalizing claims Girard has proposed may be questionable, as Mary Douglas has pointed out in a debate with Girard, and yet with regard to Milton, at least, Girard's model is helpful. Donald F. Bouchard has noticed this too in his *Milton: A Structural Reading*, though I wish to consider Girard in a way Bouchard did not. Girard is well aware that sacrifice is carried out not just in religious practice but can be deritualized and manifested in other cultural apparatuses. In *La violence et le sacré*, the alternative apparatus is ancient Greek tragedy, and in *Des choses cachées* we learn that deritualization also occurs during the Enlightenment, when rational or bourgeois desire comes to replace religious superstition: the Catholic notion of the Mass. In other words, with the splitting of religion from politics, sacrifice becomes remystified, repressed, within the political institutions themselves whose guise is always instrumental reason. It is a point made by Michel Foucault in *La volonté de savoir* when he notices how the ritual of confession returns within the very social apparatuses cleansed of so-called Catholic residues.[23]

But if we notice Milton, we see again how such a return of the repressed takes place: Milton who deritualizes, or deconstructs, the Crucifixion also recuperates it in the very political texts that he writes, for central in these texts is the decapitation of Charles I, a beheading that the Royalists correctly perceived as nothing more than a secular rite of passion with the king of England in the role of Christ or, as

Eikon Basilike puts it, royal martyr. Milton's attack on the specious *Eikon Basilike*, which was purported to be the solemn wisdom of what was after all a rather unintelligent king, was entitled *Eikonoklastes* and argued that not only was Charles I not religious himself but that he was a political traitor and a threat to true Christians who followed their individual conscience as it was informed by God rather than dogmatic church ritual whose aim was to support a corrupt state. *Eikonoklastes* places Milton in the odd position of defending reritualization and repressing the recognition of sacrifice by means of a new mystification: the instrumental reason which accompanies a politically violent takeover.

The New Philosophers read such political moves in Girardian terms (Lévy says that *Barbarism with a Human Face* is very indebted to Girard) as the beginnings of a Western fascism which negates transcendental absolutes and theologies of all sorts while reproducing them within the apparatuses of state power and thereby mystifying the mechanisms of violence and sacrifice beneath a rationalism whose purpose it is to deny vigorously the irrationality and undecidability of mimetic desire. What fascism cannot tolerate is the groundlessness of re-presentation, even while its very institutions are dedicated to uphold the triumph of a will predicated on sacrificial mechanisms whose logic is only too clear from a post-Hegelian vantage point. This is not to say, as Eric Gans seems to imply in "Scandal to the Jews, Folly to the Pagans," that with the Enlightenment comes a social violence which is more excessive because uncontrolled by a sacrificial mechanism, but that the Enlightenment is a continuation of misrecognizing sacrifice which started already with the apostles in the *New Testament*.[24] In that sense, Girard is pessimistic, not unlike the New Philosophers, because he points out that sacrifice will always be repressed and recuperated in highly displaced forms. History for him is essentially the archaeology of that displacement and return.

But if Milton is successful in covering over or displacing

sacrifice by way of legitimizing political violence, he also is willing to demystify sacrifice by recognizing the undecidable foundations upon which sacrifice is based. In fact, one could argue that because Milton took an antimetaphysical approach to the sacrificial features of a Catholicism which had denied the efficacy of sacrifice in its dogma, a denial inherited by the Anglican church, that Milton was able to make a typically Enlightenment displacement. It is this deconstruction of sacrifice, then, which I wish to explore in what remains of this section.

Milton, of course, inherited his iconoclastic perspective on the Crucifixion from the Reformation, and it is a perspective that Lévy conflates with a new political outlook in which violent revolution accompanies theological change. But against those who would simply argue that religion is merely the ideological handmaiden of an emergent class willing to break feudal ties, to kill the God of a feudal church in order to advance materially, Lévy would argue that Christianity is always more than a mere ideological apparatus. And certainly I would agree that Christianity is not reducible to mere state religion during the seventeenth century.

What is particularly interesting about Christianity is its potential for propping up a social order by means of providing stable representations of power, violence, and truth, but it also makes possible an iconoclasm by means of which such social representations of power can be deconstructed and violence resituated or freed. In this sense, Christianity is a kind of fascism which has not been deritualized. What Michael Fixler calls the "Kingdom of God" is a term which Protestants have used to conceive of a religious transformation in the sense of a political revolution, and it is this "Kingdom of God" which conceptually propped and destabilized at once the social representations of power and violence, making manifest what Girard sees as a double movement in Christianity: deconstruction-construction, revelation-concealment, antisocial-social, antimetaphysical-metaphysical.[25] In short, Protestantism by rejecting the Catholic view of sacrifice displaces it politically and in that sense will reveal and conceal a violence within this new secularized social apparatus whose aim is to bring man closer to a Kingdom of God reproducing a new absolutist state, but also detotalizing in terms of a thousand-year reign of Christ preceding the Last Judgment.

The Kingdom of God is that state which manifests an antistatism, and this Kingdom of God rests upon a rejection of the feudal mechanisms of sacrifice as transmitted by the evangelists. Milton takes this up in the epics when Satan's absolutism and tyranny are not only mocked but subjected to a critique of violence with a decidedly antimetaphysical drift. According to Satan, violence has to be reintroduced into the world in terms of sacrifice, one in which scapegoats are to be found, punished, and reconciled. And such reconciliation is important to the devils because it must include hell and the evil powers, thus stabilizing a condition which the devils fear may change for the worse. Eve, then, must fall prey to Satan in order to legitimize hell: the state of the devil. Yet this legitimation is broken up most violently in *Paradise Regained* when Christ refuses to become a culpable or sacrificial victim and the orders of heaven and hell are thereby separated. With Christ there is not only antisacrifice but a trenchant antistatism, a refusal to become a mighty ruler of the world, a totalizer of all relations. What Christ wishes to avoid are the representations which state violence elicits, representations which are sacrificial in nature to the degree that they suggest purification or violent praxis leading to peaceful stasis. This rejection by Christ extends even to the Greek notion of reason, that logocentric statism of the mind whose end is to produce transcendental categories of thought whose purpose is to support autonomous apparatuses of social power, categories which will veil and represent violence.

That the Kingdom of God is not so much a state but a quasi-Fascist antistate is confirmed in *The Reason of*

Church Government when Milton insists that the government of the gospel is "economical and paternal, that is, of such a family where there be no servants, but all sons in obedience, not in servility, as cannot be denied by him that lives but within the sound of scripture."[26] Milton, not unlike a certain right-wing Hegel in the *Phenomenology of Spirit* and the *Philosophy of Right*, situates a critique in terms of the identity and difference between family and state, though in Milton the criticism is of a Caroline monarchy which is opposed by a family allied with "the government of gospel." Here, as in Hegel, there is a violent subversion or incipient antistatism at odds with absolutism, though as we will see, what Milton is proposing, more than just subversion, is reminiscent of the deconstructive logic which Derrida uncovers in Hegel's oeuvre when he glosses the political texts in *Glas*.

In the conclusion of *The Reason of Church Government*, Milton cites Samson as the example of "the state and person of a king" who is noble in strength and perfection, but who succumbs to the flattery of the prelates who in time shear their kind of this power (his just laws) and hold him in subjection until he regains his proper stature at great cost to himself. This analogy forecasts revolution which will come only after the family (the paternal) has been corrupted by the state (the feminine), in which a king falls because of a domestic disorder in which Dalila, representative of the state, has such an important role.

What is of special significance is to what degree such a religious perspective not simply legitimizes what historians might reconstruct as materialist motives but serves to deconstruct the social relations upon which the absolutist state is founded. In an elaborate passage written in *The Reason of Church Government*, Milton is extremely close to Hegel in the *Phenomenology* with the use of sexual analogues for the purpose of deconstructing what Milton saw as the relation between a masculine family and a feminine state, and he does so in order to keep in mind a political strife which is extremely dialectical and violent, one Hegel in the *Phenomenology* sees by way of a model of the feminine family and masculine state, or what amounts to a mirror image of what Milton has in mind. In the passage below from *The Reason of Church Government,* Milton opposes an "underflowered" scripture to a "false whited" one, and reference is made to a Helena, whom Merritt Hughes identifies as the phantom Helena which is used to deceive Paris by Hera, a Helena mentioned in Euripides' *Helen.*[27] This Helena is the false scripture of the English prelates, a scripture falsified by bogus interpretation of a feminine state, and therefore she is "turned publican herself." Milton continues by insisting that she

> gives up her body to a mercenary whoredom under those fornicated arches which she calls God's house, and in the sight of those her altars, which she hath set up to be adored, makes merchandise of the bodies and the souls of men. Rejecting purgatory for no other reason, as it seems, than because her greediness cannot defer but had rather use the utmost extortion of redeemed penances in this life. But because these matters could not be thus carried without a begged and borrowed force from worldly authority, therefore prelaty, slighting the deliberate and chosen council of Christ in his spiritual government, whose glory is in the weakness of fleshly things to tread upon the crest of the world's pride and violence by the power of spiritual ordinances, hath on the contrary made these her friends and champions which are Christ's enemies in this his high design, smothering and extinguishing the spiritual force of his bodily weakness in the discipline of his church with the boisterous and carnal tyranny of an undue, unlawful, and ungospel-like jurisdiction. And thus prelaty, both in her fleshly supportments, in her carnal doctrine of ceremony and tradition, in her violent and secular power, going quite counter to the prime end of Christ's coming in the flesh, that is, to reveal his truth, his glory, and his might, in a clean contrary manner than prelaty seeks to do, thwarting and defeating the great mystery of God; I do not conclude that prelaty is antichristian, for what need I? The things themselves conclude it.[28]

Milton considers the false Helena to be the state itself as a false representation of Christ, a whorish embodiment of the glory whose "weakness of fleshly things" she mimics.

Christ is antistatist to the degree that he is unlike woman, for he does not deceive or fake something else; his glory is his own. And, more importantly, he is not interested in tyrannizing with power over the people: he does not have to. But if Christ is the antithesis of Helena, he is also a double to the extent that he is decidedly feminine in terms of the "weakness of fleshly things." We are back to a relation which we noticed in *Samson Agonistes*, one which involves a Christ figure whose "POTENCE du texte" has everything to do with the taking on of a feminine posture. In *The Reason of Church Government* the Kingdom of Heaven is also manifested in terms of a masculine figure who is in some sense castrated, weakened, feminized. The struggle in the passage above is not between man and woman so much as between feminisms, and this situates Milton somewhere within *Glas* between Hegel and Genet, for there too the sexual differences often appear as doublings which take place in the register of the feminine, a feminine that it is the male's desire to achieve at the same time that mere womanhood is rejected, the *real* woman expelled.

If this sounds odd, consider that Christianity has always attempted to become its other, and, moreover to be more authentically other than the other would originally be itself. For Christians have always played at being the Jew, have always mimicked this deviant and culpable other, taking the other's texts and claiming to belong to the other's traditions more authentically than the other himself. It is a case of mediated desire, of course, whose sacrificial scene is the pogrom. The rationale is always that the other has betrayed himself, has betrayed his own otherness and has become too much like those who are different. Christ, we are infinitely reminded by Christians, was himself a Jew, an other, and yet it is from the body of antistatist Christ that a statist Christian community founds itself, that an undecidable double scene between Jewish and non-Jewish culture manifests itself, a double scene which occurs in the *cène*, or Last Supper, that *scène / cène* in which the body is disseminated, castrated, wounded, crucified. In Milton the colonization of the other is instituted largely on a sexual register in which Jewishness itself has been displaced by the feminine. But if this surprises us, we must recall that such displacement has been instituted by the Roman Catholic priesthood centuries before Milton. The priest must be a male who cannot sexually touch women, a male who is different from women, but a male whose sexuality as male is also symbolically denied or feminized. The "POTENCE" of the priest is exactly that of a Samson or Christ which Milton has defined in *The Reason of Church Government*.

Such priestly "POTENCE" is well known too for a certain political force which has been considerable in history, for priests have always been within and without state politics. That is, they represent an antistatism analogous to the notion of a city of God, while officiating in the city of the world. Because the priest, like Christ, is not allowed to be part of a family in which he is the father who has wife and children, he is part of a collective community in which paternity is sublated in symbolic terms. He is, thus, like the eunuchs in Montesquieu, the most powerful figure in the sexual economy that is the community of men and women, because what Lacan calls the phallus has become potent on a symbolic register of experience, a register which is articulated by means of mimicking the other. In *Glas* this occurs by way of a homosexual economy that is but one modality of a deviant crossing which makes terms like phallus and vagina indeterminate sexual inscriptions. On the left side of *Glas* there is a right-wing Hegel whose theories of the family prop up National Socialism, and on the right side of *Glas* there is the antistatist (leftist?) Genet who collaborates in his imagination from within prison with the Nazis, dreaming of feminine encounters with Nazi fly boys and with Hitler in *Pompes funèbres*'s *thanatopraxie* of a flowery prose that trashes all familial relations. Ultimately we cannot tell the difference between a Hegel (*aigle*) and a Genet (*genêt*), the eagle and the flower, the masculine and the feminine. For both are invaginated in the fascism that is the modern state, a point which commentators on *Glas* often miss.

We notice that for Milton the government of gospel not unlike the fascist state in *Glas* is curiously suspended between the masculine and the feminine. Such a government knows, of course, only a symbolic power which is antherected, a topic discussed earlier. The members of the government of gospel are not heterosexual or simply homosexual, but somewhere undecidably in between. Their power is the result of a submission to the "POTENCE" of a sacrifice which yields castrated men and phallic women, a state that is not a state, a power that is its own lack, a whole which is but a part, a god which is only a dying man on a cross or in a bunker in Berlin. It is only a question of *la différance* from the standpoint of Western history and civilization, of the indeterminacy between good and evil which the *thanatopraxie* of institutions arbitrates, that death camp to which, as Lévy knows, the state inevitably returns for its "POTENCE."

By means of such deconstruction there is the recuperation of the absolute which we see once the figures of the repressed are mentioned as in Milton's religious tracts: the priests. Milton, of course, never talks about them favorably, for he knows about the advent of Jansenism, and yet however much he wishes to negate and swerve away from a church with statist priests, Milton manages to encounter the metaphysics of the church head on. In this way Milton restores the frame of power he wants to subvert. To that extent Milton's desire to break up church and state relations is saturated with an incipient absolutism which cannot be shaken off, an absolutism that appears to be inherent in Christianity itself and not merely its church politics. Milton, thus, is one of the first political thinkers to experience what we may call a proto-fascism: that is, a religious-political attitude which is radically antistatist and absolutist at the same time. To recall Lévy at this juncture, "A state is totalitarian when, by dilating the political, it claims to have annulled and abolished it; when by multiplying the centers of domination, it dissolves the image of the Master; when it proclaims simultaneously that 'everything is political,' and that the 'age of politics is at an end.'"[29]

We can appreciate Lévy's rereading of what is after all a point made by the Frankfort School critics by noting that, opposed to the masculine and centrist or absolutist notion of the state, there is the feminine and decentralized state, and together these make up a heterosexual model in which men can be castrated by women or women wholly dominated and enslaved by men. It is this dialectic which Milton has replaced with a homosexual model in which the difference between these two states is undecidable. The feminization of the gospel's government does not simply oppose absolutism but deconstructs it by means of sacrificing dialectical relations between the oppositions, thus strategically disarticulating the kind of master-and-slave duality with which Hegel, for example, begins in *The Phenomenology of Spirit*'s famous chapter on domination. Christ is the mediator between masters and slaves, the one who interrupts the historical constructions of absolutisms from on high and revolutions from below, of phallic domination and hysterical overthrow. The government of gospel, then, is what supposedly puts an end to such politics, a point stressed repeatedly in *Paradise Regained*. And yet, isn't the deconstructive solution but an intensification of the problems of masters and slaves, for does this not simply bring into the light of day but a very intense violence which results from the undecidability and radical destabilization of the difference between the absolute and the terror, erection of power and annihilation of it? And is this not, as Lévy sometimes suggests, characteristic of the modern, totalitarian states, a characteristic which is itself not discovered by Milton, Hegel, Genet, Derrida, or Lévy, but an endowment which the Reformation was given from a Christianity whose roots go back into Genesis where something is hidden in the Logos of God, in the *thanatopraxie* of creation, what Jean Genet has called "L'étrange mot d'. . . ."

"L'étrange mot d'. . ." is the title of an essay, considered in the fine print of *Glas*, whose letter has obvious fascination for Derrida. Genet uses the letter to tie together a heterogeneous skein of terms italicized in the following phrases, which are by no means exhaustive: "L'étrange mot *d'urbanisme*, qu'il vienne *d'un pape Urbain ou de la Ville*," "le crematoire, comme celui *de Dachau*," "*Dieu* vous expédie la grace: on est foutu," "la Chambre *des députés*," "*de théâtre*" ("the odd word of urbanism which comes from a pope Urban or from the city," "the crematorium, like that of Dachau," "God expedites grace: one is done in," "the Chamber of Deputies," "of theater").³⁰ The question is whether there is any difference between theater and extermination camps, representation and reality, God and murder, justice and criminality, eros and thanatos, religion and the state. Genet thinks of the catacombs in terms of the death camps, and he reminds us of Rome and the church in this context, of early Christianity and the undecidability of all the oppositions he sinisterly points out. Urbanism is the topography which deconstructs the differences as if totalitarianism were inscribed in the history of Rome, of the church, of the Reformation, of World War II. It is in this essay that Derrida hears a politics of deconstruction tolling the letter *d*, which in *Glas* signifies *dissemination*, *différance*, decapitation, double bind, *don* ("gift" in both English and German senses), deconstruction, and the proper name Derrida. For us the politics of deconstruction has already been situated in terms of Milton, who, as we have noted, is merely located somewhere in the midst of a reformulation in the seventeenth century of those undecidables which to him seem perfectly decisive from the view of revolution and regicide. If Lévy has pointed out to what extent fascism exacerbates the same kind of deconstructive oppositions, it is, not because he turns his back on the theory of deconstruction, but because he has learned so well from

Genet and Derrida what the historical significance of the political undecidabilities are, and it is in this sense that we must view Milton as part of the dark premonitions of a totalitarian rise of the modern state into whose late historical chapters we have all entered.

III

With the death of Charles I there was also the death knell for the proper name through which so much land, money, and power could pass, a name that related a state to itself, through which a state came to recognize itself, as in a mirror which was nothing less than the person of the king. "Que signifie le glas du nom propre?" That is Derrida's question, and it is apropos of the Puritan Revolution, for the death knell of Charles's name signified the possible birth of a new state founded on the relations of good and land rather than upon relations of the proper name. John Locke has heard this death knell clearly, it appears, in his *Second Treatise of Government* when he writes "that Adam had not, either by natural right of fatherhood or by positive donation from God, any such authority over his children, nor dominion over the world, as is pretended" and "that if he had, his heirs yet had no right to it."[31] So much for genealogy as the natural mode for the distribution of property, for the name as regulator of property relations, according to Locke.

But if the proper name is subjected to a *coupure,* or slashing, in the seventeenth century, it is because men like Milton fervently attacked political cratylism, opposed the proper names of kings. At one point in *Glas,* Derrida asks, "De noms peut-être, mais le nom propre est-il un signifiant linguistique?" ("Of names perhaps, but is the proper name a linguistic signifier?") And he notices that for Hegel "la lutte pour la reconnaissance n'a pas son élément dans la langue."[32] ("The battle for recognition does not have its element in language.") Language does not precede the economic and power forces of a society, but follows them, is their effect. In short, language is the idealism (*ideale Mitte*) that is produced by "la guerre pratique," or practical war, between singular forces. Language is the product of violence, of sacrifice. Thus the proper name is not merely a signifier which belongs to language as an ideal stratum but constitutes a part of the physical struggle of forces themselves; it comprises that moment by means of which the physical struggle can be idealized and posited on another plane of experience which is purely representational. And kingship marks that moment at which the outcome of a struggle is forever transcendentalized and perpetuated throughout history, though Hegel would add that kingship is vulnerable, since the proper name can always return to its original status as but a moment in a violent interchange.

A. S. P. Woodhouse is sensitive to this kind of linguistic violence in Milton even though he is not reading Milton from a Hegelian perspective. In *The Poet and His Faith*, Woodhouse singles Milton out as a writer whose language is extraterritorial, whose language is an "effect" that takes place outside what we might recognize as literary history:

It has been said that English poetry spoke one language in [Milton's] youth (the language of the poets we have been considering [Jonson, Donne, and others]) and another in his old age (the language of Dryden and emerging neoclassicism), and that Milton spoke neither of them. This is in large measure true.... There is a sense, then, in which Milton seems to belong rather to European than to English literature; and if he loses some of the beauties, he escapes the local and temporary peculiarities which mark English poetry in his day.[33]

However conservatively humanist Woodhouse sounds, there is a profound awareness on his part that Milton's voice is disembodied, extraterritorial, and beyond ordinary language. If Woodhouse suggests that is because Milton invented an artificial language cut on the ancients, we might be more inclined to argue that like Hegel, Milton breaks with cratylism, with a doctrine of proper names. A Hegelian would say, perhaps, that Milton's voice is the effect of the terror already glimpsed early in the poet's career, in the *Prolusions*, to be exact, when Milton already sings the death knell for scholasticism and the feudal conception of the state, that Milton's language is an effect of an essentially political antagonism which we see marked on the body of the young John Milton in a famous portrait wherein the child-poet appears with cropped hair, signaling a rigorous Puritan indoctrination in the vanity of names.

The proper name:

> Elle se joue entre les corps, certes, mais aussi les forces économiques, les biens, les possessions réelles, celles de la famille d'abord. L'élément linguistique implique une idéalité qui ne peut être que l'*effet* de la destruction des singularités empiriques, un effet et non un milieu de la lutte. Dans la guerre *pratique* entre les forces singulières, les lésions doivent opérer des expropriations effectives. Elles doivent arracher à l'autre la disposition de son corps, de son langage, le déloger littéralement de ses possessions.[34]

> ("It plays between the bodies, certainly, but also between economic forces, goods, real possessions, first of all those of the family. The linguistic element implies an ideality which can only be the *effect* of a destruction of empirical singularities, an effect and not a medium of combat. In the *practical* war between singular forces the wounds must produce effective expropriations, must tear away from the other the predisposition of his body and his language, literally dispossessing him of his possessions.")

The proper name is an effect of violence, the mark or space which is filled up by means of a particular relation based, not upon any inherent privilege of the subject, but upon the forces of economics, of goods, of real possessions, of this social struggle for recognition which concerns expropriation. James A. Freeman in *Milton and the Martial Muse* argues that Milton relentlessly attacked war and violence in order to make readers "withdraw their reflexive support for militarism," and yet one wonders to what extent this reflects on Freeman's humanism and impressive classical erudition rather than upon Milton's political position within an extremely turbulent historical period in which the destruction of empirical singularity and the struggle for independence from the feudal state was at issue.[35] What Milton's language represents is a position, recognized by Woodhouse, outside both the Caroline and Restoration periods, a position that can well be the effect of a dislodging of an other's possessions, a ransacking of Royalist claims to power. With such ransacking comes the inevitable expropriation of the upper class's ideological texts: its Bible, classicism, science, and customs. In the political texts of Milton, it is the bourgeoisie which takes over culture entirely, arresting it and placing it within new contexts: the justification of regicide and the installation of politics through brute force. Thus comes revolution, expropriation, and the rise of new discourses of power which even the Restoration will have to heed.

The violence of expropriation, oddly enough, is already to be glimpsed in Milton's notorious divorce tracts, which assert that "no effect of tyranny can sit more heavy on the commonwealth than this household unhappiness on the family,"[36] an unhappiness which concerns the enslavement of the master, or male, by the slave, or female, in terms of a "servile copulation." If Milton wants to break apart church and state government in the *Defence of the People of England*, in the divorce tracts he argues that no state can be free in which men are made slaves to women, in which the proper name as it circulates in civil society governs our personal relations to one another. What Milton wishes is to break the power of the proper name by invoking the sacred name of God, and, in particular, his law. The justification of divorce is what Milton terms "a greater title [which] I here bring ye [parliament] than is either in the power or in the policy of Rome to give her monarchs."[37] That is to say, by turning to Hebraic Law, as expressed in the *Talmud*, one can assert a "greater title" that serves to sunder the hold of a proper name, a hold which calls itself monarchy, genealogy, politics. Indeed, by justifying the rupture of the family name in terms of a divorce from Mary, Milton initiates the "guerre pratique" whose interest is to appeal to a language or law articulated from a position ideally outside the confines of the family, the truth of a Christian or state marriage. And this law to which Milton appeals is, of course, Hebraic or unreified, a name which cannot ever be properly named, but whose naming will necessarily fall outside or beyond the usual circulation of the name as it is conceived by the Romans, that civilization whose inheritors we are. Milton's appeal to a different or prior law works to "play among bodies," or as Derrida says, "Elle se joue entre les corps." Milton's appeal to the name implies an ideality, as Derrida says, which can be only the effect, and not a medium, of combat. And, too, the war Milton is waging in the divorce tracts serves to wound, and this wounding affects not only Caroline society, but Milton's wife Mary, and, of course, the tie which names their relation, the name of Milton itself. The tracts attempt to expropriate a name, attempt, not to erase Mary's name with regard to the house of Milton, but to sever the relationship of a Royalist to a Calvinist, to take back the wrappings of a name around a pair of citizens and to make of them a wounding which expropriates and confronts the other, as Derrida says, with the predisposition of one's body and language, literally dispossessing one of possessions.

However much Mary may usurp the role of wife, Milton makes it clear that she has been stripped of her property, her sexual appeal, that her good name has been expropriated, and by a language that pleads no mercy. With the writing of the tracts, Mary beholds her own divorce in the wake of a furious disownership, and in response she remains silent, "a mute and spiritless mate." Even if Milton takes Mary back and if the Royalists are in some way sheltered by his name, for Milton there is no doubt that a familial pact has been sundered, the genealogical imperative broken. It is the destruction of a familial mythology from which Mary's daughters will suffer in terms of so much paternal malevolence, as the "Non du Père" expressed in the sense of a "Nom du

Père."[38] And this malevolence carries over to the end, of course, for it is, not the Milton property, which these daughters are to inherit, but the dowry of the Powells which was never given to Milton, the property of the Royalists which was by the time of the Restoration expended.

Already on the level of the family, then, Milton like Flora Tristan so many decades after him, was waging revolution, appealing to the state for reform and discovering little sympathy. Is Milton to be considered a misogynist because he desired liberation from the mill that was the body of Mary Powell Milton? Or is this already a proto-feminism? For Milton's argument is that it is also the woman's prerogative to walk away from a bad relationship, that it is woman's prerogative to have access to the name which belongs to no one but herself. Such a language was incomprehensible to Milton's contemporaries and, as Woodhouse notes, is articulated outside the Caroline ambit. And yet it ought to occur to Woodhouse that such a language is an effect of revolution which in the 1650s speaks of war and the vast designs of a new state dedicated to the extinction of feudalism, though not quite sure what to do with the spoils of the aristocracy. On the one hand transformation, the end of cratylism, genealogy, proper names, the hierarchical state. On the other hand a return to a past with worship of culture, the authority of texts, the establishment of yet another bureaucracy, the continuation of Parliament and the ascent of princes. Antistatism is followed by statism, depoliticization punctuated by repoliticization in the way of property relations, passivity, cooptation, and the enlisting of the outsiders, both of the lower classes and, after Restoration, of the upper class. And language? This expropriates, confiscates, enlists, transforms, rehabilitates, recognizes, reinstitutionalizes, exacerbates, dilates, alienates. Such activities are everywhere manifest in the poetic oeuvre, of course, whose aim is to expropriate and appropriate, to dismantle the legacy of feudalism and forge with that inheritance a new bourgeois tradition, one that is announced so clearly in *Paradise Lost*, whose "Hail wedded love!" ought to be rewritten as "Vive les bourgeois!"

To expropriate the proper names of culture and dismember them, decapitate them, is already to articulate a language which denies the usual borderlines of discourse, which speaks other tongues. We must agree with Woodhouse, then, that Milton's language was indeed very different from that of his contemporaries, that the secretary of foreign tongues was a precise title for Milton, a new kind of disseminating name that yokes together the political with the cultural, Milton the revolutionary and Milton the poet. And let us agree with Woodhouse that Milton differs in the sense that he is not merely an English author but an international writer who belongs to Western culture in a very broad way. For Milton, not unlike Hegel, Goethe, Marx, Nietzsche, but also Sartre and Derrida, crosses the limits of philosophy, politics, and literature, attains a colossal, or monumentalized, writing style which speaks no ordinary language, no simple vulgar tongue of the vernacular springs of nationalism; for Milton, not unlike Hegel and others of that stature, is interested in a wholesale expropriation of language which follows upon the violence of a great revolution in the political arena, whether that be the Puritan English Revolution of the seventeenth century, the French Revolution of 1789, the Franco-Prussian war, or two world wars in the twentieth century. After the catastrophe there is an expropriation which always attempts to reconstitute the colossal writings of the past, which attempts to rewrite the past for the new orders that have taken over the seats of power. We are not speaking about mere reconstitution or return, then, but a discourse that marks a shift in the distribution of power relations. With Marx, the shift follows the way of a proletarian surge, the birth of a new class, and with Milton, similarly, a language breaks forth that is, no longer of the feudal world, but of an emergent middle class which will not make itself fully heard until the appearance in 1789 of revolution replete with its Saint-Justs and the Terror. With the new effects of language which follow economic, property, and state realignments, there occur new social recognitions, or reflexions, which manifest themselves in terms of new class relations, in terms of a new class antagonism, a new historical fault line that crosses and fractures so many social formations.

Milton's career is significant if only from the perspective that he was a literary and political writer who expressed himself just at the moment when the modern state was about to take on its capitalist appearance, a moment Milton himself seems to recognize, whereas so many of his contemporaries thought themselves living either in the past which looked back to the Elizabethan reign with nostalgia or in the eternal now of metaphysical salvation and political upheaval whose sense no one was supposed to surmise or justify. Milton, on the other hand, looks forward to the catastrophe and the terror of revolution and embraces the possibility of a new state in which the middle classes will be the determining group. But at that moment of revolution, this suspense before a new absolutism in which an old order is being broken to pieces, can we determine what the status is of the language that Milton speaks?

Can we speculate in this gap of history, this rupture, this suspension before the new absolutism, this new barbarism punctuated with a polytheism that radiates in all directions and down to our own day with the return in Nazi Germany of the woodland spirits, as Hegel called them, down to the even more crass electrified age of postmodern stars, superstars, and megastars? So many gods spread out on a pop(ular) front and all supported by worshippers, so-called dissenters all speaking a new language which is already and always the same discourse of commodity production and consumption, *l'économie libidinale?* Can we guess what Milton was speaking after what must have come as an initial shock early in life, the shock that everywhere in the industrialized zones of seventeenth-century England a bell was tolling for the end of feudalism, for the end of Renaissance, or Humanist man, and for the coming of the new set of bureaucratic orders which would have to expropriate ruthlessly the treasures of the damned within a poetics of revolution, an antagonism of an emergent class which brought to the block the heads of church and state before it realized how easily the aristocracy could be used as a blind for the machinations of capital?

Bernard-Henri Lévy may be right. "There is no linguistics that is not through and through a politics. Language is not the free murmur, the disorderly proliferation described by so many false poets and visionary apostles of the systematic disordering of words. To speak is inevitably to pronounce and articulate the law."[39] It is a law which Milton attempted to rearticulate through the apparatus of language, a society he attempted to revolutionize as much as he could. In a sense, when restoration came, Milton was himself subject to expropriation and impoverishment, though he could have been treated much worse. What saved him was the text, the rearticulation of a law that even with the shift in regimes was not incommensurate with the times. Charles II was not restored, after all, to the kind of monarchy Charles I enjoyed; Paraliament dictated that. And the middle classes never again had to worry, except briefly in the late 1680s, about being threatened by the specter of a collapsing of state, church, and civil government. Indeed, a kind of Hegelian state emerged, as well as a baroque age of the sublime. And Milton adjusted to this as he wrote his great poem on the disobedience of man. It is as if the spoils of revolution could finally be reappropriated in a cultural form which would dominate the literary and linguistic imaginations of men for centuries to come, as if revolution and politics could reassert themselves within the aesthetic as politically answerable style.

—O, Stephen will apologise.
Dante said:
—O, if not, the eagles will come
and pull out his eyes.

> *Pull out his eyes,*
> *Apologise,*
> *Apologise,*
> *Pull out his eyes.*

> *Apologise,*
> *Pull out his eyes,*
> *Pull out his eyes,*
> *Apologise.*

James Joyce,
Portrait of the Artist
as a Young Man

CHAPTER 7

Blessing the Text

This chapter introduces four more examples of Milton's *langue mineure*, of the castrated discourse whose impotence provides access to reserves of strength. I will argue first that Milton claims such a discourse for himself in *Paradise Lost*, book 3, and that he valorizes such a discourse in terms of blindness: the blind text. My second example, Christ's vehement attack on the Satanic idolatry of books in book 4 of *Paradise Regained* will show in what manner Milton conceives of a *langue mineure* in terms of a Hebraic tradition, a tradition Milton believes that Christ himself respected and upheld. Then I wish to turn to the *Areopagitica* in order to show in what way the onto-encyclopedic, or metaphysical, ideology of the book, that Satanic ideology referred to in *Paradise Regained*, is deconstructed by Milton in such a way that we see the emergence once more of a *langue mineure*, a defetishized text. And finally, I will conclude with a discussion of the relationships between Milton's "Upon the Circumcision" and Derrida's *Glas*, two texts which confront the question of the potency of the text in terms of the problematic of castration.

My purpose in presenting these examples is to show that Milton's conception of devout discourse, of true speaking, is radically opposed to the Greco-Roman ideology of the text as logos, of the word as an incarnation of the truth: in short, Milton's ideology of discourse as in direct opposition to the metaphysics of the book is what one might call a *thanatopraxie* of writing, a writing that knows it is not present, not alive, not being. This conclusion is intended to support T. S. Eliot's views on Milton, but only to the extent that they explain why Milton, unlike so many other poets, has resisted the orthodoxy of critics whose assumptions run counter to a poet who seems so much at first glance to be in accord with them.

I

It is in book 3 of *Paradise Lost* that Milton openly challenges the book of vision, the *langue majeure*, or book of knowledge fair, with his own blind text, his *langue mineure*:

> Thus with the Year
> Seasons return, but not to me returns
> Day, or the sweet approach of Ev'n or Morn,
> Or sight of vernal bloom, or Summer's Rose,
> Or flocks, or herds, or human face divine;
> But cloud instead, and ever-during dark
> Surrounds me, from the cheerful ways of men
> Cut off, and for the Book of knowledge fair
> Presented with a Universal blanc
> Of Nature's works to me expung'd and ras'd,
> And wisdom at one entrance quite shut out.
> So much the rather thou Celestial Light
> Shine inward, and the mind through all her powers
> Irradiate, there plant eyes, all mist from thence
> Purge and disperse, that I may see and tell
> Of things invisible to mortal sight. [3.40–55]

Like the blind Samson, Milton is "from the cheerful ways of men / Cut off." He is symbolically castrated, physically blinded. He can no longer read the signs which God has written into the book of nature and therefore is presented with, not a world of marks, but a universal blank from which the works or signs of nature are "expung'd," "ras'd." Unlike Adam, Milton cannot see the emblems that God has provided for man, the traces or tracks divine that Michael mentions in book 11 of *Paradise Lost*. But if the poet is severely handicapped, it is a handicap that he will turn to his advantage; for Milton has only distrust for the notion of the onto-encyclopedic book, even if that book be nature herself.

It is especially the ideology of the book as an incarnation of truth, of God, of a signified that Milton rejects, an ideology maintained by the great medieval exegetes. Hugh of St. Victor's definition of such a book is exemplary:

> For this whole visible world is as a book written by the finger of God, that is, created by divine power; and individual creatures are as figures therein not devised by human will but instituted by divine authority to show forth the wisdom of the invisible things of God. But just as some illiterate man who sees an open book looks at the figures but does not recognize the letters: just so the foolish natural man who does not perceive the things of God sees outwardly in these visible creatures the appearances but does not inwardly understand the reason. But he who is spiritual and can judge all things, while he considers outwardly the beauty of the work inwardly conceives how marvelous is the wisdom of the Creator.[1]

Hugh of St. Victor's point is that the world incarnates the logos of God. It mirrors or resembles him because it *is* him to the extent that the visible world is a figure or sign *for* him. The figures "show forth the wisdom of the invisible things of God." That is to say, they represent that wisdom by the very fact that they are logocentrically organized by the logos and have meaning only insofar as they are part of a sacred totality of relations: absolute knowledge or wisdom. Everything one sees, Hugh believes, belongs necessarily to this totality of relations, this incarnation of the logos. But to affirm such a totality of relations, such an absolute wisdom, is at once to affirm the presence of a consciousness that is omniscient and omnipresent within the totality of relations itself and comes, therefore, perilously close to pantheism, or, to put it as Milton might, to idolatry.

Hugh of St. Victor's ideology of writing, then, is an ideology of presence, incarnation, logos, and totality. In a similar vein the Thomists strongly argue for a world view in which all things figure forth God in terms of a logocentric, totalitarian structure which is metaphorically imitated by them, codified, in the *Summa*. We know from the *Prolusions* that Milton firmly rejected the books of the scholastics at an early age, and it should not surprise us that in *Paradise Lost* he once more attacks the book of knowledge fair, a concept dear to the medieval exegetes who had, after all, strong scholastic leanings.[2] What is surprising, of course, is that Milton can confront such a metaphysics of the book from a position of extraordinary weakness, from the position of the reader who cannot read the signs, since he is blind. I suggest that he can turn this "blindness" to advantage, a strategy that he uses elsewhere in *Sonnet 19* when he identifies himself with the blind man mentioned by the evangelist John:

And his disciples asked him, saying, "Master, who did sin, this man, or his parents, that he was born blind?" Jesus answered, "Neither hath this man sinned, nor his parents, but that the works of God should be showed on him."[3]

Again, in the passage quoted from *Paradise Lost* above, the argument that blindness is a blessing, because it ensures "that the works of God might be made manifest in him," is an assumption upon which the whole passage rests. Here blindness can be equated with the concept of blessing, which in English carries both the senses of wounding and consecrating.[4] It is through such a wounding, opening, or cutting that Milton discovers the penetration of celestial light, a power of vision that comes about on account of the poet's blindness to the book of nature mentioned by Hugh of St. Victor.

Instead of the book of knowledge fair, then, one has blindness. And Milton gives us an interesting image for this blindness, the "Universal blanc." In itself this image is a metaphor for the blank page of a book, for the tablet erased of all its signs. Just as Stéphane Mallarmé uses the notion of the *blanc*, or space, in his poetic to challenge the metaphysical ideology of writing, Milton uses the "blanc" in the passage quoted above to counter the scholastic's *Summa*, or onto-encyclopedic book. The blank page is meant to suggest the inadequacy of the sign as symbol, as a signifier invested with a signified. Only when one goes beyond mere symbolicity, Milton suggests, does one come in direct communication with celestial light. Here the "blanc" signifies a blind that prevents the poet from seeing the signifiers, which are, as Hugh of St. Victor insists, laden with hidden meaning, cuts the poet off from natural symbols and thereby gives access to the true light of theology. Walter Benjamin believes such an attack on the symbol is characteristic of an age that steers an allegorical course, and in *Ursprung des deutschen Trauerspiels* he writes that "symbolische Schönheit verflüchtigt sich, da das Licht der Gottesgelahrtheit drauf trifft" ("symbolic beauty takes flight where the light of divine learning (allegory) treads").[5]

If the universal blanc marks a blind spot (*tache aveugle*), it also marks the threshold where light as truth can pass through.[6] It is, in other words, a limen, or threshold, that deconstructs the symbol, puts it out of order, while at the same time preserving our ability to sight the light of theology, the light celestial. Thus what is a blind spot is also something of a passageway that allows for vision. And the "blanc" is a point of crossing, a space where blindness and insight are at once distinguished and confused, an "undecidable" liminal crossing.

To cross out the sight, or blind, is not to be dissociated from the fact that this activity, marked by the "blanc," signifies, in addition to what we have already mentioned, the cutting off of Milton from the "ways of men," from his manhood. This rupture from one's manhood is already reflected in the fact that to be blinded means that one cannot perform the Adamic task of deciphering the signs of nature, a task that falls under a husband's duty to perform not only for his own salvation but for his wife's as well. Once blinded, Milton loses this masculine privilege of interpreting the world, and like a female, he must now depend upon others to perform what once was his duty. Symbolically, Milton has been castrated, has been given a universal "blanc," a tabula rasa that is more properly a woman's possession than a man's.

And yet it is Milton's strategy to turn this "blanc," or wound, into a blessing, for Milton is not afraid to show the mark of castration and thereby display the degree to which he has overcome his fear of castration and the experience of castration as well. In elevating the *blanc*, Milton at once admits his own blessing as a wound that mutilates him, that threatens his poetic project, but at the same time exhibits his power to carry out his project, a power founded upon his overcoming the fear of castration. Symbolically, the *blanc* of the Miltonic text, the place where it is not seen, renders to Milton the power of a Medusa in the Freudian sense, that is, as a traumatizing figure who terrifies because her potency, her symbolic phallus, is imagined as being cut off. This power is represented in the snakes that are her hair, a potent displacement of the symbolic phallus that signifies the overcoming of the fear and experience of mutilation or castration. That Milton's texts have an analogous traumatizing power is evident when one reads the criticism of someone like Harold Bloom, who explains from a Freudian view a criticism founded upon the epigone's fear of castration by symbolic fathers like Milton. What makes Milton especially dangerous from this view is that he exhibits himself as weak, mutilated, and in doing so reveals vast reserves of power, what Derrida in *Glas* refers to as the "POTENCE du texte" achieved by the author with the courage to castrate himself. In *Paradise Lost*, Milton himself appears as a kind of Samson; he does not castrate himself, but is nevertheless castrated symbolically and uses a feminine strategy, the strategy of a Medusa, to overpower the masters, a strategy we have referred to earlier as a negative labor which we can see now as the effect of the blessing, the placing *sous rature*.

Milton's stress on blindness in *Paradise Lost* is significant too because it establishes a strong identification with the Old Testament and perhaps even with the Jews themselves. We recall that the medieval church doctors held the Old Testament in disparagement. To quote Henri de Lubac, the Old Testament was considered, " 'inutile,' ou 'sterile,' ou 'frivole,' ou 'sans raison,' ou 'insipide,' ou 'se détruisant elle-même,' tant qu'on n'a pas recours à l'intelligence spirituelle" (" 'useless,' or 'sterile,' or 'frivolous,' or 'without reason,' or 'insipid,' or 'destroying itself,' such that one has no recourse to spiritual intelligence"). But even worse, the church doctors believe that the Old Testament was blind. It is the "lettre d'un Testament périmé, qui ne porte plus l'esprit, qui ne le promet plus; lettre à laquelle s'attache dans son aveuglement celui qui refuse l'Evangile" ("letter of an outdated or invalid Testament which no longer carries the spirit, which no longer promises it; the letter to which clings in his blindness one who refuses the Gospel"). What is more, the church exegetes suggest that it is Christ who reveals the Old Testament as a blind text. It is Christ's appearance that makes of the Old Testament a text obviously deprived of the spirit; it is he who decapitates it. Thus: "Cette lettre-là tue, parce qu'elle est comme le corps de Jean-Baptiste décapité." ("This letter kills, because it is decapitated like the body of John the Baptist.")[7] But if Christ has decapitated the Old Testament (*decapitation:* simulacrum for castration and blinding), has, like Dalila, castrated the discourse of the Hebrews, it is a sacred condemnation that spurs the poet to accept and take on as his own a spiritual curse, a curse that Milton himself actually has to bear in a physical sense.

What I am suggesting is that when Milton chooses texts like Genesis or a section of Judges for the matter of his poems, he chooses not only texts about blindness, such as Adam and Eve's spiritual blindness and Samson's physical blindness, but also texts that in themselves are blind in the sense that they are mutilated, decapitated. Milton, the blind, cursed poet, appears to identify that curse of sightlessness with texts that share this curse, as if blindness was, finally, not so much a handicap as a spur to insight. Certainly, Milton uses the New Testament in order to prop up the Old Testament's fallen texts, but, interestingly enough, not as much as one might expect. Rather, Milton is quite willing to valorize most strongly the fallen, blind discourse of the Hebrews as he does in *Samson Agonistes*. One clear indication of this is the fact that Milton by no means fills a work like *Samson Agonistes* with numerous New Testament analogues, as his contemporaries might have filled them.[8] In *Paradise Lost* we are not, similarly, oriented primarily in terms of Christ's crucifixion, his passion, which was, again, the usual manner for Christians of all denominations to read a fallen text like Genesis. Instead, Milton accepts the blind, decapitated, fallen text in terms of a *tâche aveugle*, a blind task which is at the same time a blind spot. He eschews an *Écriture* in order that he may embrace an *écriture:* that is to say, he eschews Scripture as the language of presence, as the *langue majeure*, in order that he may embrace a fallen writing, a *langue mineure* that in the Derridean sense of *écriture* is deferred from presence. Why Milton makes this detour, this excursion through *écriture*, in order to recuperate the "POTENCE du texte," and what it means to embrace *écriture* rather than *Écriture* will be a subject that I will take up later. For now, I simply wish to establish that Milton does accept for himself a *tâche aveugle*, and that this *tache-tâche* is linked to an imitation of the Hebrews, the Jews who, similarly, travel a blind route.

II

If we have any doubts that Milton is working out of a Hebraic tradition, we have simply to turn to *Paradise Regained*, for it is here that Milton makes most explicit the superiority of the Hebraic texts which are, at once, so seemingly inferior from a classical point of view. We recall that Satan tempts Christ with worldly knowledge:

> So let extend thy mind o'er all the world,
> In knowledge, all things in it comprehend.
> All knowledge is not couch't in *Moses'* Law,
> The *Pentateuch* or what the Prophets wrote;
> The *Gentiles* also know, and write, and teach
> To admiration, led by Nature's light;
> And with the *Gentiles* much thou must converse,
> Ruling them by persuasion as thou mean'st,
> Without thir learning how wilt thou with them,
> Or they with thee hold conversation meet?
> [4. 223–32]

It is good, practical advice. But Christ is not impressed. Especially Satan's charge that the Hebraic texts are deficient in the sense that they are not encyclopedic and therefore do not contain "all knowledge" makes Christ reply most vehemently that Satan's beloved classical tradition, which Satan boasts of at length, is "little else but dreams / Conjectures, fancies, built on nothing firm." Even Socrates, "The first and wisest of them all profess'd / To know this only, that he nothing knew" (4.291–94). And Christ continues with a long speech on the classical philosophers that concludes, "Who therefore seeks in these / True wisdom, finds her not, or by delusion / Far worse, her false resemblance only meets, / An empty cloud" (4.318–21). In short, Christ dismisses Satan's logophilia in terms of denouncing the whole Greek tradition of philosophy which is founded upon an ideology of the onto-encyclopedic book, the text, or *Summa* which contains all knowledge, or the text as Logos:

> However, many books
> Wise men have said are wearisome; who reads
> Incessantly, and to his reading brings not
> A spirit and judgment equal or superior
> (And what he brings, what needs he elsewhere seek)
> Uncertain and unsettl'd still remains,
> Deep verst in books and shallow in himself,

>   Crude or intoxicate, collecting toys,
>   And trifles for choice matters, worth a sponge;
>   As Children gathering pebbles on the shore.
>   Or if I would delight my private hours
>   With Music or with Poem, where so soon
>   As in our native Language can I find
>   That solace? All our Law and Story strew'd
>   With Hymns, our Psalms with artful terms inscrib'd
>   Our Hebrew Songs and Harps in *Babylon*,
>   That pleas'd so well our Victors' ear, declare
>   That rather *Greece* from us these Arts deriv'd;
>   Ill imitated, while they loudest sing
>   The vices of thir Deities, and thir own
>   In Fable, Hymn, or Song, so personating
>   Thir Gods ridiculous, and themselves past shame.
>   Remove their swelling Epithets thick laid
>   As varnish on a Harlot's cheek, the rest,
>   Thin sown with aught of profit or delight,
>   Will far be found unworthy to compare
>   With *Sion's* songs, to all true tastes excelling,
>   Where God is prais'd aright, and Godlike men,
>   The Holiest of Holies, and his Saints;
>   Such are from God inspir'd, not such from thee.
>   [4.321–50]

Christ charges that, if anything, the Greek, or classical, tradition is but a pirated discourse, a gross parody of the Hebraic tradition, "That rather Greece from us these Arts deriv'd / Ill imitated, while they loudest sing / The vices of thir Deities." The classical tradition is nothing more than a gross, Satanic idolatry or worship of books, of genres perversely modeled upon the Hebrew Scriptures in the same way that Greek gods are idols "personating / Thir gods ridiculous," copying and defiling their model, the Hebrew God. What Satan valorizes as the books of wise men, Christ admonishes here as "varnish on a Harlot's cheek," as mere eloquence which prostitutes itself to whoever wishes to see it. Christ insists, "Thir Orators thou then extoll'st . . . But herein to our Prophets far beneath, / As men divinely taught, and better teaching / The solid rules of Civil Government / In thir majestic unaffected style / Than all the

Oratory of *Greece* and *Rome*" (4.353–60). If the prophets are "beneath" the Greek and Roman philosophers, it is to their advantage, since the prophets can think clearly, plainly, straightforwardly. The temptation is always to let the mind wander, to err, and Adam notes this when he says in *Paradise Lost:*

> But apt the Mind or Fancy is to rove
> Uncheckt, and of her roving is no end;
> Till warn'd, or by experience taught, she learn
> That not to know at large of things remote
> From use, obscure and subtle, but to know
> That which before us lies in daily life.
> [8.188–93]

Ironically, it is the rational, or logical, text of the Greeks, the learned texts disciplined by the speculations of great intellects, that amount to nothing more than toys, the sterile stones found by children on the shore, or the cosmetics of whores. Suddenly it is the *langue majeure,* the rational text of powerful men, that turns into the *langue mineure,* a feminine and weak discourse; and it is the Hebraic *langue mineure,* the blind, ignorant text of the Hebrews, the feminine hysterical outbursts of the prophets, the unpremeditated verse of intuitive men who do not think in terms of rational systems, but who transmit inspired messages, that is seen as the *langue majeure.*

The emphasis upon a powerful discourse that is spontaneously sung is strong in the passage cited above. Christ says, "All our Law and Story [is] strew'd / With Hymns, our Psalms with artful terms inscrib'd / Our Hebrew Songs and Harps in *Babylon,* / That pleas'd so well our Victors' ear" (8.334–37). Such is the discourse of praise, prayer, and thanksgiving, a discourse that offers thanks in return for heavenly gifts. It has been observed that in *Paradise Lost* prelapsarian man's central occupation is the spontaneous recitation of a discourse that is occasional and answerable to the modes of order that surround man, an order that is itself Edenic, or sacred.[9] It is the occasional, prelapsarian verses, the spontaneous discourse of Adamic praise and thanksgiving, that is exemplary for fallen, Hebraic man. What is characteristic of such a discourse is that it does not lay claim to reason, to logos, to scientific data about the modes of order that surround us. Rather, it lays claim to another significant distinction from all other discourse: that it is considered by God to be a proper offering to him and is, therefore, sacred, privileged, and blessed. In this, of course, the Hebraic Scriptures are radically opposed to the Greek texts of the philosophers.

Christ himself is exemplary of such a Hebraic text, since he is the Word, the crucified Word, to be exact. He is the offering that will be sacrificed, the text that has to be divested of its presence in order that it can be offered up to God. Similarly, the prayer, the psalm, the hymn are offerings that must be subjected to an economics of sacrifice. If Milton divests his "present" to Christ of its "presence" in the "Nativity Ode," the humble or plain songs that Christ cites in the passage from *Paradise Regained* can also be considered in terms of being stripped of their logocentricism, their rational eloquence, to put it in further classical terms. In short, if the Hebraic Scriptures are ignorant, as Satan insists, then that is fine, since that is the sacrifice that God exacts from the offering that is to be given him, a sacrifice that impoverishes only to restore thousandfold. Again, the word *blessing* is relevant for us, since this word puns on the sacrifice, the wound, that marks a restoration, a glorification.

III

A great stumbling block to the critic who would claim that Milton himself sides unequivocally with a Hebrew tradition throughout his poetic career is the famous passage on the book in the *Areopagitica*. It would seem to any intelligent reader that in this passage Milton is strongly arguing for logophilia, for a conception of the onto-encyclopedic book, and that he is doing so in a Neoplatonic way. However, I think that a close examination of the passage will reveal that, although Milton refers to the book in a Neoplatonic context, he uses that very context to deconstruct the kinds of books Satan values in *Paradise Regained*. Here is the passage in question.

> For books are not absolutely dead things, but do contain a potency of life in them to be as active as that soul was whose progeny they are; nay, they do preserve as in a vial the purest efficacy and extraction of that living intellect that bred them. I know they are as lively and as vigorously productive as those fabulous dragon's teeth; and being sown up and down, may chance to spring up armed men. And yet, on the other hand, unless wariness be used, as good almost kill a man as kill a good book: who kills a man kills a reasonable creature, God's image; but he who destroys a good book, kills reason itself, kills the image of God, as it were, in the eye. Many a man lives a burden to the earth; but a good book is the precious lifeblood of a master spirit, embalmed and treasured up on purpose to a life beyond life.[10]

At first sight, one would assume that this master spirit, this absolute knowledge, was the Logos itself, a presence completely present to itself. Milton suggests that the book contains a spirit or life that can be executed or killed. Books are "lively and vigorously productive." Thus: "As good almost kill a man as kill a good book." Again: "A book is the precious lifeblood of a master spirit." And: "He who kills a good book, kills reason itself." It is as if Milton were arguing that signs contain their signifieds, that the book is written out in symbols or words that incarnate logic, reason, truth, and being. Yet such metaphysical optimism is strongly checked by other statements in the same passage. For example, Milton suggests the book is not completely alive when he says, "For books are not absolutely dead things." In other words, they *are* dead, but *not absolutely dead*. Again, the master spirit is "embalmed and treasured up"; it is subject to the sustaining powers of the embalmer's craft, a craft that is itself a technics and in no way a natural or metaphysical life support.

The book: *économie de la mort*, the crossroads where spirit and the letter overlap. In the *Areopagitica*, it is clear that writing is involved in a praxis of death, the embalmer's art, and that it preserves truth, meaning, and being only at the price of fixing or fastening in the alchemical sense of fastening a volatile spirit, or essence, by combination with a tangible solid or fluid: in this case, writing. The suggestion that the text embalms or fixes is important, for a learned reader of Milton's time might have immediately made the connection between the idea of "fixing" and its related alchemical terms, "dyssolve," "dystill," or "sublyme." That Milton does, indeed, suggest these latter terms becomes likely when one considers his use of the "vial" image. Books "do preserve as in a vial the purest efficacy and extraction of that living intellect that bred them." In other words, if the book embalms a master spirit, it thereby fixes or distills it. The book itself is the vial; it is the substance to which the essence is fastened or held.

Again, the outward appearance of such a metaphorical connection between composing books and performing the embalmer's art is strictly metaphysical, for Milton appears to be saying that signs, or writing, can incarnate truth, that we can in some sense make the book a body that houses a soul through the technics, ironically enough, of the chemist who can cleverly mix or fuse them with his special miraculous arts. Here necromancy or sorcery wins the day. The maker of the book, like the chemist who holds the vial, has succeeded in capturing the Logos, the divine extract of that living intellect whose power can be of use to us.

However, it is also clear that if the efficacy and potency of a master spirit is embalmed, this process of embalming entails a certain loss or fading of the original power that the process attempts to maintain. The book does not capture or incarnate the fullness of being, but some kind of extract that has been subjected to a technics, that has been processed, in the modern sense of the word. That is to say, if the extract is potent, it is also devitalized or corrupted. Moreover, the process of embalming suggests not so much an incarnation of truth as it does a medium to which truth is artificially fastened or fixed. In other words, truth is again mixed with something base (a base, actually) that corrupts or kills it. The script, or writing, to which the Logos is attached is not transformed necessarily into a symbol that contains the spirit naturally, but an allegorical sign that merely attaches itself to the spirit artificially. It is a foreign substance, an artificial glue, or base, which makes only artificial, alchemical attachments. In this sense, writing is not like a man's body, which is the natural house for the soul; it is not a product of nature, but the product of man's technics, which in this case is not only unnatural but supernatural. In this sense Milton can assert that books constitute a supernatural *thanatopraxie*, that they are the precious lifeblood of a master spirit, a spirit that is, by way of the text, "embalmed and treasured up on purpose to a life beyond life."

There is a question whether Milton could approve of valorizing the book positively as an act of sorcery when one looks at how he considers writing elsewhere. That is, it seems unlikely that Milton is presenting a Neoplatonic version of writing that we are to accept without a certain skepticism. What he is doing, it seems to me, is rhetorically appealing to an audience with Neoplatonic sympathies, while at the same time leaving room for more enlightened readers, perhaps of Milton's Protestant persuasion, to detect certain disturbing checks. If Milton allows a Neoplatonic reader to enjoy the book as a material that can appropriately house the reason as the body houses the soul, he also shows in what way such a literary conjunction of mind-body or signifier-signified is extremely unnatural and, moreover, closely associated with the notion that the book is really nothing more than a tomb, a necropolis of signs, a *thanatopraxie* of writing.

The latter suggestion in the passage from the *Areopagitica* is most significant, for it develops a Renaissance topos that was well known in Milton's time, the book as tomb. Sir Thomas Browne's *Hydriotaphia; or, Urne Buriall,* which was published in 1658, some fourteen years after the *Areopagitica* first appeared, indicates that during Milton's time the equation of book as tomb was not necessarily considered in a positive light by intellectuals. Thus when Milton made such a connection, he may very well have been trying to make a negative suggestion. To be "but Pyramidally extant, is a fallacy in duration," Browne writes, and the thrust of his argument is that all monuments, whether they be pyramids, urns, or tombstones, are but a vain technics of stone and signs made to preserve man longer than God has ordained. According to Browne, "The Platonicks rejected not a due care of the grave, though they put their ashes to unreasonable expectations." What Browne finds particularly amusing is that men use writing to continue themselves in our memories and that they vainly believe that this writing can be monumentalized for all time upon the monument that marks their grave. "Five Languages secured not the Epitaph of *Gordianus.*" And: "Time hath spared the Epitaph of *Adrians* horse, confounded that of himself." Browne concludes:

The man of God lives longer without a Tomb than any by one, invisibly interred by Angels; and adjudged to obscurity, though not without some marks directing humane discovery. *Enoch* and *Elias* without either tomb or buriall, in an anomalous state of being, are the great Examples of perpetuity, in their long and living memory, in strict account being still on this side death, and having a late part yet to act upon this stage of earth.[11]

Browne's point is that writing is not suitable as a vehicle for spirit. Those who make use of the letter, of the technics of writing and funereal pomp, will be subject to the ruins of time, for the "iniquity of oblivion blindely scattereth her poppy, and deals with the memory of men without distinction to merit of perpetuity."[12] That is, those who use the technics of the letter will become subject to its dissemination, its violent erosion which makes a mockery of all funereal pomp, of all vainglory and pride. Better that one should die without graves, for at least then one's markers will not survive in order to disgrace one centuries later.

Browne's *Urne Buriall* is largely a critique of symbolicity, of what Browne terms the enigma, the emblem, the symbol. What one finds in the funerary inscriptions of the pagan dead and what Browne believed to be the urns of the primitive Christian church are nothing more than indecipherable designs whose keys are lost. They are inscriptions without meanings. They are nonsense. What Browne suspects is that all symbols, whether modern or ancient, are really nonsense and that if they have meaning, it is only because men artificially attach meaning to these symbols, signs, or emblems. Once these men die, as they must eventually, these meanings are slowly lost. Thus one views hieroglyphics in Egypt, but has no way of telling what they say, since it was never in their power to say anything in the first place. For these are just dumb signs, to which meaning was attached artificially by convention.

In the *Areopagitica,* the suggestion that a master spirit is fixed or fastened to script may have had from a viewpoint such as that of Browne's a definite negativity, for that connection is artificial; it is made through the technics of the funeral pomp and makes of the book a monument whose meaning is, not intrinsic, but extrinsic. There is a sense in which the book is, not to be seen as a symbol, but to be seen as an allegory, a technics in which signifier and signified are brought together unnaturally. To recall a phrase of Walter Benjamin's: "Soviel Bedeutung, soviel Todverfallenheit" ("So much meaning, so much falling into death"). Indeed, this negativity underscores the optimism which appears in terms of a Neoplatonic certainty, a certainty Milton here makes ambivalent when he introduces the trope of the book as tomb.

The tomb, of course, is itself a liminal site, a place where life and death cross, and if Milton's passage is in any sense ambivalent, this is by no means surprising, for he is describing the book in terms of a necropolis of signs, in terms of a threshold that continues life after it has terminated and begs off death, into whose hands the spirit is now to enter. Up to this point we have seen that Milton suggests such a liminality between life and death in terms of the ambivalent crossing of spirit and the embalmer's craft. But the ambivalence is carried further in Milton's curious handling of the Cadmus myth.

Books are as "lively and as vigorously productive as those fabulous dragon's teeth." More importantly, they "may chance to spring up armed men." Milton's reference to the Cadmus myth presupposes an emphasis upon the hero, Cadmus, as an emissary of writing, a culture hero who presents the invention of the alphabet to a foreign people. Here again, the opposition of writing in terms of life and death presents itself again in terms of analogous oppositions: the conflict between man and dragon, creation and destruction, sowing and violence, terrestial and chthonic. In terms of the myth itself, the fundamental opposition is that of two different ontological orders, the order of men and the order of chthonic beings. In Milton's reading of the myth, the book is a crossroads where these two orders meet, a rapprochement between these two different orders, though not in any way a synthesis of them. Like the dragon who zealously protects the sacred spring, the book is a sterile guardian of mysterious sources of power. It is a writing that is implacable and immovable precisely because the springs of thought it guards are not meant to be defined by errant signification. Like the hero, however, the book is a vital cultural force, a dynamic authority that founds culture and changes thought. The book cannot be said to be at once immovable and changing, though in some sense we must admit that it has qualities of both, that it can in some sense relate to each order: human (changing, founding) and chthonic (static, protecting).

The opposition between men and monsters is complicated further by Milton's reference to the dragon's teeth, which can be opposed to their metamorphosis into men, the Spartoi. The dragon's teeth are sown, and allegorically we may take this to represent a sowing of the alphabet. That the teeth might represent letters is not entirely a fanciful notion once one realizes that, like teeth, letters are nothing more than an inanimate series, or row, of identical objects whose shape varies somewhat. It is precisely by sowing the teeth or disseminating the letters that Cadmus composes the book which is now figured forth in terms of the armed men, the Spartoi. What was initially a dark, sterile row of letters, a technics known as the alphabet, has now been transformed into life, into logos, into man. The letter has been given spirit.

And yet, if the emergence of the Spartoi signifies the transition of technics (the series, the teeth) to being (man, culture), the Spartoi also have the power to signify the intrusion of a lifeless, or supernatural, order into our world, the intrusion of death itself. For we recall that in the Cadmus myth, the Spartoi engage in killing each other off. What Cadmus has reaped is not so much an army of cultured beings but an array of hideous corpses. If books are like the armed men who chance to spring up, they cannot be optimistically hailed as anything but destructive, dangerous, and sinister. On the other hand, in Ovid's telling of the story, we read that a few of the armed men do survive, and it is they who, together with Cadmus, founded Thebes, that city which inspires the great tragedians to compose their books about blind heroes and seers.

Especially in the reference to the Cadmus myth, then, the stress between seeing the book as a technics of signs, or letters, and the logos of men, between the letter and the spirit, is noticeable. Again, the book appears to be a threshold that separates the underworld, the world of death, from the world of man; and, at the same time, the book manages to confuse these two orders, to mix them. It serves as the crossing point, the limen where letter and spirit are twisted around each other and yet deviantly separated too.

IV

By now it should be evident that Milton has, even in the least likely of places, the *Areopagitica,* mounted an attack upon the classical ideology of the book as a metaphysical instrument, of writing as logos. As we have noted in the first chapter, T. S. Eliot felt the wound but misinterpreted the cause, as did Samuel Johnson before him in the "Life of Milton." There are, of course, numerous other critics, especially formalist ones, who have refused even to feel the wounds, as Eliot and Johnson did, and it is they who have read Milton as if he maintained an ideology of writing or verse that centers around an intellectual will to power that is based upon the presupposition that this will can be carried out most strongly in terms of the onto-encyclopedic ideology of the *Summa,* or book.

Northrop Frye is one of these formalists, and his collection of essays on Milton, *The Return of Eden,* is exemplary of how the presupposition that Milton respected a metaphysical ideology of writing leads to very inadequate readings. Frye's insistence that Milton structures his epics in terms of typological closure because he wanted to imitate the encyclopedic scope of the Old Testament and the New Testament (a Pauline scope, really), leads Frye to look for "archetypal patterns" that many might argue are not "archetypal" (that is, privileged, central, germinal, or latent) for Milton as they might be for poets like Samuel Austin or Edmund Spenser.[13] To assume, as Frye does, that Milton is using the same archetypal grammar as Malory or Spenser may be a great mistake, for it leads to the assumption that Milton's verse is far more eschatological and epiphantic than it really is. That Frye's concept of the "archetype" is that of a symbol that contextualizes a plot, image, setting, or character in terms of a "total action," a story with a beginning and an end, only reinforces the eschatological drift. I have already shown in what manner Milton differs from a Samuel Austin who explicitly reads the Christian tradition in terms of Pauline types, how Milton sacrifices the New Testament for the Old Testament's blind scripture. And I wish to briefly explain here how Milton dispenses with anything that could be construed as an archetype, by which I mean a deep structure or source that has the double duty of determining the total action of a new poem at the same time that it reproduces the total action of an ur-text from which it is quarried.

When elaborating upon the Miltonic inclusion of the sacred command that the seed of Adam shall bruise the serpent's head, Frye begins to make many archetypal connections. "The imagery suggests the romance theme of a knight-errant killing a dragon."[14] He is thinking of Spenser, of course, not Milton. He continues, "Besides the serpent in Eden, the Old Testament speaks of a dragon or sea monster, called 'leviathan,' or 'Rahab.'" Now he is thinking of Blake. "Or, in the metaphor of the sea serpent, hooked and landed, on the day of judgment," Revelations comes to mind. In fact, Frye likes this association best, for he elaborates it in terms of the seven-headed monster of Revelations and shortly in terms of Spenser's Saint George's dragon. Lastly, the serpent is to be equated with the Nile or Egypt. We are now considering the prophets. It is clear that for Frye the archetype of the serpent links together three important moments in the encyclopedic Christian tradition: Genesis, Exodus, and the Last Judgment. It reproduces the ur-text, the Bible, at the same time that it determines the total action of *Paradise Lost*.

Now, no one is going to refute Frye's canny observations. But if one looks closely, one does find that Milton himself frustrates such observations a good deal. Satan is not compared to any apocalyptic dragons, and when, in book 1, Satan is equated with Leviathan, it is within the context of classical monsters, Briareus or Typhon and Dipsas. Furthermore, when the Leviathan image is expanded, it is not in Biblical terms. Rather, it is in terms of a pilot who on the Norway foam makes the error of taking Leviathan for an island. Again in book 9, just at that point when one would expect the serpent equated with an apocalyptic monster, the context is once more a classical one:

> And lovely, never since of Serpent kind
> Lovelier, not those that in *Illyria* chang'd
> *Hermione* and *Cadmus*, or the God
> In *Epidaurus;* nor to which transform'd
> *Ammonian Jove*, or *Capitoline* was seen.
> [9.504–8]

And in book 10 Satan is changed to "A monstrous Serpent on his Belly prone, / Reluctant, but in vain" (10.514–15). All the devils are then changed, and hell becomes thickly swarming with "complicated monsters." If ever Milton had a chance to imitate Revelations, it is here, but again we get a classical catalog: Satan is like "*Amphisbaena* dire, *Cerastes* horn'd, *Hydrus*, and *Ellops* drear." Finally, Milton writes,

> But still greatest hee the midst,
> Now Dragon grown, larger than whom the Sun
> Ingender'd in the *Pythian* Vale on slime,
> Huge *Python*, and his Power no less he seem'd
> Above the rest still to retain. [10.528–32]

Is this the dragon with seven heads Frye speaks of? Apparently not, for even here the reference is to Python in Ovid's *Metamorphoses*.

It is true that Milton does not prevent us from *associating* Python with the dragon in Revelations, but, curiously enough, he does not go much out of his way to encourage it either. Rather than reproducing the ur-text of the Bible, as an archetype is expected to do, the image of the serpent appears to make nothing more than a cluster of allusions, and not even to the Bible. It does not secure a prefabricated total action, but tries to fragment, to break apart a total action by its errant associations to all kinds of classical texts which together do not make up a single, unified book or secular scripture, to say nothing of an encyclopedic tradition. In fact, one could go so far as to say that the image of the serpent does not determine the text of *Paradise Lost*, but overdetermines it in the Freudian sense. It overloads the text with references, associations, and glosses to the point that an archetypal critic might be hard put to say with integrity that "this" is what the image "means." In short, Milton has let the image of the serpent disseminate, or cross-breed, with so many literary monsters that to look for its archetypal meaning, much less its archetypal source (the generating myth, the ur-text, the privileged place of origin), becomes a rather futile effort. Indeed, in terms of such intertextuality, myth criticism, like its distant cousin, historicism, is what one might call capsized in its own search for the rock bottom of the text.

This difficulty bothered T. S. Eliot, who perceived it some years before Frye began writing archetypal criticism. Milton, Eliot says in *On Poetry and Poets*, lacks "depth." One cannot find the sources for the verse, either in Milton's personal writings or in Renaissance tradition. Even when Milton provides us with classical allusions, they are usually multiple allusions, and often one cannot decide which is the stronger one, the one Milton or the one his texts believe to be most important. If Milton is encyclopedic in the sense that he covers all the classical allusions of an image or phrase at once, he is antiencyclopedic at the same time in the sense that he works against semantic closure, against the confines of encyclopedic grids. In this he is close to Montaigne, Rabelais, Browne, and Burton, not to mention lesser known figures like Alexander Gil. Like the texts of so many of Milton's contemporaries and near contemporaries, Milton's texts are not encyclopedic in the sense that they work centripetally to pull texts and traditions together in a logocentric structure, but are antiencyclopedic in the sense that they work centrifugally, dispersing and proliferating information everywhere, overwhelming the reader and overstraining his rational capacity to comprehend, to enclose in formal grids that which he is reading.

There have been formalists, like Isabel MacCaffrey, Anne Ferry, John Steadman, Louis Martz, Arnold Stein, and Christopher Ricks, who have consistently failed to perceive Milton's antiformalism; yet others, like Christopher Grose and Geoffrey Hartman, have not failed in this way. What is odd is that Harold Bloom, who is in many ways close to Hartman, has also been insisting in recent years that Milton is the poet of a text that "absorbs its precursors," an ontoencyclopedic text that cannibalizes all prior texts. Perhaps he should be arguing, as Hartman would, that Milton is a poet, not of the book, but of a Derridean *dissémination*, an *écriture*.[15]

Of all the critics who can help us gain access to Milton's poetry, none is more important than Jacques Derrida (something I have tried to demonstrate in this study), for it is in his *Glas* that problematics also found in Milton are broached. Derrida too is working very much out of a Hebrew tradition, and some of this is made very clear in *Glas*. It is a point made by Susan Handelman, and I wish to expand upon this point here in my own way, because the issue involved is very close to those issues we have already encountered in Milton.[16]

In *Glas*, Derrida considers the texts of Hegel, as we have mentioned in earlier chapters, a Hegel concerned with the family, and it is while considering these Hegelian texts that Derrida breaks into a discourse on Jewish culture, since he takes up Hegel's criticism that Jews are incapable of loving, that they are blind and are cut off from the truth. For Derrida, the criticism is turned upon itself once one understands it in terms of the problematic of symbolic castration with all of its Freudian resonances. Derrida writes:

Le Juif opère (sur) lui-même un simulacre de castration pour marquer son propre, sa propriété, son nom, fonder la loi qu'il subira pour l'imposer aux autres et se constituer en esclave favori de la puissance infinie. En entamant son gland, il se défend d'avance contre la menace infinie, châtre à son tour l'ennemi, élabore une sorte d'apotropaïque sans mesure. Il exhibe sa castration comme une érection qui met l'autre au défi.¹⁷

("The Jew operates (on) himself a simulacrum of castration in order to mark what is his own, his property [propriety, ownership], his name, founding the law to which he will submit in order to impose it on others and to constitute himself as the favorite bondsman of an infinite power. By way of cutting his penis, he defends himself in advance against an infinite menace, castrates the enemy in his turn and elaborates a sort of the apotropaic which is without measure. He exhibits his castration as an erection which serves as a challenge to the other.")

In this passage castration is taken somewhat metaphorically, for Derrida stresses that it is upon himself that the Jew produces an imitation of castration. That is, we are really talking about the circumcision as a representation of castration. Through the rite of circumcision, the Jew symbolically castrates himself in order that he can have the power of a Medusa, of a woman, which is the power, Freud tells us in the note on Medusa, to instill fear in one's enemies by raising or elevating the trauma of castration, a trauma the Jew overcomes by submitting himself willingly to it. In a textual context this means that *Glas* symbolically mutilates itself, submits to a "blessure" (wounding which gives way to power unequaled by other texts).

In the column on Genet, Derrida calls this exhibition of the castration an erection that places the other on the defensive, that gives him the challenge, the *anthérection*. "L'érection [qui] ne se produit qu'en abyme" ("the erection [which] only produces itself in the abyss").¹⁸ Yet we have to ask what this signifies in terms of the logocentric, onto-encyclopedic ideology of books, of texts. It means, as we have seen in this chapter, that the poet flaunts his blindness, his woundedness, but in doing so flaunts his superiority, his compensatory insight. It means one metaphorically embalms the presence of the living word, that one reveals the book as a necropolis of signs and, in the very act of asserting its death, assures its perpetuation, its afterlife which is now an undecidable, neither fully dead nor fully alive. In one sense, castratedness is a ruse, even if it is not a lie, because it is through mutilation that one gains access to a "POTENCE du texte." Derrida explains how this is so in *Glas* when he meditates on his own text, which is divided in two, which is a double session or scene:

Si j'écris deux textes à la fois, vous ne pourrez pas me châtrer. Si je délinéarise, j'érige. Mais en même temps, je divise mon acte et mon désir. Je—marque la division et vous échappant toujours, je simule sans cesse et ne jouis nulle part. Je me châtre moi-même—je me reste ainsi—et je "joue à jouir."[19]

("If I write two texts at the same time, you will not be able to castrate me. If I de-lineate, I erect [exalt, establish, raise up, elevate]. But at the same time, I divide my act and my desire. I—mark the division and, always escaping you, I simulate without cease and come nowhere. I castrate myself—I thus remain myself—and I 'play at coming.'")

It is because the poet is willing to geld himself that no one else can castrate him or rob him. My text is already castrated, Derrida says; therefore, you cannot harm me. You cannot go to my text and attack its meaning, its presence, its author, its ideas, or thoughts. There is no locus that you can attack, no center you can debunk, no place where you can go to mount your offensive. If "I" de-lineate (erect columns and tear them down, write in two columns), "I get a rise out of it," Derrida insists. But at the same time, "I" divide my acts and my desires, which is to say the "I" never gets to participate in what it is saying, since the event of castration makes the realization of the presence of the author in the text, that free play of signs, impossible. The "I" never gets to erect itself in the text, for the "I" has cut itself off. "I" am impotent; therefore, my text is virile. But conversely, my text is cut up, gelded; therefore, "I" am still standing erect and intact. With Derrida this contradiction maintains itself in a suspended relation throughout *Glas*.

We have seen that Derrida's strategy in *Glas* is related in the column on Hegel to the Hebrews who practice the simulacrum of castration, circumcision, in order to frighten off their enemies. Again the logic is similar. The Hebrews are already castrated, so what greater harm can befall them? How can they be unmanned? If the phallus is gelded, the "I" is still standing erect. Yet, if the mark terrifies the enemy, if it is virile, that means the "I" is less than powerful. For Derrida, this economics of castration is the economics of the Hebraic text, the economics of the Jewish thinker whose thought is always flawed, illegitimate, dangerous, divisive, deconstructive. Derrida himself is such a thinker, as Philippe Boyer in "Le point de la question" shows:

> Hasn't Judaism left its mark as a subversive force of separation and of rupture in Marx, Freud, or Einstein? . . . We find in them the same work of separation and of cutting—a work within separation and within cutting—this same double articulation of tradition and of narration (or fiction), and even more generally still of a reference and of a loss, of a residence and of an exile where one finds them again just today, provided one takes the time to read them, in those works already evoked by Blanchot, Jabès, Derrida, and Levinas.[20]

What Boyer cites as the rupture is in *Glas* radicalized in terms of castration, which Derrida relates to the thought of Freud, a modern Jewish hero, and, as we see in the passage above from the Hegel column, to the Hebraic tradition as a whole.

Milton, it could be argued, is not only aware that such a Hebraic tradition exists but, himself a Christian, identifies with this tradition in somewhat the same way that Derrida as a Jewish thinker wishes to establish certain connections with it when he writes on Jabès, Levinas, Freud, and the ancient Hebrews. Protestants of the seventeenth century like Milton, of course, were very anxious to make ties with the Hebrews of the Old Testament, because they wanted to show that they were, indeed, the remnant of the chosen people, a remnant that did not, as the Roman Catholics did, worship idols. If one reads the works of William Perkins, William Ames, Abraham Darcie, Alexander Gil, and countless other Protestant treatises on theology, of which Milton's *Christian Doctrine* is but one, that were written during the seventeenth century, one quickly perceives that central to each document is the insistence on defetishizing the sacraments, on defetishizing Christ, on defetishizing the Scriptures. Zwingli began this Protestant labor of defetishization when he suggested that when Christ says, "This is my body," the disciples were to understand that the bread was not literally Christ's body, but only a metaphor for it. In other words, Zwingli suggested that there was a rupture, or *coupure*, in the Scriptures, or, to be more precise, in the language of Christ himself.[21] To say that something is is not to make a literal identification, even when it is Christ who is the one being identified or represented in terms of something else.

My argument is that Milton not only emphasizes this rupture in his verse but that he does so in terms of the thematic of wounding, cutting, castration, and blinding. What Derrida has termed the simulacrum of castration, a simulacrum practiced by the Hebrews, is directly addressed by Milton in his poem "Upon the Circumcision." Like the "Nativity Ode," this poem celebrates the coming of Christ into the world. However, unlike the ode, "Upon the Circumcision" is slightly more elegiac and stresses the equation *circumcision = wound = smart = crucifixion*. As in the ode, however, Christ is seen in "Upon the Circumcision" in terms of a self-emptying, or *kenosis*. The final lines reinforce this thematic of sacrifice when Milton states that Christ

> seals obedience first with wounding smart
> This day; but Oh! ere long
> Huge pangs and strong
> Will pierce more near his heart.

The Christian context for a Derridean theory of symbolic castration could not be much stronger, given Milton's seventeenth-century background and training in the Christian tradition. Milton is aware, it seems to me, that Christ's strength is inscribed in the simulacrum for castration, circumcision, the "wounding smart," which is identified as a sign or type for the Crucifixion itself. This "smart" is what is said to seal obedience; it marks Christ's commitment, even as an infant, to suffering and pain which in manhood will be enacted in another scene of cutting and wounding, the Crucifixion. Like the Hebrews that Derrida describes in *Glas*, Christ subjects himself to a painful humiliation which turns out to be the seal of his superiority, his divinity. Like the author of *Glas*, the Christ willingly subjects himself to a sacrificial scene of cutting, of torture, in order that no one will henceforth be able to attack him, to mutilate him. Thus the Christ is always already mutilated (*kenosis:* "self-emptying, crucifixion, circumcision"), metaphorically castrated. And he is, therefore, untouchable. But like the author of *Glas*, the God, Christ, is always out of the picture, so to speak. He is never really on earth in the fullest sense of the word. For Christ has come here only by means of laying aside his divinity. If such symbolic castration is powerful, as Milton suggests, it is also a signification of a limit, a sign where a God's power ends, where it cannot go.

As in *Glas*, the thematic of castration in "Upon the Circumcision" affects the form of the poem itself, since it is prematurely cut off at the end, clipped, as Tillyard mentions in his *Milton*. "There is something very unsatisfactory in a poem consisting of two stanzas of equal length. A third stanza is needed; or if there are two divisions only, they should be of equal length."[22] Admittedly, it is hard to refute criticism like this on its own grounds, and yet it is easy to agree with Tillyard that there is something unnaturally abrupt about the end. It is not that the stanzas are not balanced well, or not numerous enough, but that Milton prepares us for an event that never takes place in the poem: crucifixion. He mentions it, but does not dramatize it or describe it much. And yet this is a poem, curiously enough, about Christ's great sacrifice, which is only adumbrated in the marginal ritual of circumcision. One wonders why even the sacrifice is sacrificed, finally. Why does it not present itself? We wonder how Milton can leave us in what seems mid-sentence. "Huge pangs and strong / Will pierce more near his heart." One expects the poem to continue, but it does not. We only witness the pangs, not the nails, not the thorns, not the loss of blood on the cross. We are never told what the pangs are, or what is causing them. Pain? Despair? Sadness? Perhaps the poem stops abruptly in order to reinforce the manner in which the word is placed in ex-communication, the manner in which it is symbolically castrated or put to the death. In "Upon the Circumcision" the text itself is forced to suffer the wound (*blessure*), the crucifixion of Christ, that blessing of the text which can only end abruptly and violently. As in *Glas,* one has the simulacrum of castration not only in terms of circumcision but in terms of the mutilated text as well.

The wounded or mutilated text is, Walter Benjamin tells us, characteristic of seventeenth-century Protestant poets and dramatists. Such a text in Benjamin is termed *Allegorie.* In Derrida this is translated in terms of what he calls *écriture:* writing as an aphoristic force. Rupture, castration, *thanatopraxie:* these are the metaphors that trace the relays of *écriture,* which Derrida in "Tors" has appropriately termed the "crypt," the tomb that is also a script, a writing inscribed within the economics of death.[23] In this study I have concentrated on the theatrical representations, as Derrida might call them, of the crypt, and have attempted to show how such a crypt reveals itself in terms of a table of synonyms: castration, blindness, fall, death, *Allegorie, écriture, anthérection, langage mineure, thanatopraxie.* But to suggest that Milton's writing is, in fact, a species of *écriture,* what Derrida has more recently called a "cryptonomie," is only the first stage of a much longer investigation that must eventually decryptify Milton's crypts in ways that take us beyond mere theatrical representations, beyond a terminology, such as I have presented it here. What is needed is a conversion from themaphor to alloseme, a conversion from a discourse that considers the metaphoric displacements created to describe a complex, such as the complex related to rupturing, to a discourse that traces the isomeric variations of a signifier (the alloseme) through a table, or "verbier," of metonymic displacements and deformations, a table that does not metaphorically thematize or represent any complex or constellation but metonymically slides over all signifieds. This discourse, Nicolas Abraham has called *cryptonomie*, an *écriture* unmoored from the metaphysics of presence, a *thanatopraxie* of sound which is everywhere haunted by a returning voice, a deconstructive ricorso of sorts.

NOTES

Introduction

1. Lord Macaulay, *An Essay on Milton* (New York: American Book Company, 1894), p. 46.
2. Ibid., p. 45.
3. "We often hear of the magical influence of poetry. The expression in general means nothing; but, applied to the writings of Milton, it is most appropriate. Its merit lies less in its obvious meaning than in its occult power." Ibid., p. 33. Also see Winfried Menninghaus, *Walter Benjamins Theorie der Sprachmagie* (Frankfort on the Main: Suhrkamp, 1980).
4. Jacques Derrida, *L'écriture et la différence* (Paris: Seuil, 1967), p. 34. The English translation is by Alan Bass: *Writing and Difference* (Chicago: University of Chicago Press, 1978), pp. 19–20.
5. Bass, trans., *Writing and Difference*, by Derrida, p. 305.
6. Geoffrey Hartman, *Saving the Text* (Baltimore, Md.: Johns Hopkins University Press, 1981); Louis Martz, *Poet of Exile* (New Haven, Conn.: Yale University Press, 1980), pp. 64–65; Jacques Derrida, *Glas* (Paris: Galilée, 1974), p. 7a.
7. Jean-Luc Nancy, *Le discours de la syncope* (Paris: Aubier-Flammarion, 1976), p. 7. "Cette transsubstantiation est inévitable (et c'est aussi pourquoi cette digression s'imposait . . .): cette conversion est prescrite dans l'économie même des tout premiers discours qui avancent ces index, et pas seulement dans les répétitions ou les pillages des épigones."

Chapter One

1. T. S. Eliot, *On Poetry and Poets* (New York: Farrar, Straus and Giroux, 1961), pp. 159, 161, 162, 175 (emphasis added).

2. See Jacques Derrida, "La pharmacie de Platon," *La dissémination* (Paris: Seuil, 1972), pp. 71–197. It suffices, Derrida says, to lend systematic attention to the "permanence d'un schème platonicien qui assigne l'origine et le pouvoir de la parole, précisément du *logos*, à la position paternelle" ("permanence of a platonic scheme which assigns the origin and power of speech precisely of the logos, to the paternal position") (p. 86). Opposed to this is the son, "le fils perdu" ("the lost son"), who writes that "le père n'est pas, c'est à dire n'est pas présent" ("the father is not, that is to say, is not present") (p. 169). Unlike Lacan, Derrida finds this family squabble between father and son as but another bit of foolishness in the history of metaphysics. (The degree to which this family romance is important in Derrida's later writings is clear in the "legs" of Freud [that is, his legacy], which Derrida considers at length in *La carte postale* [Paris: Aubier-Flammarion, 1980].) For the Derrida of *La dissémination*, "L'écriture et la parole sont donc maintenant deux sortes de trace, deux valeurs de la trace" ("writing and speech are then two sorts of trace, two valorizations of the trace") (p. 176). The question of paternity is nothing other than the space that gives rise to difference, to value, to the possibility of an economy of signification. Only in this sense is it to be taken seriously.

3. See Jacques Derrida, *De la grammatologie* (Paris: Minuit, 1967), pp. 15–41, in which the concept of the book as a summa or logocentric totality of signs incarnating spirit is placed in jeopardy by "writing" or "style," what Derrida calls *écriture*. For Derrida the concept of *écriture* describes an economics of signification that destructures the closed form of the book by introducing certain "undecidables" or "liminal structures" that frustrate metaphysical determinacy: limits, centers, meanings, binary oppositions. According to Derrida, the binary opposition of a living sign to a dead sign is always frustrated by the notion of the "trace," a liminal term that insists upon what Jacques Lacan calls "le fading," the fact that presence is always deferred, is always where we are not, "échappant" or escaping the sign.

4. Stéphane Mallarmé, *Selected Prose*, trans. Bradford Cook (Baltimore, Md.: Johns Hopkins University Press, 1959), p. 40; Michel Foucault, *The Order of Things* (New York: Random House, 1974), p. 306 (translation of *Les mots et les choses*).

5. The word *shifter* was originally a term introduced by Otto Jespersen, but used later by Roman Jakobson in order to describe in what way a pronoun like *I* is merely a "formal indicator" determined by language, not the ego of man, the self. See "Les embrayeurs, les catégories verbales et le verbe russe," *Essais de linguis-*

tique générale I: les fondements du langage (Paris: Seuil, 1963), pp. 167–96.

6. Eliot, *On Poetry and Poets*, p. 175; Mallarmé *Selected Writings*, p. 38.

7. "On sait maintenant que l'être du langage est le visible effacement de celui qui parle." Michel Foucault, "La pensée du dehors," in *Critique*, no. 229 (1966), p. 543.

8. Eliot, *On Poetry and Poets*, pp. 156, 157.

9. Eliot's protests are again echoed in Christopher Ricks's *Milton's Grand Style* (London: Oxford University Press, 1963), pp. 47–57. Here too there is the charge that Milton transgresses the concept of a "living text," that he is inferior to Shakespeare, because he is deaf to idioms, living metaphors, qualities of speech. For Ricks the text should ideally be a "living tissue" or organism that preserves life in all of its parts. And it is this notion that is fundamental to the "metaphysics of the book." To quote Derrida, "L'idée du livre, qui renvoie toujours à une totalité naturelle, est profondément étrangère au sens de l'écriture. Elle est la protection encyclopédique de la théologie et du logocentrisme contre la disruption de l'écriture." ("The idea of the book, which always refers to a natural totality, is profoundly alien to the sense of writing. It is the encyclopedic protection of theology and of logocentrism against the disruption of writing.") See *De la grammatologie*, pp. 30–31; and the English translation: *Of Grammatology*, trans. Gayatri Chakravorty Spivak (Baltimore, Md.: Johns Hopkins University Press, 1976), p. 18.

10. Harold Bloom, *A Map of Misreading* (New York: Oxford University Press, 1975), p. 125.

11. Christopher Grose in *Milton's Epic Process* (New Haven, Conn.: Yale University Press, 1973) stresses Milton's iconoclasm when he says, "As Milton's writing frequently suggests, the trouble with images was their tendency to become self-sufficient, their almost corpuscular discreetness as 'things'" (p. 18). Grose suggests that Milton was sensitive to the possibility of a text that could invite "irrational admiration," that might lead to a "literary form of worship or even idolatry," the type of thing Roland Barthes flaunts in *Le plaisir du texte* (Paris: Seuil, 1973) (*The Pleasure of the Text*, trans. Richard Miller [New York: Hill and Wang, 1975]). Milton's desire was to defetishize the image, to empty words of their corporeality, their *parousia*, which to Milton was but an illusion to begin with. (This interpretation complicates a Marxist approach to Milton, which would attempt to show via Benjamin that Milton's words are subject to a certain commodification. See Chapter 2, n. 11). Also see Christopher Hill's *Milton and the English*

Revolution (Middlesex: Penguin, 1979), pp. 171–81, for a more political reading of Milton's iconoclasm.

12. Derrida, *Glas*, p. 223b.

13. Ibid., p. 100b.

14. See Maria Ruegg, "Metaphor and Metonymy: The Logic of Structuralist Rhetoric," *Glyph 6* (Baltimore, M.D.: Johns Hopkins University Press, 1979): 141–57. "Despite their repeated insistence that the new theoretical age—inaugurated by Saussurian linguistics, Freudian analysis, Nietzschean 'symptomology' and Mallarméan poetics—constituted a 'radical epistemological rupture' with the 'pre-scientific' past, a large number of structuralists were, at the same time, strangely attracted to the antiquated, elaborately constructed systems of tropes and figures offered by classical manuals of rhetoric, from Quintillian to Fontanier" (p. 141). Ruegg points out that structuralists like Roman Jakobson and poststructuralists like Jacques Lacan are highly classical in their approach to critical theory and, moreover, prescientific in their outlooks, which are, for the most part, difficult to defend. This is particularly true, Ruegg feels, of the metaphor-metonymy distinction, whose classical difference both Jakobson and Lacan try to negotiate. Those who side with the Jakobsonian point of view argue that in fact Jakobson does not attempt to maintain any clear distinction between such classical terms and that Ruegg's complaints depend upon a very overreductive reading of what is at issue. Nevertheless, no one can deny the importance, perhaps even the priority, that classical thought has for such postmodern figures as Jakobson, Lacan, Derrida, Irigaray, and Serres.

15. That the rhetorical tradition in the Renaissance is essentially one that praises the blending of poetry with argument, beautiful tropes with sententiae, and reason with lyricism is clear in texts such as the following of Niccolo degli Oddi: "And now as to the rest, what Latin or Italian poem is richer in precepts, more copious in reasons, more pregnant with beautiful sententiae, more abundant in figures, painted with more lovely words, more full of the purest passions, gayer in most beautiful sayings, graver in mature arguments? With these things it frequently passes through our feelings, arousing anger, awakening pride, inflaming love, spurring hatred, making envy grow pale, tinging shame and humiliating pity, just as it pleases." Of this passage from the *Dialogo in difesa di Camillo Pellegrini contra gli Academici della Crusca*, Bernard Weinberg comments, "Both the methods employed here—the isolation of the particular rhetorical device and the indication of the particular passions aroused—fall completely within a critical tradition which is concerned neither with poetic form nor with the

special effects produced by the poetic form." That is to say, for Weinberg it is strange to conceive of an approach to poetry, in this case that of Tasso, which is so aware of "rhetorical" concerns, which wants to cross philosophy with poetry, argument with lyric. Oddi's quotation and Weinberg's comment appear in Bernard Weinberg, *A History of Literary Criticism in the Italian Renaissance*, vol. 2 (Chicago: University of Chicago Press, 1961), p. 1034.

16. See Marjorie Perloff, *The Poetics of Indeterminacy* (Princeton, N.J.: Princeton University Press, 1981), p. 17.

Chapter Two

1. Walter Benjamin, *Ursprung des deutschen Trauerspiels, Gesammelte Schriften* (Frankfort on the Main: Suhrkamp, 1974), vol. 1, no. 1, p. 343. Translation by John Osborne, *The Origin of German Tragic Drama* (London: New Left Books, 1977), p. 166.

2. Paul de Man, "The Rhetoric of Temporality," in *Interpretation: Theory and Practice*, ed. C. S. Singleton (Baltimore, Md.: Johns Hopkins University Press, 1969).

3. Benjamin, *Ursprung des deutschen Trauerspiels*, p. 343.

4. Michael Murrin, *The Veil of Allegory* (Chicago: University of Chicago Press, 1969), p. 8. Also see pp. 3–20.

5. *The Oxford English Dictionary* defines the word *portent* with the analogues "sign," "omen," "monster," "marvelous tale." A "portent" is "that which portends or foretells something momentous about to happen, esp. of a calamitous nature; an omen, significant sign or token." Example: "1671, Milton, *P.R.* 4. 491. 'As false portents not sent from God, but thee.'"

6. To the fallen reader, this negative meaning of "portentous" as an omen of ill is uppermost, since he, unlike the innocent angels, is painfully aware of what the wages of sin is, and in the passage above experiences dramatic irony as he sees the angels perplexed before what he already knows is a portent of evil to come.

7. Gilles Deleuze, *Proust and Signs*, trans. Richard Howard (New York: Braziller, 1972), pp. 93–157.

8. Sigmund Freud, "Mourning and Melancholy," *The Standard Edition of the Complete Works*, ed. and trans. James Strachey, Anna Freud, Alix Strachey, and Alan Tyson (London: Hogarth Press and Institute of Psychoanalysis, 1953–74), 17:245. "Aber die freie Libido nicht auf ein anderes Objekt verschoben, sondern ins Ich zurückgezogen. Dort fand sie aber nicht eine beliebige Verwendung, sondern diente dazu, eine *Identifizierung* des Ichs mit dem aufgegebenen Objekt herzustellen. Der Schatten des Objekts fiel so

auf das Ich, welches nun von einer besonderen Instanz wie ein Objekt, wie das verlassene Objekt, beurteilt werden konnte. Auf diese Weise hatte sich der Objektverlust in einen Ichverlust verwandelt, der Konflikt zwischen dem Ich und der geliebten Person in einen Zwiespalt zwischen der Ichkritik und dem durch Identifizierung veränderten Ich." ("Trauer und Melancholie," *Gesammelte Werke*, vol. 10. [Frankfort on the Main: S. Fischer Verlag, 1946], p. 435.)

9. Freud, "Mourning and Melancholy," *Complete Works*, 17:245.

10. Benjamin, *Ursprung des deutschen Trauerspiels*, p. 339.

11. On "Schriftcharakter der Allegorie," see ibid., p. 359. Fredric Jameson, *Marxism and Form* (Princeton, N.J.: Princeton University Press, 1971), p. 72. Jameson's argument that this notion of allegory represents a "pathology" of the modern world is most intriguing and points out indirectly the important affinity Milton has with modern writers like Derrida who take up "script," or "écriture," in works like *Glas* in order to expose this "pathology."

Terry Eagleton in *Walter Benjamin* (London: New Left Books, 1981) develops an interesting hybrid reading of Benjamin in which Derrida and Lacan are very influential figures, extending some of Jameson's earlier leads. Also, Eagleton's reading of Milton within the Benjaminian perspective is congruent with the approach I have taken in this chapter, though where Eagleton differs from me is in his consideration of the commodification of the sign, the materialism of the signifier, a topic which receives much more treatment in England than it does in America or on the Continent. It is interesting that Eagleton does not wish to employ Lukács's perspectives in *Theory of the Novel* (trans. Anna Bostock [Cambridge, Mass.: M.I.T. Press, 1971]) to explore the relations better between commodification and consciousness at a time when the bourgeoisie is coming into its own and epic forms, from Lukács's line of thinking, are possible no longer as such, but only as modalities of middle-class tragedy, such as a domestic falling out in a prelapsarian garden.

12. Herbert Heckmann, *Elemente des barocken Trauerspiels: Am Beispiel des "Papinian" von Andreas Gryphius* (Darmstadt: H. Gentner Verlag, 1959).

My thesis that Milton's epic is fundamentally close to the *Trauerspiel* tradition ("The Uncouth Swain: A Post-Structuralist Reading of Milton" [Ph.D. diss., University of California at Irvine, 1978]) differs considerably from the dramatic studies of *Paradise Lost* that have been advanced by other Miltonists. Closest to this approach is Frank Kastor's *Milton and the Literary Satan* (Amsterdam, 1974) which surveys "sacred representations" such as Giambattista Andreini's *L'Adamo* and Joost van den Vondel's *Lucifer* in order to study the figure of Milton's Satan and its literary origins. Helen Gardner in *A Reading of "Paradise Lost"* (New York: Oxford, 1965) sees the epic as an extended drama which centers on the Fall; and John M. Steadman in *Epic and Tragic Structure in "Paradise Lost"* (Chicago: University of Chicago Press, 1976) develops Gardner's points by way of situating Milton's theatrical heritage in Italian tradition and the Aristotelian tragic model outlined in the *Poetics*. More interesting is John G. Demaray's well-documented *Milton's Theatrical Epic* (Cambridge, Mass.: Harvard University Press, 1980), which also turns mainly to Italian tradition in order to situate Milton's scenic devices. What concerns Demaray is the question of spectacle, and this leads him seriously to consider a kind of drama close in spirit to the *Trauerspiel:* the "sacra rappresentazione." Needed now is a better understanding of how the kinds of theatrical representations which depend largely upon emblematic visual devices, representations which are not simply masques, relate to German tragic drama of the period, especially in light of Benjamin's theories. Again, Terry Eagleton in *Walter Benjamin*, like some other Marxist critics, has been interested in applying Benjamin's theories to poets of the seventeenth century, and, in particular, Milton. For him the interest is mainly semiotic, however, and he does not really advance any kind of interpretation of Milton based on what Benjamin has to say, except a broad social theory which relates the rise of the commodity in the West. In this way, Eagleton makes his link with problematics related to Charles Baudelaire, a writer Benjamin also studied in detail with regard to some issues which can be traced back to his study on the baroque period.

13. Fredric Jameson, *Marxism and Form*, p. 61.

14. Benjamin, *Gesammelte Schriften*, vol. 1, no. 3, p. 938. This quotation comes from Benjamin's manuscript of the introduction to *Ursprung* (bracketed emendations supplied by editors). The final version is far more compressed:

"Das adamitische Namengeben ist so weit entfernt Spiel und Willkür zu sein, dass vielmehr gerade in ihm der paradiesische Stand sich als solcher bestätigt, der mit der mitteilenden Bedeutung der Worte noch nicht zu ringen hatte. Wie die Ideen intentionslos im Benennen sich geben, so haben sie in philosophischer Kontemplation sich zu erneuern. In dieser Erneuerung stellt das ursprüngliche Vernehmen der Worte sich wieder her. Und so ist die Philosophie im Verlauf ihrer Geschichte" (vol. 1, no. 1, p. 217).

15. Paul Ricoeur, "Religion, Atheism, and Faith," in *The Re-*

ligious Significance of Atheism, by Paul Ricoeur and Alasdair MacIntyre (New York: Columbia University Press, 1969), p. 94.

16. Benjamin, *Ursprung des deutschen Trauerspiels*, p. 352.

17. Benjamin, "Das Kunstwerk im Zeitalter seiner technischen Reproduzierbarkeit," *Gesammelte Schriften*, vol. 1, no. 1, pp. 431–71.

Chapter Three

1. Jean Genet, *The Thief's Journal*, trans. Bernard Frechtman (New York: Grove Press, Inc. 1964), p. 9.

2. See Jacques Derrida, *La dissémination* (Paris: Seuil, 1972).

3. In *A Dictionary of Puns in Milton's English Poetry* (New York: Columbia University Press, 1981), Edward Le Comte misses this rather crucial pun altogether.

4. Ibid., p. 115.

5. Donald F. Bouchard, *Milton: A Structural Reading* (London: Edward Arnold, 1974).

6. Derrida, *La dissémination*, p. 240.

7. Derrida, "La mythologie blanche," in *Marges de la philosophie* (Paris: Minuit, 1972), p. 308.

8. See Millicent Bell, "The Fallacy of the Fall in *Paradise Lost*," *PMLA* 68 (1953): 863–83. Also of importance is Wayne Shumaker's response to Bell in "Notes, Documents, and Critical Comment: The Fallacy of the Fall in *Paradise Lost*," *PMLA* 70 (1955): 1185–87. Texts which are relevant to the debate are Douglas Bush, *Paradise Lost in Our Time* (Ithaca, N.Y.: Cornell University Press, 1945); A. J. A. Waldock, *Paradise Lost and Its Critics* (London: Cambridge University Press, 1947); and E. M. W. Tillyard, "The Crisis of *Paradise Lost*," *Studies in Milton* (London: Collier, 1951).

9. Quoted by Bell in response to Shumaker in "Notes, Documents, and Critical Comment," *PMLA* 70 (1955): 1194. According to Bell, the extended passage to which the above quotation belongs "entered the bloodstream of Western thought and flowed" in Milton's veins (p. 1195).

10. Stanley Fish, *Surprised by Sin* (Berkeley: University of California Press, 1971), p. 136.

11. Sigurd Burckhardt, *Shakespearean Meanings* (Princeton, N.J.: Princeton University Press, 1968), pp. 22–46. Also see Murray Krieger, *Theory of Criticism* (Baltimore, Md.: Johns Hopkins University Press, 1976), pp. 17–22.

12. In *Seven Types of Ambiguity* (New York: New Directions,

1947), William Empson goes so far as to cite Freud in order to show how the seventh type of ambiguity is a function of the poet's unconscious "desire" to bring two conflicting systems of judgment into reconciliation, "exhausting satisfaction." Here Empson's stress on a kind of textual "jouissance" which satisfies the "desire" of the poet, and vicariously the reader as well, is part of a process that "could pierce to regions that underlie the whole structure of our thought: could tap the energies of the very depths of mind." In other words, "ambiguity" is the key that unlocks the mystery of the origin of thought. It is the trope within which is contained truth, the signified, the origin of thought. That is to say, for Empson ambiguity, or confusion of opposites, is merely an appearance or effect produced by levels of consciousness that are "wishing" for unification, for the reconciliation of opposites, of different desires which all demand gratification at the same time. Clearly, Empson sees even his most violent type of ambiguity, the ambiguity of contradiction, to be an effect of a totalizing, logocentric drive that asserts its will to power at the expense of what the New Critics valorize in terms of the "aesthetic." See ibid., p. 224.

13. Francis Ponge, *Le parti pris des choses*, ed. Ian Higgins (London: Athalone, 1979), p. 70; *The Voice of Things*, trans. Beth Archer (New York: McGraw-Hill, 1972) p. 66.

14. Georges Bataille, *Oeuvres complètes*, 9 vols. to date (Paris: Gallimard, 1976—).

15. Ibid., "L'economie à la mesure de l'univers," 7:12.

16. Ibid., "Sacrifices," 1:89. "*Moi*, j'existe,—suspendu dans un vide réalisé—suspendu à ma propre angoisse—différent de tout autre être et tel que les divers événements qui peuvent atteindre tout autre et non *moi* rejettent cruellement ce *moi* hors d'une existence totale. Mais, en même temps, je considère ma venue au monde—qui a dépendu de la naissance et de la conjonction de tel homme et de telle femme, puis du moment de cette conjonction—il existe en effet un moment unique en rapport avec la possibilité de moi—et ainsi apparaît l'improbabilité infinie de cette venue au monde."

17. Ibid., 1:89–90. "L'improbabilité totale de ma venue au monde pose sur un mode impératif une hétérogénéité totale."

18. Ibid., 1:93. "Le moi s'élevant à l'impératif pur, vivant-mourant pour un abîme sans paroi et sans fond, cet impératif se formule 'meurs comme un chien' dans la partie la plus étrange de l'être."

19. See Maurice Blanchot, *L'arrêt de mort* (Paris: Gallimard, 1948), and Derrida's working over this pun in "Living On: Border

Lines," *Deconstruction and Criticism*, ed. Geoffrey Hartman (New York: Seabury, 1979). In "Living On: Border Lines," Derrida's indebtedness to both Blanchot's and Bataille's critical perspectives becomes of major interest with respect to *Glas* and the earlier essays, in which that filiation does not appear so prominently, particularly with respect to the idea of the suspension which informs so much of Blanchot and Bataille's thinking.

20. Alastair Fowler, ed., *Paradise Lost*, by John Milton (London: Longman, 1968), p. 482.

21. Derrida, *La dissémination*, p. 238; *Dissemination*, trans. Barbara Johnson (Chicago: University of Chicago Press, 1981), p. 210.

22. Derrida, *La dissémination*, p. 239; *Dissemination*, trans. Johnson, p. 210–11.

23. T. S. Eliot, *On Poetry and Poets* (New York: Farrar, Straus and Giroux, 1961), p. 162.

24. Sanford Ames, "Killer Bees: An Ontology in Abeyance," *Visible Language* 14 no. 3 (1980): 241–49.

25. Jacques Lacan, *Écrits* (Paris: Seuil, 1966), pp. 408, 411; my translation is based on that in *Ecrits*, trans. Alan Sheridan (New York: Norton, 1977), pp. 121, 123.

26. Louis Marin, *Le portrait du roi* (Paris: Minuit, 1981). Essentially, the précis I give from Marin's work is a distillation of an argument one sees in works like *Le portrait du roi* as well as in his other numerous works on visibility and painting. See *Détruire la peinture* (Paris: Galilée, 1977) and *Le récit est un piège* (Paris: Minuit, 1978).

27. For a discussion of Descartes in this respect, see Jean-Luc Nancy, *Ego Sum* (Paris: Flammarion, 1979), pp. 63–94.

28. Michel Foucault, *The Order of Things* (New York: Vintage, 1970), p. 5; see also *Les mots et les choses* (Paris: Gallimard, 1966), pp. 20–21. ("Nul regard n'est stable, ou plutôt, dans le sillon neutre du regard qui transperce la toile à la perpendiculaire, le sujet et l'objet, le spectateur et le modèle inversent leur rôle à l'infini. . . . obstinément invisible, elle empêche que soit jamais repérable ni définitivement établi le rapport des regards.")

29. Both Edgar Wind in *Pagan Mysteries in the Renaissance* (New York: Norton, 1968), and Charles Dempsey in "Mercurius Ver: The Sources of Botticelli's Primavera," *Journal of the Warburg and Courtauld Institutes* 31 (1968): 251–73, note this reference in Ovid.

30. Jan Kott, *Shakespeare Our Contemporary* (New York: Doubleday, 1964), p. 301.

31. Ibid., pp. 287–342.

32. Derrida, *Marges de la philosophie* (Paris: Édition de Minuit, 1972), p. 130.

Chapter Four

1. Sigmund Freud, "Analysis Terminable and Interminable," trans. Joan Rivière, *International Journal of Psychoanalysis* 18 (1937): 380. *The Standard Edition of the Complete Works*, ed. and trans. James Strachey, Anna Freud, Alix Strachey, and Alan Tyson (London: Hogarth Press and Institute of Psychoanalysis, 1953–74), 23:222, uses the word "topic" instead of "theme." Freud's German expression is "Thema" (*Gesammelte Werke*, vol. 16 [London: Imago, 1950], p. 67).
2. The Derridean problematics are taken largely from *Glas* and the Lacanian perspectives can be found throughout the *Écrits*, but mainly in the "Purloined Letter" essay that initiates that collection. Derrida and Lacan, of course, have very different views on the question of the castration complex. However, as I have tried to show in my article, "Lacan Disbarred: Translation as Ellipsis," *Diacritics* 6, no. 4 (Winter 1976), Lacan and Derrida are very compatible on the issue of what Lacan would term *béance*, and many of Derrida's ideas are in some way indebted to Lacan's earlier formulations concerning gaps which are undecidable, not the least of which is that of castration: *coupure, écart*.
3. Jacques Derrida, *Glas* (Paris: Galilée, 1974), p. 223b. A modern French reader will think of *potence* primarily in its meaning as "gallows." But the structure of the sentence will also suggest the word "potency," which in Old French was the meaning for *potence*.
4. Jacques Lacan, *Écrits* (Paris: Seuil, 1966), pp. 11–61.
5. Derrida, *Glas*, p. 80b.
6. Derrida, *Glas*, p. 157b. Translation by Gayatri Spivak in "Glas-Piece," *Diacritics*, September 1977, p. 29. "*Anth:* Often in Mod. Scientific words, written analytically anti-" (*Oxford English Dictionary*). Anther: "Bot. a mod. Fr. *anthère*, and mod. L. *anthēra*, in cl. L. 'a medicine extracted from flowers.' a. Gr. [anthera], fem. of [antheros] flowery, f. [anthe-] ([anthos]) flower. As these medicines often consisted of the internal organs of flowers (*e.g.* saffron, one of the chief *anthērae* was the stigma), the name *anthēra* was specially applied by the early pharmacists to these parts, and at length confined by the herbalists, c. 1700, to the pollen-bearing organ."

Derrida uses the word, *anthérection* in the sense of an "antierection," except that by "anti-" we should not simply think of the opposite of erect. The floral associations are important here, for they suggest that the cutting of that which is erect, the cutting of stems, for example, results in exfoliation. The pharmaceutical references also tip us off to the fact that Derrida may be thinking that the word *anthérection* should recall his previous use of *pharmacie* in his essay on Plato in *La dissémination* (Paris: Seuil, 1972). That is, like the *pharmacie* of remedies and poisons operative in Plato's texts, one has a similar *pharmacie* of flowers, of erections, in *Glas*. What this latter *pharmacie* proves is that the binary opposition potency-impotency is deconstructed through a careful reading of Genet's dramas and novels.

7. Derrida, *Glas*, p. 156b.

8. Derrida, *La dissémination* (Paris: Seuil, 1972). See particularly the essay on Philippe Sollers entitled "La dissémination." We have already touched on this subject in Chapter 1, in which I discussed T. S. Eliot's charge that Milton's poetry commits "original acts of lawlessness." This notion and the one that such deviant acts consign a text to death are central to Derrida's reading of texts in terms of the verbal economy he calls "dissémination." Again, in *Glas* the association of flower-anther-cutting provides a further example of dissemination in the work of Genet and relates somewhat to the material on Hegel as well. To disseminate means not only to transgress but to fall, to rupture, to cut.

9. Wayne Shumaker, "Flowerets and Sounding Seas," in *Milton*, ed. Alan Rudrum (Nashville, Tenn.: Aurora, 1970), p. 96.

10. Notice Johnson's antipathy to Milton's "Babylonish dialect," which nevertheless manages to recuperate itself as a grand English style at every turn in Johnson's "Life of Milton."

11. Jacques Lacan has, more than any other psychoanalyst, stressed the importance of the castration complex in terms of an Oedipal scene. Anthony Wilden summarizes one of Lacan's positions vis à vis the Oedipal and castration when he writes, "Thus castration (which is neither real, nor really potential) is part of the child's relationship to the father, that of the 'symbolic debt'" (*The Language of the Self* [Baltimore, Md.: Johns Hopkins University Press, 1968], p. 187). In my analysis of *Lycidas* the "symbolic debt" is paid through "plucking" the berries and leaves. What is "paid back" to the father is homage, of course, but ironically this "paying back" works to enhance the power of the son, in fact, to assert the son's superiority to the father. In this sense the "symbolic debt" is but a ruse, yet a necessary one. Further, one could say its precarious

nature (lie, ruse, or counterfeit) serves to ensure there will always be anxiety and guilt on the part of the Oedipal child.

12. Derrida, *Glas*, p. 17b.

13. It is in this context that one should read Derrida's repeated insistence that the antherection is always a simulacrum, a prothesis, a disguise. That is, the process of impairing-repairing always happens in terms of metaphor. See Sigmund Freud, "The Uncanny," *On Creativity and the Unconscious*, ed. Benjamin Nelson (New York: Harper and Row, 1958), pp. 122–61.

14. Edward Le Comte, *Milton and Sex* (New York: Columbia University Press, 1978), p. 20.

15. Renato Poggioli, *The Oaten Flute* (Cambridge, Mass.: Harvard University Press, 1975), p. 96.

16. Freud, "Das Medusenhaupt," *Gesammelte Werke*, vol. 17 (1950), p. 47.

17. Derrida, *La dissémination*, p. 337; translation by Barbara Johnson, *Dissemination* (Chicago: University of Chicago Press, 1981), p. 304; *Glas*, p. 27b.

18. Derrida, *Glas*, p. 8a.

19. Derrida, *De la grammatologie* (Paris: Minuit, 1967), p. 59. See *On Grammatology*, trans. Gayatri Chakravorty Spivak (Baltimore, Md.: Johns Hopkins University Press, 1976), p. 39.

20. The question of insincerity in *Lycidas* has been raised with some force by Samuel Johnson in his "Life of Milton." Twentieth-century critics like Douglas Bush in *English Literature in the Earlier Seventeenth Century* (Oxford: Oxford University Press, 1945) and E. M. W. Tillyard in *Milton* (New York: Collier, 1966) tend to dismiss the question of sincerity too easily. For example, Bush writes, "The degree of the author's sorrow for Edward King is quite irrelevant" (p. 386). Tillyard argues that King is merely an excuse for Milton to write about himself (p. 70). My argument would be that Milton's poem is "insincere," but that "insincerity" is itself akin to the kind of *coupure* (*anthérection*) we are analysing, an impairment that repairs.

21. Indeed, the word "hearse" could be explicated as a very ambivalent term, for it means *castrum doloris*, scaffolding of pain, that is, the framework or fortress that surrounds the casket and upon which candles could be placed. But the "hearse" is also synonymous with *corpse* and with *bier* in Milton's time. The common modern meaning of *hearse* is less well known in the seventeenth century than one might suspect. See entries under "hearse" in the *Oxford English Dictionary*.

22. Jacques Derrida, "Fors: Les mots anglés de Nicolas Abraham

et Maria Torok," in *Cryptonomie: le verbier de l'homme aux loups*, by Nicolas Abraham and Maria Torok (Paris: Aubier Flammarion, 1976), p. 25; translated by Barbara Johnson in "Fors," *Georgia Review* 31, no. 1 (1977): 78.

23. Ibid., pp. 27, 29.

Chapter Five

1. Friedrich Nietzsche, *The Gay Science*, trans. Walter Kaufmann (New York: Random House, 1974), p. 124. "Der Zauber und die mächtigste Wirkung der Frauen ist, um die Sprache der Philosophen zu reden, eine Wirkung in die Ferne, eine *actio in distans*: dazu gehört aber, zuerst und vor allem—*Distanz!*" (*Die fröhliche Wissenschaft* [Munich: Carl Hanser, 1955], p. 80).

2. Nietzsche, *The Gay Science*, pp. 123–24. "Hier stehe ich inmitten des Brandes der Brandung, deren weisse Flammen bis zu meinem Fusse heraufzüngeln—von allen Seiten heult, droht, schreit, schrillt es auf mich zu, während in der tiefsten Tiefe der alte Erderschütterer seine Arie singt, dumpf wie ein brüllender Stier: er stampft sich dazu einen solchen Erderschütterer-Takt, dass selbst diesen verwetterten Felsunholden hier das Herz darüber im Leibe zittert. Da, plötzlich, wie aus dem Nichts geboren, erscheint vor dem Tore dieses höllischen Labyrinthes, nur wenige Klafter weit entfernt—ein grosses Segelschiff, schweigsam wie ein Gespenst dahergleitend. Oh diese gespenstische Schönheit! Mit welchem Zauber fasst sie mich an! Wie? Hat alle Ruhe und Schweigsamkeit der Welt sich hier eingeschifft? Sitzt mein Glück selber an diesem stillen Platze, mein glücklicheres Ich, mein zweites verewigtes Selbst? Nicht tot sein und doch auch nicht mehr lebend? Als ein geisterhaftes, stilles, schauendes, gleitendes, schwebendes Mittelwesen? Dem Schiffe gleichend, welches mit seinen weissen Segeln wie ein ungeheurer Schmetterling über das dunkle Meer hinläuft! Ja! *Über* das Dasein hinlaufen! Das ist es! Das wäre es!—Es scheint, der Lärm hier hat mich zum Phantasten gemacht? Aller grosse Lärm macht, dass wir das Glück in die Stille und Ferne setzen. Wenn ein Mann inmitten *seines* Lärms steht, inmitten seiner Brandung von Würfen und Entwürfen: da sieht er auch wohl stille zauberhafte Wesen an sich vorübergleiten, nach deren Glück und Zurückgezogenheit er sich sehnt—*es sind die Frauen*. Fast meint er, dort bei den Frauen wohne sein besseres Selbst: an diesen stillen Plätzen werde auch die lauteste Brandung zur Totenstille und das Leben selber zum Traume über das Leben. Jedoch! Jedoch! Mein edler Schwärmer, es gibt auch auf dem

schönsten Segelschiffe so viel Geräusch und Lärm, und leider so viel kleinen erbärmlichen Lärm!" (*Die fröhliche Wissenschaft*, pp. 79–80).

3. The image of the butterfly is similar in that the butterfly can glide over existence, but only at the cost of having in an earlier stage to cling to matter in the form of a caterpillar or worm.

4. See Sigmund Freud, "The Uncanny," *The Standard Edition of the Complete Works*, ed. and trans. James Strachey, Anna Freud, Alix Strachey, and Alan Tyson (London: Hogarth Press and Institute of Psychoanalysis, 1953–77), vol. 17.

5. See Jacques Derrida, "La question du style," *Nietzsche aujourd'hui?* (Paris: U.G.E., 1973), pp. 235–99. The essay appears slightly altered in *Éperons* (Paris: Flammarion, 1977), which has an English translation by Barbara Harlow. A rather loose translation, Derrida's piece in English becomes feminized and intriguingly taken over by a woman writing in a foreign tongue. Whether Harlow intentionally subverted the piece or simply translated it too loosely is difficult to determine and perhaps irrelevant to ask from a deconstructive standpoint. What matters is that, considering the misogyny in Nietzsche and its fascination for Derrida, the essay receives from a feminist perspective a rather just fate. One might say Harlow's mistranslation was written in the letter of the texts and is itself part of a feminine (and justifiable) resistance, part of what Nietzsche himself calls the "battle of the sexes."

I am, of course, applying much of what Derrida says in this essay on spurs to the analysis of Dalila, though I am not doing so in order to deconstruct the notion of castration, a definite aim of Derrida's piece. I side with Lacan in noting that the castration complex as a stage in child development is quite undeconstructable, that it is a metaphor which describes a sudden feeling of powerlessness, an awareness on the part of the small child that it is not the object that mother really needs to fulfill all her desires, that it is in some sense alone and supplementary, that mother and father comprise the nexus of the family circle, and not baby. But Lacan knows too that castration, like so much else, is part of a knot in which the simple presence-absence type of distinctions do not hold, that castration is, like everything else in psychoanalysis, deconstructed in the Derridean sense of failing to obey metaphysical oppositions. This is taken for granted in Lacanian analysis, then, and Derrida's objections to Lacan's metaphysical psychoanalytical assumptions (*Éperons* is an implicit critique of Lacan) are the result of so many refusals to see Lacanian analysis in its broader dimensions.

6. *Samson Agonistes*, l. 748. See Pliny's *Natural History* for the observation that the hyena was androgynous.

7. Friedrich Nietzsche, *Ecce Homo*, trans. Walter Kaufmann (New York: Random House, 1967), p. 57. "Euch den kühnen Suchern, Versuchern, und wer je sich mit listigen Segeln auf furchtbare Meere einschiffte" ([Munich: Carl Hanser, 1960], p. 1103).

8. Nietzsche, *Ecce Homo*, trans. Kaufmann, p. 265. "Man weiss vor mir nicht, was man mit der deutschen Sprache kann—was man überhaupt mit der Sprache kann. Die Kunst des *grossen* Rhythmus, der *grosse* Stil der Periodik, zum Ausdruck eines ungeheuren Auf und Nieder von sublimer, von übermenschlicher Leidenschaft, ist erst mir entdeckt" ([Munich: Carl Hanser, 1960], p. 1104.)

9. Gilles Deleuze, "Preface" in *La quinzaine*, no. 232, 15 May 1976. Deleuze's "Preface" is to Henri Gobard's *Aliénation linguistique* (Paris: Flammarion, 1976) and introduces Gobard's sociological study of intralanguages (the vernacular, the vehicular, the referential, and the mythical). Deleuze stresses here that Gobard prefers to resist the dichotomy of high and low, major and minor languages, and therefore posits four or more categories. Yet it is clear in Gobard himself that the topic under discussion is precisely that of privileged versus underprivileged languages. It is, as Deleuze himself notes, largely the question of "l'impérialisme anglais ou plutôt d'americain d'aujourd'hui." That is, the imperialism of English and American languages. It is in this sense that I wish to use Deleuze's distinctions of a "langue haute et d'une langue basse, d'une langue majeure et d'une langue mineure, ou bien d'une langue de pouvoir et d'une langue de peuple" ("a high language and a low language, a major language and a minor language, or else a language of power and a language of the people"). In my analysis of *Samson Agonistes*, I will proceed to augment this recovery of Deleuze's distinction between a *langue mineure* and a *langue majeure*, a distinction that, as we shall see later, is endemic to the problematic of valorizing an uncouth or alienated discourse. Too, the word *langue* is preserved in the French, because it represents a language distinction between *langage* and *parole:* the notion of language as a finite set of signs and rules of combinations which in itself cannot ever be made manifest, that sum from which we fashion our speech, and the individual utterance or speech which is idiosyncratic in each one of us. *Langue* represents a particular form of *langage* (in English the word *dialect* comes to mind) which a particular group uses to constitute its *parole*, or utterances. *Sociolect* might be an English equivalent, though *langue* is really a more general term.

10. Bernard Pautrat, "Nietzsche Médusé" in *Nietzsche aujourd'hui*, (Paris, U.G.E., 1973), pp. 9–30. Pautrat explores further

the relationship between style and woman, but does so largely through a reworking of Freud's note entitled "Medusa's Head."

11. Julia Kristeva, *Des chinoises* (Paris: des Femmes, 1974), pp. 21–28.

12. See *Des chinoises*, p. 25.

13. "Thy fair enchanted cup, and warbling charms / No more on me have power" (*Samson Agonistes*, ll. 934–35.) The lines not only recall the figure of Circe but also allude to Milton's Comus as well: Circe is Comus's mother, and Dalila is figuratively identified with them and their sorcery. However, whereas the victims of Circe and Comus do not perceive their "foul disfigurement," Dalila's victim is only too aware that he has been horribly changed.

14. Homer, *The Odyssey*, trans. Robert Fitzgerald (New York: Doubleday, 1963), 11.217–23.

15. Ibid., 11.243–45.

16. Ibid., 11.103–7. Emphasis added.

17. Ibid., 11.339–41.

18. Not only is Dalila reminiscent of Circe, but of other castrating females as well, particularly Salomé (who beheads John the Baptist) and Judith (the slayer of Holophernes). Although these two figures, who are part of, not a Greek, but a Hebraic culture, decapitate their lovers instead of actually castrating them, their actions could be called symbolic acts of castration, displaced acts which stand for or represent castration. (Again, "The Uncanny" of Freud is most important for showing in what manner the castration complex is repressed only to recur in displaced terms: *decapitation, blinding, mutilation.*) In Renaissance paintings of Judith, and especially in that of Lucas Cranach the Elder, one sees Judith sumptuously dressed, sword in hand, and toying with the curls of the decapitated head. Cranach and others who painted Judith probably thought of this image as depicting the uncanny connection between frivolity and violence, refinement and power, femininity and brutality. Cranach's wistful Judith toying with a decapitated head whose expression is extremely tortured, while holding a massive, ornate sword in her right hand, became a familiar Renaissance topos of which Dalila is but another representation. Surely, the cutting of Samson's hair and his blinding, coupled with his many references to his own unmanning, clearly show how strong the thematic of castration runs in Milton's play, a thematic well represented in European art of the Renaissance.

19. Sigmund Freud, "Medusa's Head," *International Journal of Psychoanalysis* 22 (1941): 69; *Gesammelte Werke*, 17:47. The manuscript is dated May 14, 1922, and is a sketch, probably, for a more extended piece. Again, see Pautrat, "Nietzsche Médusé," as

well as Jean Michel Rey, *Parcours de Freud* (Paris: Galilée, 1974), pp. 15–55, for another reworking of the famous Freud note.

20. See Jacques Lacan, "La signification du phallus," *Écrits* (Paris: Seuil, 1966).

21. Germaine Greer, *The Female Eunuch* (New York: Bantam, 1971). Of women, Greer writes, "Her essential quality is castratedness. She absolutely must be young, her body hairless, her flesh buoyant, and *she must not have a sexual organ*" (p. 57). Greer's point is that man cannot have woman sexually unless she is castrated, unless she accedes to the condition of a desexed male, a eunuch. This interesting rereading of Freud's note on the Medusa, which states already in brief that castration is the prerequisite for the male's erection, has been largely misunderstood or neglected by feminists. See, for example, Juliet Mitchell, *Psychoanalysis and Feminism* (New York: Random House, 1974), pp. 340–45. In terms of our analysis it can be argued that Samson's castration at the hands of Dalila is, also, an ironic means of potency.

22. Hesiod, *The Theogony*, trans. Hugh G. Evelyn-White, Loeb Classical Library (Cambridge, Mass.: Harvard University Press, 1914), p. 123.

23. Christopher Ricks, *Milton's Grand Style* (Oxford: Oxford University Press, Clarendon Press, 1963), p. 52.

24. Eugene McCarthy, "Metaphor and Plot in *Samson Agonistes*," 6, no. 4 (December 1972), p. 88.

25. Ricks, *Milton's Grand Style*, p. 49.

26. Merritt Hughes traces the comparison of woman to a ship back to Plautus's *Poenulus* 1. 2 in his edition of *Samson Agonistes*. But the connection is already clear in a less satirical manner in the plays of Euripides, especially the *Medea*.

27. Roman Jakobson, "Linguistique et poétique," in *Essais de linguistique générale, I: les fondements du langage* (Paris: Minuit, 1963), pp. 209–48.

28. We recall that *ship = feminine = loquacious* is already an associative trope Milton inherits.

29. Ricks, *Milton's Grand Style*, p. 50.

30. Nietzsche, *Ecce Homo*, trans. Kaufmann, p. 266.

31. The severe prejudices Hegel holds against Jews are brought out by Derrida in *Glas*, as well as other petty themes that run throughout Hegel's philosophy of right. If I am reading Derrida correctly, he is making a point that it is these very flaws in Hegel that constitute his strengths, the philosophical watersheds from which we should be drawing philosophical sustenance. In Genet, Derrida maintains there is "le procès d'une écriture style anale,"

and much of Derrida's work in *Glas* is to show how a base style that rejects woman even as it uses her in principle forms part of a textual economy of the sublime.

As for Derrida's conception of the *anthérection*, it consists of the Freudian suspicion that potency is predicated upon the fear of castration, that, finally, the difference between potency and impotency is a false distinction, that, finally, the difference becomes *différance:* undecidability. Those writers who recognize this truth, which is anything but a truth in the ordinary sense of the word, reach to the sublime even while they appear to be submitting to the worst of tortures, to the insurance that the sublime will never be achieved.

32. Derrida, *Glas* (Paris: Galilée, 1974), p. 148b.
33. Derrida, "La question du style," p. 283.

Chapter Six

1. Georg Lukács, *The Destruction of Reason*, trans. Peter Palmer (Atlantic Highlands: Humanities Press, 1981). Jürgen Habermas, *Theory and Practice*, trans. John Viertel (Boston: Beacon, 1973).
2. Joyce Oldham Appleby, *Economic Thought and Ideology in Seventeenth-Century England* (Princeton, N.J.: Princeton University Press, 1978), p. 51.
3. Ibid., p. 99.
4. Lucien Goldmann, *Le dieu caché* (Paris: Gallimard, 1947), p. 41.
5. John Milton, *A Defence of the People of England*, trans. Donald Mackenzie, *Complete Prose Works of John Milton*, vol. 4, pt. 1 (New Haven, Conn.: Yale, 1966), pp. 457–58.
6. V. I. Lenin, *The Lenin Reader*, ed. Stefan Possony (Chicago: Henry Regnery, 1966), p. 350. See "The Revolutionary Army and the Revolutionary Government," *Selected Works of Lenin* (Moscow, 1943), 3:312–17.
7. Lenin, *The Lenin Reader*, p. 351.
8. Herbert Marcuse, *One-Dimensional Man* (Boston: Beacon, 1964); "Repressive Tolerance," *A Critique of Pure Tolerance* (Boston: Beacon, 1965). Also see Jean Baudrillard, *Le système des objets* (Paris: Denoel Gonthier, 1968), *L'échange symbolique et la mort* (Paris: Gallimard, 1976), and *De la séduction* (Paris: Galilée, 1981).
9. Perry Anderson, *Lineages of the Absolutist State* (London: New Left Books, 1974), p. 27.

10. Christopher Hill, *Milton and the English Revolution* (London: Penguin, 1978), pp. 93–116.

11. Milton, *Defence of the People of England*, p. 508.

12. See Gayatri Spivak and Michael Ryan, "Anarchism Revisited: A New Philosophy," *Diacritics* 8, no. 2 (Summer 1978), pp. 66–79.

13. Bernard-Henri Lévy, *Barbarism with a Human Face*, trans. George Holoch (New York: Harper and Row, 1979), p. 137. ("Soit et c'est plus grave, le déchaînement barbare d'un État qui ne répond à rien, qui ne répond de rien, qui n'a plus de répondant ni d'impératif transcendant: on n'entend rien à l'hitlérisme par exemple si on oublie qu'une de ses cibles était l'au-delà justement, comme recours du sujet et borne du souverain, la figure de la transcendance comme limite à la toute-puissance et aux délires meurtrièrs du pouvoir." (*La barbarie à visage humain* [Paris: Grasset, 1977], p. 161.)

14. Karl Marx and Friedrich Engels, *The Communist Manifesto* (New York: Washington Square, 1964), pp. 61–62.

15. Marx and Engels, *The Communist Manifesto*, pp. 62–65.

16. John Milton, *Areopagitica, John Milton: Complete Poems and Major Prose*, ed. Merritt Y. Hughes (New York: Odyssey, 1957), p. 741. Emphasis added.

17. Lévy, *Barbarism with a Human Face*, p. 112. ("Le fascisme ne bloque pas, n'empêche pas, n'interdit pas; il pousse au contraire, il pousse le pouvoir à l'extrême de ses tendances. Il ne censure pas, ne tait pas, ne bâillonne pas, il déchaîne au contraire, il force à dire et à parler. Dépensière, follement dépensière, la barbarie n'est pas la *transfiguration* mais *l'exaspération* du Capital,—le pouvoir ne *renonçant* pas, mais *persévérant* dans son oeuvre." [*La barbarie*, p. 134.])

18. Milton, *Areopagitica*, p. 728.

19. Jacques Derrida, *Glas* (Paris: Galilée, 1974), p. 99b.

20. Bernard-Henry Lévy, *The Testament of God*, trans. George Holoch (New York: Harper and Row, 1980), pp. 20–21. ("Dieu est mort? La belle affaire pour qui a lu Pascal, Maître Eckart et surtout Luther où l'on trouve le mot écrit en toutes lettres. La nouvelle est connue, parfaitement connue de tous, traînant depuis le Moyen Age dans le moindre traité de catéchisme, au chapitre du Calvaire, et de la Résurrection. La catastrophe n'en est pas une pour peu que l'on sache l'interpréter en son sens classique et liturgique de la reconnaissance, sous la dépouille et l'avatar, de la figure du Dieu Nouveau." (*Le testament de dieu* [Paris: Grasset, 1979], p. 32.)

21. René Girard, *Des choses cachées depuis la fondation du monde* (Paris: Grasset, 1978).
22. Alexandre Kojève, *Introduction à la lecture de Hegel* (Paris: Gallimard, 1947), p. 13.
23. Michel Foucault, *La volonté de savoir* (Paris: Gallimard, 1976).
24. Eric Gans, "Scandal to the Jews, Folly to the Pagans," *Diacritics* 9, no. 3 (Fall 1979), pp. 43–53.
25. Michael Fixler, *Milton and the Kingdoms of God* (Evanston, Ill.: Northwestern University Press, 1964).
26. John Milton, *The Reason of Church Government*, *John Milton: Complete Poems and Major Prose*, ed. Merritt Y. Hughes, p. 683.
27. Ibid.
28. Ibid, pp. 683–84.
29. Lévy, *Barbarism with a Human Face*, pp. 148–49. ("Un État est totalitaire quand, diluant de politique, il feint de l'annuler et de l'abolir; quand, multipliant les foyers de maîtrise, il dissout la figure du Maître: quand il proclame conjointement que 'tout est politique' et que 'l'ère de la politique s'achève'" [*La barbarie*, p. 174].)
30. Jean Genet, "L'étrange mot d' . . .", *Tel quel*, no. 30 (Summer 1967), pp. 3–11 (italics mine). In many ways this is one of the most interesting nonfiction texts Genet has ever written, and Derrida takes it up in *Glas* in a very marginal way. See pp. 258–59b.
31. John Locke, *Second Treatise of Government*, in *The English Philosophers from Bacon to Mill*, ed. Edwin Burtt (New York: Random House, 1939), p. 403.
32. Derrida, *Glas*, p. 156a.
33. A. S. P. Woodhouse, *The Poet and His Faith* (Chicago: University of Chicago Press, 1965), p. 90.
34. Derrida, *Glas*, p. 156a.
35. James A. Freeman, *Milton and the Martial Muse* (Princeton, N.J.: Princeton University Press, 1981).
36. John Milton, *The Doctrine and Discipline of Divorce*, *John Milton: Complete Poems and Major Prose*, ed. Merritt Y. Hughes, p. 700.
37. Ibid., p. 701.
38. See Michel Foucault, "Le 'Non' du Père," *Critique*, no. 178 (1962), for the play on "nom" / "non."
39. Lévy, *Barbarism with a Human Face*, p. 34. ("Il n'y a pas de linguistique qui ne soit de part en part une politique. La langue n'est pas ce bourdonnement libre, cette prolifération désordonnée

que décrivent tant de faux poètes et d'apôtres illuminés du dérèglement de tous les mots. Parler c'est, inévitablement, dire et articuler la loi." [*La barbarie*, p. 50.])

Chapter Seven

1. Hugh of St. Victor, quoted in C. S. Singleton, *Commedia: Elements of Structure* (Cambridge, Mass.: Harvard University Press, 1964), p. 25.

2. Milton wrote the *Prolusions* in Latin and delivered some of them at Cambridge while still a student there and others in the public schools. This Third Prolusion, *Contra Philosophiam Scholasticam*, is a blistering attack on Thomistic metaphysics and scholastic methods of disputation, both of which the Cambridge system of education upheld to a large degree. Milton's attack is firmly grounded upon the presupposition that the scholastic's ideology of the text as onto-encyclopedic book is dangerous, since it fosters endless disputes which circle around self-evident truths. The *Prolusions* are important in that they demonstrate the extent to which the young Milton rejected logocentric textual models, or, in scholastic terms, the notion of the *Summa*. Also see Christopher Hill, *Milton and the English Revolution* (London: Penguin, 1978), p. 34.

3. John 9:2 (Geneva Bible).

4. The word *bless* is etymologically linked to the Old Teutonic word *blodisojan* (Old English: *blod*), which means "to bloody." Another satisfactory derivation stems from the Old English *blot*, which stems from *blodisojan* and signifies "sacrifice." *Bloedsian, bledsian, bletcaen, blecen, blissen, bleese* (that is, "bless") signify, according to the *Oxford English Dictionary*, the notion of "marking" with "blood" ("sacrifice"), or "consecrating." The meaning of *bless* is further enhanced by the fact that it was used during the English conversion to Christianity to render into the vernacular the Latin word *benedicere*, "to speak well, to praise." And finally, *bless* is associated with the Hebrew "to bend at the knee, to praise, to invoke blessings on." The concept of blessing taken in these etymological senses all at once is useful for us at this point, because it indicates a kind of writing or marking that is at once sacrificed, wounded, cut and at the same time a marking that speaks well, a text that consecrates, that blesses. In book 10 of *Paradise Lost*, Milton appears sensitive to the complex etymological background of the word bless when he lets Adam say, "Fair

Patrimony / That I must leave ye, Sons; O were I able / To waste it all myself, and leave ye none! / So disinherited how would ye bless / Me now your Curse!" (10.818–22). Adam is mocking the inheritance he leaves his not yet begotten children. Could he consume that inheritance, he would be blessed by his future progeny: praised. But the truth is that Adam cannot consume that inheritance and is condemned to be cursed. Yet we know that this curse is ironically to be a blessing, that the sacrifice of Adam's reputation, the sacrifice of Adam and Eve's innocence, is finally to work itself out historically in terms of the blessing of Christ, his coming which is, again, to reinscribe the dialectic of wounding-mending. My argument is that Milton himself finds he is situated within the ambiguity of the blessing, that he must sustain the curse (just as Samson did) in order to be consecrated.

5. Walter Benjamin, *Ursprung des deutschen Trauerspiels, Gesammelte Schriften*, (Frankfort on the Main: Suhrkamp, 1974) vol. 1., no. 1, p. 352.

6. The blind spot is similar to the Derridean notion of crossing out or placing *sous rature*. In " + R (par dessus le marché)," *Derrière le miroir*, May 1975, Derrida shows how such cancellations function at once as devices that dissociate, truncate, uncouple, that break the text out of line (out of column), while at the same time ("sur l'autre scène") constituting a cohesion, joining, integration, propping up. The "X," or *chiasme*, is the sign for such a crossing out, such a blind spot. It is the limen, or threshold, at which blindness and insight distinguish and confuse themselves.

7. Henri de Lubac, *Exégèse médiévale* (Paris: Aubier, 1959), vol. 1, pt. 2, pp. 444, 446. Lubac cites numerous examples of medieval metaphors for Old Testament blindness. The letter of the Jews is but a shadow, "l'ombre des mots" (p. 447). Moses' face is veiled (p. 341). Christ brings illumination to the Old Testament words which are shrouded in darkness, and so on.

8. This lack of typological significance in *Paradise Lost* has not been considered seriously enough by most critics, and, therefore, we must give some space to it here. For, if one looks at a poem like *Austin's Urania; or, The Heavenly Muse: Being a Story of Man's Fall and Redemption in a Poem Containing Two Books—Whereof One Resembles the Law, the Other the Gospell*, by Samuel Austin, one is struck by a poem very much like *Paradise Lost* in theme and execution, except for one major difference (discounting, of course, poetic quality). Austin's poem explains the Fall and its meaning for mankind by means of reading the Old Testament by way of the New Testament. His poem focuses upon the Crucifixion and the

Resurrection and sees the Fall entirely in those terms. Here Austin preserves the Pauline distinction between the letter (the book of the law) and the spirit (the book of Christ), because he never wants us to forget that the events and stories of the history he is presenting must be understood in terms of eschatology. Like the medieval church doctors, Austin believes the Old Testament is essentially blind and needs the sight of the New Testament. The beginning (Genesis) has to be reinterpreted in terms of present "revelations." Thus Austin depends almost entirely upon a typological grid.

Such a view supports the medieval churchmen who considered the Old Testament "useless" or "sterile" or "without reason" or "se-détruisant elle-même, tant qu'on n'a pas recours à l'intelligence spirituelle," (Lubac, Exégèse médiévale, vol. 1, pt. 1, p. 444). As Lubac notes, the Scriptures of the Hebrews are not considered part of a living discourse of God, but a dead script, a technics which is only good for recalling the historical events of the time. It was the task of the church exegetes of the Middle Ages, and poets like Austin, to interpret these signs in terms of the living text, of the New Testament, which could be read allegorically or in terms of similitudes. Only in this way could history be given meaning: spirit.

Milton offers the Pauline distinction between letter and spirit, law and grace, and the shadowy text of the Old Testament and the truth of the New Testament in book 12 of *Paradise Lost:*

> So Law appears imperfet, and but giv'n
> With purpose to resign them in full time
> Up to a better Cov'nant, disciplin'd
> From shadowy Types to Truth, from Flesh to Spirit,
> From imposition of strict Laws, to free
> Acceptance of large Grace, from servile fear
> To filial, works of Law to works of Faith
> [12:300–306]

But it is clear from the very positioning of this passage in book 12, as opposed to book 9 or 1, for instance, that Milton is not interested in giving any great, structural, poetic priority to this Pauline distinction. Milton does not think of *Paradise Lost* mainly as a pleasing revision of Genesis from an eschatological perspective, though one could, like W. G. Madsen in *From Shadowy Types to Truth* (New Haven, Conn.: Yale University Press, 1968) find enough matter in the poem to make such a reading work. For, unlike Austin, Milton is not constantly seeing the events of the Old Testament from the mount of Calvary. This is not to say that felix culpa does not play an important role in *Paradise Lost* or that we must discount the force of the last two books. It is to say, however, that *Paradise Lost* cannot be centered in terms of the thematics of eschatology, for *Paradise Lost* is essentially a book about loss, about falling, about suffering. It is a text about blindness, and it is itself a blind text. As we will see, *Paradise Lost* is conscious about its own blindness, conscious of the fact that it does not revise Genesis with typological overpasses, that it is not retelling Genesis from the mount of Calvary, as is *The Heavenly Muse*, but is a return, an actual going back to the letter, a reconstruction of Old Testament blindness. Such is Milton's *tâche aveugle*, his blind task which is at the same time a blind spot. It is a task, I submit, that broaches even an identification between Milton and the Jews.

9. Harold Toliver, "Symbol Making and the Labors of Milton's Eden," *Texas Studies in Literature and Language* 18, no. 3 (Fall 1976).

10. John Milton, *Areopagitica, John Milton: Complete Poetry and Selected Prose*, ed. Merritt Y. Hughes (New York: Odyssey, 1977), p. 720.

11. Sir Thomas Browne, *Hydriotaphia; or, Urne Buriall, The Prose of Sir Thomas Browne*, ed. Norman Endicott (New York: New York University Press, 1967), pp. 273, 282, 284.

12. Ibid., p. 282.

13. Northrop Frye, *The Return of Eden* (Toronto: University of Toronto Press, 1967), pp. 9–10.

14. Ibid., pp. 118–19.

15. This position can already be glimpsed in Geoffrey Hartman, *Saving the Text* (Baltimore, Md.: Johns Hopkins University Press, 1981), pp. 1–66.

16. Susan Handelman, *The Slayers of Moses* (New York: State University of New York, 1982). See especially pp. 163–78.

17. Derrida, *Glas*, pp. 55a–56a.

18. Ibid., p. 80b.

19. Ibid., p. 77b.

20. Philippe Boyer, "Le point de la question," *Change* 22 (1975): 47.

21. See Martin Luther, "Sacrament of the Body and Blood of Christ against the Fanatics," *Luther's Work*, trans. F. C. Ahrens, vol. 36 (Philadelphia: Fortress Press, 1969), pp. 329–62.

22. E. M. W. Tillyard, *Milton* (London: Book Circle, 1948), p. 54.

23. Jacques Derrida, "Fors: Les mots anglés de Nicolas Abraham et Maria Torok" in *Cryptonomie: le verbier de l'homme aux loups*, by Nicolas Abraham and Maria Torok (Paris: Aubier Flammarion, 1976), pp. 8–73.

INDEX

Abraham, Nicolas, 239; *Cryptonomie*, 124
Ames, Sanford: "Killer Bees," 89
Appleby, Joyce O.: *Economic Thought and Ideology in Seventeenth-Century England*, 169
Augustine, Saint: *City of God*, 70
Austin, Samuel, 229; *Austin's Urania; or, The Heavenly Muse*, 263–65

Barthes, Roland: *Leçon*, 166
Bass, Alan, 6
Bataille, Georges, 63, 74, 80, 85; "L'économie à la mesure de l'univers," 75; *La part maudite*, 74; "Sacrifices," 76–78
Baudelaire, Charles, 55, 59
Baudrillard, Jean, 174
Bell, Millicent: "The Fallacy of the Fall in *Paradise Lost*," 70
Benjamin, Walter, 185, 238; *Ursprung des deutschen Trauerspiels*, 22–56, 213, 225
Blanchot, Maurice: *L'arrêt de mort*, 77, 78; *Le très haut*, 77
Bloom, Harold, 111, 214; *A Map of Misreading*, 16
Botticelli, Sandro, 60–63, 82; *Primavera*, 93, 94, 95, 96–99
Bouchard, Donald F.: *Milton: A Structural Reading*, 66, 188
Boyer, Phillippe: "Le point de la question," 235
Browne, Sir Thomas: *Hydriotaphia; or, Urne Buriall*, 224–25
Burckhardt, Sigurd, 73
Bush, Douglas: "*Paradise Lost* in Our Time," 171–72
Butler, Samuel: *Hudibras*, 10, 14

Charles I, 118, 167, 176, 178, 188, 189, 199
Cranach, Lucas (the Elder), 62, 257; *Adam and Eve*, 62; *The Judgement of Paris*, 62

Deleuze, Gilles, 30, 31, 141
Dempsey, Charles, 94
Derrida, Jacques, 3, 18–21, 32, 45, 61, 62, 75, 93, 97, 104, 109, 112, 117, 123–25, 126,

Derrida, Jacques (continued)
128, 141, 179, 203; *La carte postale*, 242; *La dissémination*, 4, 56, 60, 63, 66–67, 72, 80, 81, 82–83, 84, 90, 91, 120; *L'écriture et la différence*, 5–6; *Glas*, 4, 7, 8, 17–18, 20, 33, 45, 60, 63, 99, 102, 105, 107–8, 113, 114, 116, 118, 120, 121, 130, 161, 162, 168, 173, 183, 192, 194, 195, 196, 198, 199, 201, 214, 232–35, 237, 238; *De la grammatologie*, 12, 45, 56, 75, 122, 161; *Marges de la philosophie*, 69, 98; "+R (par dessus le marché)," 263; "La question du style," 161, 162, 163

Descartes, René, 92

Donne, John, 67; "Good Friday, 1613: Riding Westward," 184–86; "Valediction Forbidding Mourning," 68

Eagleton, Terry: *Walter Benjamin*, 246, 247
Eliot, T. S., 35, 111, 160; *On Poetry and Poets*, 11–21, 85, 231
Empson, William, 73, 249
Engels, Friedrich: *The Communist Manifesto*, 179, 180, 181

Ficino, Marsilio, 30
Fish, Stanley: *Surprised by Sin*, 71, 72
Fixler, Michael, 190
Foucault, Michel, 181; "Les mots et les choses," 14, 92, 93; "La pensée du dehors," 14, "La volonté du savoir," 188

Fowler, Alastair, 79
Freeman, James A.: *Milton and the Martial Muse*, 201
Freud, Sigmund, 55, 123, 135, 137, 160; "Analysis Terminable and Interminable," 103; "The Uncanny," 115, 136, 139, 150; "The Medusa's Head," 119, 150; "Mourning and Melancholia," 34–35, 42
Frye, Northrop, 228–30

Gadamer, Hans Georg: *Wahreit und Methode*, 24
Gans, Eric: "Scandal to the Jews, Folly to the Pagans," 189
Genet, Jean, 59–61, 93, 95, 96, 99–100, 120, 162, 163; "L'étrange mot d'. . .", 198; *Pompes funèbres*, 59, 195
Girard, René, 88; *Des choses cachées*, 186–88; *La violence et le sacré*, 188
Glucksmann, André, 177
Gobard, Henri, 256
Goldmann, Lucien: *Le dieu caché*, 171
Gombrich, E. H., 94, 97
Greer, Germaine: *The Female Eunuch*, 152
Grose, Christopher: *Milton's Epic Process*, 243
Gryphius, Andreas, 50, 52

Habermas, Jürgen, 169, 170; *Theory and Practice*, 168
Handelman, Susan, 232
Harlow, Barbara, 255
Hartman, Geoffrey, 232; *Saving the Text*, 7
Heckmann, Herbert: *Elemente*

des barocken Trauerspiels, 51
Hegel, G. W. F., 195, 200; *Phenomenology of Spirit*, 121, 186, 187, 192, 193, 197; *Philosophy of Right*, 168
Heidegger, Martin, 25, 46, 54, 55
Hesiod: *Theogony*, 153
Hill, Christopher: *Milton and The English Revolution*, 176
Hobbes, Thomas, 167, 178
Holbein, Hans (the Younger): *The French Ambassadors*, 93
Homer: *Odyssey*, 148–49
Hugh of St. Victor, 211, 212
Hughes, Merritt, 193

Jameson, Fredric: *Marxism and Form*, 40, 52
Jay, Martin: *Dialectical Imagination*, 52
Johnson, Samuel, 110, 111
Jonson, Ben, 26; *Epicoene; or, The Silent Woman*, 142

Kierkegaard, Søren, 46, 56
King, Edward, 123
Knox, John, 168
Kojève, Alexandre: *Introduction à la lecture de Hegel*, 186–87
Kott, Jan: *Shakespeare Our Contemporary*, 94, 95
Krieger, Murray, 73
Kristeva, Julia, 107, 144; *Des chinoises*, 142, 156

Lacan, Jacques, 81, 82, 83–84, 85, 89–90, 104, 105, 107, 119, 127, 128, 151, 187
Laud, William (archbishop), 176

Le Comte, Edward, 65; *Milton and Sex*, 116
Lenin, V. I., 173, 174, 178
Lévy, Bernard-Henri, 167, 176, 177, 178, 179, 190, 198; *La barbarie à visage humaine*, 181, 196–97, 207; *Le testament de dieu*, 166, 183–89
Locke, John, 86; *Second Treatise of Government*, 199
Lohenstein, Daniel Caspar von, 50, 52
Lubac, Henri de: *Exégèse médiévale*, 215
Lukács, Georg: *The Destruction of Reason*, 168

Macaulay, Thomas Babington, 4, 8, 9; *An Essay on Milton*, 2–3
McCarthy, Eugene: "Metaphor and Plot in *Samson Agonistes*," 156
Mallarmé, Stéphane, 13–14, 16, 212
Man, Paul de, 24; "The Rhetoric of Temporality," 23
Marcuse, Herbert: *One-Dimensional Man*, 174; "Repressive Tolerance," 174
Marin, Louis, 91
Martz, Louis, 7
Marx, Karl: *The Communist Manifesto*, 179, 180, 181
Misselden, Edward, 169
Montesquieu, Charles, 195
Mun, Thomas, 169

Nancy, Jean-Luc: *Le discours de la syncope*, 8
Nietzsche, Friedrich, 135, 162, 163, 164; *Ecce Homo*, 140–41, 161; *The Gay Sci-*

Nietzsche, Friedrich (*continued*)
ence, 131, 132–33, 134, 136, 137, 139, 140, 183, 184

Opitz, Martin, 52
Ovid, 148; *Fasti*, 94, 95; *Metamorphoses*, 113

Pautrat, Bernard, 141, 150
Perloff, Marjorie, 21
Pico della Mirandola, 25
Poggioli, Renato, 118
Ponge, Francis: *Le parti pris des choses*, 74, 75, 80
Poussin, Nicolas, 92
Powell, Mary, 202–3, 204
Puttenham, George, 26

Rembrandt van Rijn, 92
Reynolds, Henry, 30
Richard, Jean-Pierre, 1
Ricks, Christopher, 161; *Milton's Grand Style*, 155–60
Ricoeur, Paul, 46; "Religion, Atheism, and Faith," 53–54
Rist, Johann, 50, 52
Rucgg, Maria: "Metaphor and Metonymy: The Logic of Structuralist Rhetoric," 244
Ryan, Michael, 178

Saenredam, Pieter, Jr., 92
Samuel, Irene, 2
Shakespeare, William: *Macbeth*, 154
Sheridan, Alan, 90
Shumaker, Wayne, 70
Sollers, Philippe: *Paradis*, 66
Spenser, Edmund, 25
Spivak, Gayatri C., 178

Thom, René, 61, 77
Tillyard, E. M. W.: *Milton*, 237
Torok, Maria: *Cryptonomie*, 124
Tristan, Flora, 204

Van Eyck, Jan: *Giovanni Arnolfini*, 93
Velázquez, Diego Rodriguez de Silva y: *Las meninas*, 92, 93
Vermeer, Johannes, 92

Waldock, A. J. A., 37
Wilson, Thomas, 26
Wind, Edgar, 94
Woodhouse, A. S. P., 200; *The Poet and His Faith*, 204, 205

Zwingli, Ulrich, 236